Erzabt

Bonifaz Wimmer, O.S.B.

Prämie
zum
Wahrheitsfreund.

The original book, *Boniface Wimmer, Abbot of Saint Vincent in Pennsylvania,* was a case bound (hardcover) book, printed in German, with the pages sewn or stitched together. The hard-cover book had an intricately drawn cover, with mitre and crozier, to match the intricately drawn illustrations inside. However, through time, the stamped drawing became lost in the the linen covering as its black outlines melded with the deep brown color of the linen, which had darkened with age. It is likely that the linen covering was a deep gold or similar color, which would have set off the illustration. The illustration is reproduced on the previous page and new "outside" cover art created for this publication.

PREFACE

It would be impossible to say anything substantial about Saint Vincent Archabbey in Latrobe, Pennsylvania, or, for that matter, of Benedictine monasticism in North America, without some mention of Archabbot Boniface Wimmer. Extensive books and intensive articles over recent years have provided a wealth of information, commentary, and perspective on the essential role of this nineteenth century monastic missionary and founder in the unfolding of American Benedictine history.

In one way or another, these studies have also drawn on the first biographical sketch of Boniface Wimmer, published just a few years after his death. But the original modestly sized sketch itself has become increasingly inaccessible or, at least, neglected, due to the fact that it was originally published by Benzinger Brothers of New York, Cincinnati and Chicago in 1891 and in the German language. The present volume therefore has no more ambitious purpose than to provide an English translation of this first biographical portrait of this key figure in American Benedictine history.

While there are no major differences in content from what is recorded in the more recent publications, and certainly no new or surprising revelations, there are some personable details not recounted elsewhere. And there are also some letters cited, from or to Abbot Boniface, whose whereabouts are otherwise unknown. Perhaps the most palpable quality is that the original book was written at a time when the Benedictine community had laid to rest its fatherly founder and was facing decisions on how to continue his legacy while modifying it to meet new challenges and opportunities.

The translation was almost totally provided by Dr. Maria von Mickwitz. Some small portions of the translation were done by Fr. Warren Murrman, O.S.B., who also served as editor. Accordingly, he is also the one responsible for the explanatory footnotes. The book is produced by Archabbey Publications. Most of the etchings of the original edition were reproduced as best as possible. The original was published in octavo, and in very small eight-point Gothic print; the current volume appears in a more generous format. It is hoped that the retrieval of this first biographical sketch of Archabbot Boniface by one of his most trusted protégés, namely Fr. Oswald Moosmüller, will find a thankful readership.

Bonif. Wimmer
OSB.

Boniface Wimmer

Abbot of Saint Vincent
in Pennsylvania

A Biography for Our Time

by

Father Oswald Moosmüller, O.S.B.,

Prior of Saint Vincent, Pa.

Premium of the 55th year of the "Wahrheitsfreund"

Translated

by

DR. MARIA VON MICKWITZ

and

FATHER WARREN MURRMAN, O.S.B., editor

Archabbey Publications, © 2019
Saint Vincent Archabbey
Latrobe, Pennsylvania

INTRODUCTION[1]

In these pages, an attempt will be made to present the life of a man of our days, whose robust appearance and vigorous manner are, no doubt, still vivid in the memory of the majority of the readers of this publication. Whoever was personally acquainted with the late Archabbot Boniface Wimmer will say: if this book offers even a remotely faithful picture of the original, it will certainly offer interesting reading. For the life of a man who pioneered his path in spite of manifold obstacles put in his way by both friends and enemies, the life of a man who did not let himself be stopped, neither by hardships nor failure and misfortune, from pursuing his calling with unshakable trust in assistance from on high, has to afford many an instructive experience as well as extraordinary guidance from Providence to the one who takes the effort to get acquainted with it.

Even though one may rightfully assert that a man like Abbot Wimmer, who erected so many monuments to himself on his life's way by the founding of monasteries, schools, and churches, needs neither pen nor press to leave good memories of his name to posterity; yet it should not prevent us from mobilizing our weak efforts also in order to erect a modest memorial of honest thankfulness to him by way of this writing.

Besides this, the author is encouraged by another motive: for who is there who has not experienced that nothing works so powerfully, so uplifting, so inspiring as a biography from the present time. As once Abbot Boniface came to a consciousness of his own calling through reading the reports in the *Annals of the Missions*, so perhaps the reading of this biography will awaken in many a young person a slumbering vocation to the missionary life or to join a religious order, and in this way become the basis for much unforeseeable good.

If even only one generous act can instill respect in us, should we not even more so be impressed by a life which for a half century knew no other endeavor than to work and sacrifice for the honor and service of God and to care for the temporal

---

[1]The first two paragraphs of this Introduction were translated by Dr. Maria von Mickwicz; the rest were translated by Fr. Warren Murrman.

and eternal well-being of his neighbor. Should we not respect even more a life whose calling it was to join others to itself and to lead them to the same noble purposes.

The world and public opinion measure the praise and esteem that they pay to their heroes according to the success of their undertakings; but the wise person also understands to honor as well the vigor, the effort, the persistence, the willingness to sacrifice, and above all the pure and good intention.

If the author was intent only to offer a panegyric and could not find enough words of praise for his hero, there would be room for doubt about his love of the truth. But since he considers it his duty, however, to express honest, though discreet criticism in judging main aspects, he sees cause right at the beginning to preface things with a sort of apology. He must expect to encounter questions, without whose answers the value of his whole work could be placed in doubt; he must expect to encounter objections, without whose resolution the service of the blessed Archabbot could be misinterpreted. In order to meet these challenges to some extent, he should first answer those who ask why Fr. Boniface Wimmer introduced the Benedictine Order into America at all, whether or not another Order could have done just as well as the Benedictines, whether or not new Orders would be better suited for a new land, whether or not the Benedictine Order has not outlived itself, whether or not it has had its time and fulfilled its duty, reaped its fame, so that it now could consequently step back from the scene and leave the work to others while it rests on its laurels. Secondly, he should explain to others in all possible brevity, why so many different Orders exist in the Catholic Church and whether there is any other difference among them besides the name and dress, since they all have the same occupation, in that they teach classes in school, seminaries, and colleges, in that they are engaged in pastoral work, staff parishes, conduct missions, etc. By answering the second question, the first will be answered of itself.

The differentiating characteristics among the various Orders appear in the most obvious way at the time of their origin. One only has to read the history of the establishment of an Order, for instance of the Franciscans, Dominicans, or Jesuits, and one will already recognize the higher influence that put it in place in the battle against a predominant evil or against an enemy of the truth. It is Divine Providence that calls new Orders into existence at the appropriate time and makes use of them in the Church militant, in the Kingdom of God on earth, in ways similar to how a circumspect general knows how to utilize to his advantage against his foe the different kinds of weaponry and military units on the battle field, each according to what is required at the right moment and at the proper place. Seen from this perspective, the stable Benedictines appear like the artillery with heavy guns; where they were established, they built extensive abbeys, like fortresses and advance posts of religion and culture. The Franciscans, who could say with the ancient Greeks, *Omnia mea mecum porto,*[2] are according to their holy rule the

---

[2] Latin: I carry all my belongings with me.

poorest in earthly goods, but the richest in the number of members; they are similar to the infantry, the poor foot soldiers of the army who are pushed into the forefront at every battle. The Jesuits, established by a knight, are ready to march and fight at any moment; and they surprise the foe by means of their winged movements like rapid cavalry that the field commander always sends where the danger is the greatest.

In regard to the Benedictine Order, many maintain the view that it has already fulfilled its purpose, in that in times of the collapse of states at the end of an ancient epoch and of the beginning of a new one in the history of the world, it did unmistakable service teaching rough tribal peoples about the material things of this world and educating yet unlearned peoples in spiritual matters. Whoever considers the fostering of sciences, literature, agronomy, or even pastoral care and education of youth as the main purpose of the Benedictine Order is in error and has not rightly understood and appreciated the essence of this Order. Surely, one praises the Benedictines for rendering great service to humanity and having earned its admiration and gratitude for cutting down the forests, drying up the swamps, copying and preserving the works of the Latin and Greek classical writers and Church Fathers, as well as for the great amount of literary work. Only for one who has delved deeply into the spirit of the Benedictine Order will this all appear as a coincidental by-product, while he directs his eye predominantly if not exclusively on the actual purpose, point, and life of the Order, which consists in the liturgy, the Divine Office to praise God day and night.

Saint Benedict deals with no subject in greater length in his *Rule* than communal prayer, which he wants his disciples to know as their main duty, in that he establishes the principle for them: "nothing is to be preferred to the Work of God" (RB 43:3).[3] From chapter eight to twenty the *Rule* of Saint Benedict speaks exclusively about prayer in choir; moreover, chapters 43, 45, 47, and 52 refer to the same subject. Correspondingly, in all the more significant abbeys not only a part of the prayer in choir is sung by the monks but also a solemn high Mass. Whoever correctly understands the main task of the Benedictine Order will doubtlessly come to the conclusion that its introduction into America was timely and that the monks also of our time justifiably exist, especially if they have chosen the clever house rule of the ancient Romans as their own maxim: *bene vixit, qui bene latuit,* happy is he who lives in obscurity.

This was the ideal that was always in the mind of Abbot Wimmer. But he had the experience of that artist of whom it is said, "he strove for the ideal, and it was his grief that it could never become reality;" so one should never forget that, under the sun, nothing is perfect. The honorable Abbot Boniface Wimmer, whose life will be recounted in this book, occupies an eminent place not only in the narrower history of the Order, of which he has been a member for fifty-five years; and his name is not only most profoundly connected with the Abbey of Saint Vincent in Pennsylvania, which he founded and personally led throughout a period of forty-one years; but

---

[3]Translation of this and other passages of the *Rule* of Saint Benedict are according to *RB 1980,* Collegeville, MN: The Liturgical Press, 1981.

his name deserves also an honorable place in the history of the Catholic Church in America.

Just as we recognize certain outstanding characteristics in the life of all men of significance, whether they have distinguished themselves as scholars, war heroes, or statesmen, so we make this observation also in the life of Abbot Boniface.

If it would be left to the whim of the author to determine the scope of this book, he would wish for twice the extent. But since the limits were set for him right after the start of the work, so he had to strive to imitate the ability of the painter who understands how to present the face of a person in a portrait in just a few highlighting strokes. To the extent that the author has succeeded, on the one hand, in portraying for the reader in this biographical portrait the resemblance of the original through a few strong lines in true-to-life freshness and, on the other hand, to report only facts in an impartial and faithful manner, may competent judges decide.

Saint Vincent, Pennsylvania, on the feast of Saint Benedict 1889.

The author
Oswald Moosmüller

A BRIEF BIOGRAPHY OF
OSWALD MOOSMÜLLER

By Fr. Warren D. Murrman O.S.B

When Archabbot Boniface Wimmer died on 8 December 1887, the monastic community of Saint Vincent Archabbey found itself at the crucial point that any group, certainly any religious group, encounters at the death of its founder. In what ways in the coming years would Saint Vincent continue and develop the heritage of its revered founder and in what ways would it see fit or deem necessary to alter or adapt it? In February 1888, Fr. Andrew Hintenach, who had been serving as superior for the past eight months in the Alabama missions, was elected as the successor abbot. It appears that the mood of the electors was for placing a greater emphasis upon an improved spirit of monastic observance at the home abbey and in its dependencies, and upon a lessening of the thrust of external missionary activity. Accordingly, although he only "very reluctantly" accepted the election, Abbot Andrew began a program of monastic reform and spiritual renewal in the community. To assist him, he also called back Fr. Oswald Moosmüller from the southern missions and appointed him to be prior.[1]

Fr. Oswald, one of the greatest of the missionary monks during the decades of apostolic engagement in Abbot Boniface's time, had developed into an advocate of consolidating the community's resources at home and shifting the focus to communal prayer and literary endeavors. One of the first tasks that Abbot Andrew gave to Father Oswald was that he should write a history of Boniface Wimmer and, therefore of course, of the Bavarian Benedictine Mission to America. Fr. Oswald was ideally suited to the task, having been a student at Saint Vincent since 1852 and then a professed member of the community since 1855. As an active missionary, after ordination to the priesthood in 1856, he had first-hand knowledge of many of the community's pastoral and missionary engagements, both far and near. He was, moreover, a trained historian.[2]

---

[1] See the section from chapter four: "Consolidation and Renewal" in Jerome Oetgen, *Mission to America* (Washington, D.C.: The Catholic University of America Press, 2000) 175-183.

[2] Perhaps his most significant work, beyond that done in immediate relationship to Saint Vincent, was *Europäer in Amerika vor Columbus*, Regensburg: G.J. Manz, 1879. Even so, his interest was to determine what involvement monks may have had in the exploration and tentative settlement attempts of North America undertaken by Scandinavians in the centuries before "discovery" of the New World was credited to Christopher Columbus.

He set about at once to gather documents and other materials, including his own earlier history of Saint Vincent, published for the occasion of the twenty-fifth anniversary of the establishment of the monastery.[3] His new book therefore would include the twenty years of history since that earlier study. It was published as a premium for Cincinnati *Wahrheitsfreund*, a Catholic newspaper in the German language. Fr. Oswald's introduction as well as the content of the book leave no doubt of his admiration and esteem of Abbot Boniface, yet he also wished to provide "honest, though discreet criticisms" of the emphasis on external outreach, which criticisms reflected what he now saw as a necessary transitioning of the American Benedictines to a more balanced life of prayer and work. He considered the biography of Abbot Wimmer as potentially capable of awakening religious vocations in the young, of providing an argument for the lasting place of the charism of the Benedictine Order in the Church's militant struggle in the world, and as an argument that the main purpose of the Order consisted "in the liturgy, the Divine Office to praise God day and night."[4]

Oswald Moosmüller had been born in the village of Aidling, near Murnau in Southern Bavaria, on 26 January 1832, where at Baptism he was given the name William. He attended the monastery school at Metten, where he learned of Boniface Wimmer and the Bavarian Benedictine Mission in the New World. At the age of 20 he arrived at Saint Vincent in May 1852. He made monastic profession on 14 January 1855. To leave home, he had had to post bail of 1000 florins, since he was subject to military draft in Bavaria; but his inheritance from his deceased father, who had served as a Royal Bavarian Game Warden, had to remain in Europe due to an old Bavarian law which forbade transfer of personal fortunes to monasteries outside of the country. Boniface Wimmer had appealed to his great benefactor King Ludwig I, now an abdicated monarch, to exercise his influence in the matter.[5] But the matter dragged on for several years, until Oswald was ordained to the priesthood in 1856.[6]

The list of Fr. Oswald's activities during the 45 years following his ordination to the priesthood on 18 May 1856 is remarkable; and not everything is noted here. Recourse must be made to other sources.[7] He first was sent to help at the parish of St.

---

[3] *St. Vincenz in Pennsylvanien*, New York and Cincinnati: Fr. Pustet & Co., 1873.

[4] The quotations in this paragraph are taken from Fr. Oswald's Introduction to *Bonifaz Wimmer, Erzabt von St. Vincent in Pennsylvanien*, New York, Cincinnati and Chicago: Benzinger Brothers, 1891. His Introduction is on pages V to VIII and was written in 1889.

[5] For a fuller account, see the letter B.W. to Ludwig I, in *Boniface Wimmer: Letters of An American Abbot*, ed. Jerome Oetgen (Latrobe, Pennsylvania: Saint Vincent Archabbey Publications, 2008) 133-135.

[6] Court Chaplain Joseph Ferdinand Müller reported on his efforts and frustrations in the matter, in at least eleven letters over the course of more than two years (letters 34, 35, 36, 41, 42, 45, 46,49, 51, and 52; the first dated 10 June 1854 and the last 15 January 1857).

[7] For instance: Fidelis Busam, "In Memoriam: Very Rev. Oswald Moosmüller, O.S.B." in *St. Vincent's Journal*, X,6 (March 1901) 217-230; editor, "Obituary: Very Rev. Oswald Moosmüller, O.S.B.," in *St. Vincent's Journal*, X,6 (March 1901) 243-244; Jerome Oetgen, "Oswald Moosmüller, Monk and Missionary," in *American Benedictine Review* (ABR) 27:1 (March 1976) 1-35; Oetgen, *Mission to America*, in particular the many references given in the index under the name Moosmüller.

Benedict in Carrolltown, PA. In 1858 he was sent to establish a priory in Covington, and he worked as a missionary throughout northeastern Kentucky. In 1862 he led a group of monks to London, Ontario to take over Assumption College in Sandwich, which would also serve as a refuge for those young confreres threatened by military conscription during the American Civil War. He then spent an extended time in Brazil to study the condition of the Benedictine monasteries and the circumstances of German immigrants there. In December 1863 he returned to Saint Vincent but by November 1864 he was sent as prior to Newark, New Jersey, where he remained until October 1866 when he was sent to Rome as superior of Saint Elizabeth's House of Studies for the American Benedictines.

He returned in 1871 to serve as prior under Abbot Boniface. It was during this time, to mark the twenty-fifth anniversary of the foundation at Saint Vincent, that he was commissioned to write the history of the American Benedictines. Later in the decade he is found in the Alabama missions where he helped to lay the foundation for the future Saint Bernard's Abbey. Later still, 1875-77, he was sent to help the community in St. Benedict's in Kansas and then in February 1877 to Savannah, Georgia, where he took over a school and established a parish for African-Americans. After a decade there, he was brought back to Saint Vincent to be prior for the second time, during which he wrote the biography of the recently deceased Boniface Wimmer. In the last phase of his life, he was prior of New Cluny Priory at Wetaug in Southern Illinois, from 1891 until his death in 1901. There he tried to promote a monastery of strict monastic observance and a literary apostolate. The small community struggled through those years but was unable to manage in the isolated region, where there were few Catholics, great difficulty in retaining candidates in the austere conditions, and little prospects of financial sustenance.[8] The remnants of the little community soon relocated as members of a new foundation, Saint Peter's, to serve German immigrants in Saskatchewan, Canada.[9]

---

[8]See Oetgen, *Mission*, 216-218.
[9]See Colleen Fitzgerald, *Begin a Good Work, Muenster, Saskatchewan:* St. Peter's Press, 2003. This history of St. Peter's Abbey, published on the occasion of the community's centennial, provides an account of the "Foundations," pages 9-32, including the transfer of the remnant community at Wetaug to Canada in 1903. While concluding that to name a single founder would be problematic, Fitzgerald writes: "The source of the monastic tradition came from both St. Vincent's Archabbey and St. John's Abbey, but the time spent at Cluny under the leadership of Moosmueller also played an essential part in shaping their future" (31-32). Certainly his memory is honored and his spirit continues there. At some unspecified time the remains of Fr. Oswald were transferred and reinterred in the monastic cemetery at St. Peter's.

TABLE OF CONTENTS

CHAPTER ONE
Youth and Student Years 1809-1829

About eight English miles south of Regensburg lies the village of Thalmassing, the birthplace of Archabbot Boniface Wimmer. A still existing excerpt from the parish baptismal register reads:[1]

Thalmassing, July 12, 1828

"In the year one thousand eight-hundred nine (1809), on January 14, was born Sebastian Wimmer, legitimate son of Peter Wimmer, innkeeper of Thalmassing, and his wife Elizabeth, née Lang from Langmerling."

Witnessed by
Royal Deanery Thalmassing
A. Kaemel, Dean

The childhood of young Sebastian came at a time of unrest. During his boyhood years he often was told of the calamitous blows that the neighboring city of Regensburg had suffered shortly after his birth. It was April 23, 1809, when the city, bravely defended by the Austrians, fell into the hands of the French. About two hundred buildings were destroyed during a terrible fire. The flames shot so high that night that even the house in which little Sebastian's cradle stood was frighteningly illuminated. The proud city, which from 1663 to 1806 had been the permanent seat of the German Reichstag (parliament) which had met there 62 times, was now humiliated to the extreme.

War and earthquakes have often taught many an indifferent person to pray. Public calamities also serve to enliven the faith of believing Christians that may have weakened a little in times of rest. This was also the case in the family of innkeeper Wimmer, where the seeds for his future vocation were to be planted in the heart of

[1]For this and for the documents referred to later, Fr. Oswald does not provide footnotes; but the wording of the text gives some indication where he found the information.

young Sebastian. However, this should in no way suggest that his parents, or anyone else in his environment, was already expressing any intimations or hopes that the lively boy would one day pursue a vocation to be a monk. The times were less than favorable for this to occur. For it was less than six years before his birth, that the Bavarian government had closed all the monasteries in the land and confiscated their properties, though the ruling house of Wittelsbach was actually considered to be favorably disposed toward the Catholic Church. Nevertheless that did not stop the spread of Encyclopedian and Febronian ideas, which were advancing from the West across the Rhine River. Nor did it stem the Josephinian influence that was already gradually being hitched to the wagon of the state, with the intention of making it a complete state institution. Bishops and priests were only to be officials of the state. Indeed, priests actually seemed to find it appropriate to call themselves "royal priests."

An example of the Zeitgeist prevailing in Bavaria at the time is offered by a booklet printed in 1805, entitled, "Progress of the Light in Bavaria." In a letter from Munich of July 4, 1803, p. 79, the author expresses the following, as the monastery-closing decree was being made public:

> "There were politicians who criticized our administration for starting with the mendicant monks. [But taking] the fat established monasteries, that would really help finances! Just this circumstance witnesses loudly to the pure intentions of our government: They were concerned about something loftier than mere finances! And what these politicians criticize, actually bestows on the government its greatest honor. . . . There were among these prelatures a few courageous men, who welcomed the dissolution as representing a progressive spirit and an improvement ... however, among the majority of the people this was not so! ... The educational system was mostly very badly neglected (and these were supposed to be men of God!) ... Added to this is the present and long-standing damage of centuries, the damage to the population, the culture of the land, industry, and especially to the genuine, moral enlightenment. What a happy prospect that these properties are now being distributed as much as possible everywhere! Because of all this, restitution will be nearly impossible if (*dii meliora*) the spirit of superstition or blind, one-sided politics should return."

Only a miracle would make it possible to stem this tide of the Zeitgeist and bring about a reaction toward starting any improvement. But the counsels of God are unsearchable. For this herculean task Providence chose a man, who like Moses, was the most gentle among his contemporaries. Michael Wittmann is the name of the celebrated one, whose task it was for almost half a century to form, by word and example, a clergy inspired by apostolic fervor. Since Sebastian Wimmer was also counted among his students, we will have further opportunities to refer to him.

What is known to us from Sebastian's boyhood, is that his mother diligently encouraged him in prayer. From early on, he also demonstrated signs of courage and determination. His closest friend reported the following story from his tenth year of life. One day Sebastian was bothered by a loose tooth in his mouth. Out on the pasture, where he was watching the horses, he thought about how he could rid himself of this bothersome tooth. Finally, the ingenious thought occurred to him to have one of the tamest horses pull it out for him. For this purpose, he approached the horse so closely that he was able to wrap a few long hairs from the tail around the tooth. As soon as that was done, he hit the horse with his switch, and the operation was a success.

Sebastian took school very seriously; he did not consider it a playground. From the parochial school of his hometown, he went on to the Latin school in Regensburg. At the age of 12½, according to his report card of August 30 for the 1820-1821 school year, he placed 15th among his 88 classmates. His teacher, Mayrhofer, made the following comments:

"Sebastian Wimmer has attained the same rank as his predecessor and joins the group of praiseworthy students in his class. Nature has equipped him with excellent intellectual potential. He has a lively temperament, grasps things well, and demonstrates quick and good judgment to a high degree. Given so many and such good traits, which many of his predecessors possess only to a lesser degree, he probably would have achieved a higher rank among the scholastic prize winners, if he had come to this class with the necessary prerequisites from his private tutoring. His diligence was untiring and steady, and his attention during class, undivided. Never did he come to class unprepared, especially in the second half of the year, when his mind awoke even more. He learned the rules of the Latin language excellently, though he did not always have that much success in their application. In his oral responses he shows thoughtfulness and mental maturity. Equally deserving of praise is the virtuous behavior of this student. His morals are unspoiled, and his overt behavior is open, relaxed, and more settled than one might expect of someone of his years. May the good boy continue on his commendably started way of life, and

Regensburg

combine his lively eagerness for knowledge with an equally keen appreciation for virtue, and may he always maintain this."

Regensburg, August 30, 1821
Mayrhofer

After this fine report card from Professor Mayrhofer, it was justifiable to have high hopes for young Sebastian, the fulfillment of which the venerable teacher was able to experience at least in part. Five years later his colleague, Rector Saulfrank, agreed with the above evaluation, with the following commendation:

"Sebastian Wimmer. This very talented young man has made an honest effort to increase his talents. The reward of his striving was very good progress in all areas. Only mathematics put him in 30th place. With a grade of II, and with excellent morals, he is being transferred for instruction at an institution of higher learning."

Regensburg, September 7, 1826
Saulfrauk
Co-Rector & Professor

In the academic year 1826-1827, Sebastian studied philosophy at the Lyceum at Regensburg with Professors Denk and Fr. Emmeram Salomon, O.S.B. After that, he entered the University in Munich. Here he took philosophy with Schelling, history of philosophy with Reubel, science with Oken, secular history with Görres, mathematics with Mangold, O.S.B., physics with Sieber, O.S.B., church history and church law with Döllinger, Hebrew with Mall, O.S.B., exegesis, hermeneutics, and introduction to Sacred Scriptures from Allioli, Moral Theology with Aman, and dogmatics with Buchner.

A very sad experience for Sebastian was the death of his elderly father in 1827. And he feared this sad occurrence might result in an unwelcome break in his academic career, if not in a total change in his vocation. The only source of support from which he could now expect any help was his pious mother. She, however, soon withdrew from their business, transferring it to her oldest son, Georg Wimmer, and requesting only a small amount of money for her own needs. Because of this, Sebastian had to depend pretty much on himself, as can be gleaned from the following document:

> From the Royal County Court of Stadtamhof
> "This is to state that, according to an accounting presented by his brother, Georg Wimmer, property owner, Sebastian Wimmer, candidate in philosophical and theological studies, son of an innkeeper in Thalmassing, can expect to receive only 315 florins and 10 kreutzer after payments already received from his inheritance.[2] As a result, he is not in a position to continue his studies and to pay for his tuition. Furthermore, neither his mother, nor his brother, the above mentioned Georg, nor his sister Anna, married to hunter Mathias Schmid in Alteglofsheim, are in a position to support their brother, Sebastian Wimmer, financially."
>
> Stadtamhof, January 23, 1828
> Royal County Court Stadtamhof
> Fr. Widam
> County Judge

As far back as the Middle Ages, associations had been established among university students, partly for the purpose of mutual encouragement and ongoing growth of their intellectual development, and partly also for the purpose of the common management of their expenses for the necessary material sustenance. However, by the time Sebastian Wimmer entered the university, these associations had moved far away from their original purpose. Only the derived title "fellow" recalled the common purse. In actuality, these associations seemed only to pursue amusements, and anyone who did not join in, was considered odd. This moral coercion was at least part of the reason why Sebastian joined one of these organizations, one which was known as "Bavaria." As identification, the members of this organization were in the habit of wearing white caps, similar to our baseball players, with the difference,

---

[2] At that time, before 1837, a florin, also called Gulden, contained 3.5g of gold. A Kreutzer was 1/60 of a florin. A laborer earned approximately 20 Gulden a year.

Munich

however, that they wore this identification even outside of their meetings. With this white cap Sebastian also made his appearance in Thalmassing during his next vacation, which did not particularly please his mother. She was equally displeased about his announcement that he wanted to devote himself to the study of law. She did not place any obstacles in his way, but prayed all the more fervently to the Lord for the grace that He would influence her son toward a vocation for the priesthood.

Sebastian Wimmer rented a room near the Sendlinger gate in Munich, in the house of a certain Bartholomäus Grundner. Due to the fact that Dr. Döllinger had also rented an apartment in the same house, Sebastian attended the lectures of this professor fairly regularly. Because of his special love for the study of history, he rarely missed the lectures of the famous Görres. In contrast, the rest of the professors had entered him on their class rosters but did not know him personally, since he appeared in their lecture halls only a few times at the beginning of the academic year. All the more diligently and regularly, Sebastian, in the company of his speckled poodle, Phylax,[3] appeared at the meetings of the fraternity brothers of the "Bavaria." These meetings had such a strong attraction for him that he even no longer found time for the pious practice of praying the rosary, to which his mother had always held him back home.

The wild goings-on of the fraternity made time fly for him, in great contrast to his time in Regensburg, where one year in school had often seemed to last endlessly long. However, one day when he consulted his calendar in order to organize his financial affairs, he realized in panic that only one month was left before he would be

---

[3]The name may refer to Philoctetes, loyal friend of Hercules. See Bullfinch, Mythology (Philadelphia: Running Press, 1987) 120, 177.

faced with final exams. His conscience now started to bother him. What was he to do, he asked himself? "Study" was the answer. Quickly he made a decision: now it had to be done, and he settled down to serious studying. Without delay, he looked up some of his friends who were known to be good students and borrowed their notes, and from a used bookstore he obtained textbooks. Every morning he arose at three o'clock and studied furiously.

The time for the exams approached quickly. Sebastian presented himself quite appropriately at his place in the classroom and actually passed most of the exams with "excellent." Only the professor of mathematics, Dr. Mangold, showed him the door. Encouraged by this unexpectedly favorable success, he dared yet more. Connected with the university, there is a college in Munich for candidates in Theology, called the "Georgianum." It is funded to offer sixty full scholarships, which can be obtained through a competitive examination. A test for thirty of the scholarships was being announced just at that time, and so Sebastian Wimmer applied. He registered for the required examinations, but thereupon learned that 120 candidates were competing for the 30 places. The information about the large number of competitors discouraged him considerably. Afterwards, he felt entitled to very little hope for success, because he had a strong suspicion that he had by no means done very well on this examination. Nevertheless, he wanted to wait for the announcement of the results and made no plans to start on his vacation trip back to his hometown until he had learned the 30 names. However, an unmerciful misfortune forced him to change his plans. For when he checked out his finances, it turned out that his whole supply of cash consisted of 18 Kreuzer. There was no time to lose. Therefore, he started immediately for home. Needless to say that on this hasty trip, the loyal Phylax also observed *magro stretto,*[4] like his owner. When he arrived in Thalmassing, Sebastian announced to his dear mother that he was thinking of becoming a priest, provided that he would get accepted at the Georgianum. However, she was not very convinced by this statement, as much as she wished for it to be true, for the white Bavaria cap and the well-manicured trace of a beard on his face weakened her trust in this declaration.

His mother did inform him at this time that a son of the Seidenschwarz family from their village had been accepted at the Georgianum in the past year, and that his parents had already received several letters from him. He was very pleased with this news, since he was eager to learn how a compatriot was faring at the Georgianum, and if it was at all tolerable to live there. He immediately paid the family a visit and presented his concern. They handed him the letters and he read them with eager haste. However, what did he find in them? Veritable jeremiads of the most discouraging kind. The result was that what he read, along with the uncertainly about being accepted, gradually made it seem probable to him that he would not be entering the Georgianum.

---

[4][original footnote:] Strict fasting.

CHAPTER TWO

**Sebastian Wimmer decides
to become a soldier and go to Greece.
His matriculation at the Georgianum.
The call to priesthood. Benedictine at Metten.**

From time to time the Greeks would experience anew the painful awareness of their humiliating oppression. Young Greeks attended European universities and the political movements in the rest of Europe did not fail to arouse the Greeks' longing for political independence. At the same time, the interest and sympathy of their Christian brothers in the West became more and more evident. In spite of being poorly organized, they rallied their energies in 1821 in order to throw off the unbearable yoke of the Turks. Sultan Mahmud II called upon all Muslim men to go against the Greeks. Wherever any Greeks were found, they were massacred by the Turks. Within three months, 30,000 Greeks lost their lives. In 1822, the Turks had created such a bloodbath among the Greek inhabitants of the island of Chios (Scio), that nearly 40,000 of them were massacred. A cry of indignation was raised throughout the West. As is being done today on behalf of the abolition of the slave trade in Africa, so at that time associations were founded everywhere on behalf of the liberation of Greece. Contributions were being solicited and many brave young men from Germany, France and England volunteered to join the Greek multitude.

The Greeks achieved brilliant victories at sea near Lesbos, Samos, and the island Zante, and a victory on land near the Thermopylae. The deeds of the heroes Miaulis and Canaris at sea and of the brothers Marko and Noto Bozzaris on land were celebrated in song, and King Ludwig I had them depicted in beautiful fresco paintings on the walls of the arcades in the royal gardens (Hofgarten) in Munich.[1]

On October 20, 1827, the Turkish-Egyptian fleet was destroyed by the allied superpowers near Navarino,[2] and the independence of Greece was recognized.

The enthusiasm of the academic young people of Munich for the classical land grew ever stronger, especially when it became known that the powers intended to place the Bavarian prince Otto on the Greek throne. Several of our Sebastian Wimmer's fellow students had already enrolled in the volunteer army for Greece, and now he himself made the

---

[1] Admiral Andreas Miaoulis; Constantine Canaris was a naval officer during the war of independence, 1821-1829, and later Prime Minister.
[2] Great Britain, France, and Russia.

firm decision to follow their example. So one day, after serious reflection, he actually started to make his way to the Greek recruiting office. As if by chance, one of his colleagues ran into him on the street, who told him he was coming to see him in order to give him an important message regarding a meeting of their fraternity. As they were talking, a third fraternity brother joined them, and so their conversation stretched until the hour when the recruiting office customarily closed. Soon afterward, on his second trip to this office, a delay of a similar nature occurred, and again seemingly quite "by accident," as Sebastian believed at the time, while he later could not thank Divine Providence enough for this turn of events. In his opinion at the time, however, he believed he had been delayed only for that day in carrying out his intentions and said to himself, "a delay is not a cancellation." For the next while, he devoted himself completely to the exuberant activities of his Bavaria brothers, until the serious reminder that exams were approaching forced him to study, as mentioned above.

When Sebastian started his return trip to Munich after summer vacation, he had about as little hope as desire to be accepted at the Georgianum. For that reason, he now had firmly made up his mind to volunteer for the Greek army as soon as he arrived in the capital city. The students joked "*ultima spes, miles*"[3]; however, a higher power directed differently. Upon arrival in Munich, Sebastian marched toward the Sendlinger gate, tired and not in the best of spirits, when he met Herr Grundner, his landlord, at the door. The latter greeted him kindly with the words: "Herr Wimmer, you have been accepted into the Georgianum!" However, these words came to Sebastian like a bolt out of the blue. "What?!," he said and his knees started to shake. "How do you know that?" Grundner showed him the *Intelligenzblatt* (newspaper). Yes, it was true beyond all doubt, but he was not happy about it; he had by now already made other plans.

He was afraid of the Georgianum and was tempted to abandon the whole thing and to give up this privilege. He stood there like Hercules at the crossroads. He struggled long within himself, until finally the grace of God helped him to victory, undoubtedly due to the prayers of his pious mother. He pulled himself together, upset about his own cowardice, and made the decision to persevere at least one year, consoling himself with the thought, "It won't cost you your head."

With this [decision], Sebastian had arrived at the most important turning point of his life. He had to change completely, even in his outward appearance. In only two days, he was to report to the Rector of the Georgianum, who had been described to him as a strict and ascetic man. This step, however, must not be taken in his free and easy student attire; the little beard had to disappear, and he borrowed a top hat from a friend. Everything went very well. Indeed, he was more than a little pleased when he learned that in addition to his acceptance, he would also be entitled to a sum of money from the foundation.

---

[3]Latin: the last hope, [become a] soldier.

He hurried to write to his beloved mother about his happy news. However, she was still not able to overcome her concerns and doubts, until a week later, when a messenger brought her son's bed and his loyal dog, Phylax, to her from Munich. Only now did she thank the dear Lord a thousand times for the blessing she had longed for so long, that he had called her son to the priesthood.

Once Sebastian Wimmer had entered the seminary of the Georgianum, it became evident that over summer vacation all the knowledge he had acquired in the few weeks before exams had evaporated like smoke. As a result, he was forced to repeat the same studies that year. Therefore, he applied himself with great zeal to the study of all the pertinent subjects in theology, while at the same time, the grace of his call to the priesthood exerted an ever stronger influence on him from day to day. After two years he had to proceed to the diocesan seminary in Regensburg and at the same time obtained the following stipend:

Ludwig, by the Grace of God
King of Bavaria

Since the Candidate in Theology and alumnus of the Georgianum, Sebastian Wimmer of Thalmassing is planning to enter the priesthood, and for this reason, has most humbly requested our stipend, We grant him the same most graciously, so that if he were, without having a church benefice or other maintenance, to become unsuitable for pastoral ministry, or due to sickness or other legal impediments would no longer be able to preside over the responsibilities of his office, but would not have the necessary means for his support, the use of this stipend would commence. For the confirmation of this, we have had this document prepared and delivered to the theological student Sebastian Wimmer.

Regensburg, February 16, 1830
In the name of his Royal Majesty the Royal Government of the
Regen District,
Department of the Interior
Niem. Geraunauer[4]

---

[4][orig. footnote:] The names of the officials may have been as given here; but on the documents they are not clearly legible.

Sebastian's friends said of him that he was definitely of strong character, and did not let any obstacle get in his way once he had made a decision. At the same time, he was always cheerful, full of unshakeable trust in God and most loyal dedication to his set goal, and he also had the gift of quickly winning the full trust of all who came in contact with him.

At the theological seminary in Regensburg, Sebastian had the invaluable good fortune to come under the mentorship of the enlightened and holy Georg Michael Wittmann. The teachings, principles, and above all the admirable example, which he absorbed here, stayed with him all the days of his life. Even though Wittmann was named coadjutor to Bishop Sailer of Regensburg already in the year 1829 and was himself elevated to the dignity of the episcopacy, he nevertheless kept the rectorship of the theological seminary until his blessed death on March 8, 1833. After obtaining a papal dispensation due to not yet having attained canonical age, Sebastian was ordained a priest on August 1, 1831. Eight of the newly ordained priests went to help out in the Diocese of Passau for one year, where four of them received positions as vicars, while the rest, among them also Sebastian Wimmer, were to minister at the pilgrimage shrine of Altötting.

A quarter century had elapsed since the dissolution of the monasteries, when the star of the spirit of Enlightenment, which had caused this horror of devastation, gradually began to grow dim in Bavaria and to lose its power. King Ludwig I became more inclined to carry out Article VII of the *Concordat* which his father, Max Joseph, had made with Pope Pius VII on October 24, 1817. In it, the Bavarian government agreed to restore several monasteries for the instruction of the young, for assistance in pastoral ministry, and for care of the sick; moreover it agreed to endow them sufficiently.

The first step to bring about this happy event was taken by Herr von Pronath, who owned an estate in Offenberg. In 1819, he had acquired through purchase a large part of the Metten monastery after it was dissolved in 1803. The Metten Abbey, founded by Emperor Charlemagne in 791,[5] had existed for a thousand years as a bastion of the holy faith, as a school of learning, and as a rich fountain of charity.

Since Herr von Pronath perceived the change in attitude in higher circles at this time, and encouraged by Bishop Sailer, he made an offer to the king to relinquish the former cloister building free of charge in case the monastery was to be re-established. This offer was accepted; and already on March 31, 1830, two of the old Benedictines appeared who had served in parish ministry since the dissolution of the monastery, Fr. Ildephons Nebauer and Fr. Roman Raith.

---

[5] The traditional date for the founding of the monastery at Metten actually is 766. Or this is at least the first sure date of its existence. A church synod held at Dingolfing in that year lists among its participants a certain Abbot Utto of Metten. See Michael Kaufmann, *Chronik der Abtei Metten, 766-2016.* (Sankt Ottilien: EOS, 2016) 17-34 (concerning the eighth century), here 29. This book is the sixth in the series on the *Entwicklungsgeschichte* of the abbey. Fr. Oswald's later date might be related to the fact that in 788 Bavaria came directly under the dominion of the Carolingians, and therefore the monasteries were placed under Charlemagne's protection and enjoyed immunity from other lesser members of the nobility (see Kaufmann, *Chronik*, 30-33).

Fr. Ildephons Nebauer[6] was born in Brennberg on January 27, 1768, made solemn vows at Andechs on June 29, 1788, and was ordained a priest on March 27, 1791. After the dissolution of his monastery, he became a professor at Straubing, and later city pastor. After the restoration of the Abbey at Metten, he resigned his pastorate, renewed his vows at Metten, and became prior.

Roman Raith[7] was born in Wörth on the Danube in 1778, received his education at the seminary of St. Emmeram and at Straubing, made profession on October 28, 1800 at Metten, and was ordained a priest on September 8, 1802. He served as choir director and inspector at the monastery's school. After the secularization, he became pastor of the parish at Oberwinkling. With joy he returned to his beloved monastery as soon as it was reopened. These two fathers were thus the bearers and transmitters of the rights and privileges, as well as the practices and way of life of the Bavarian Benedictine Congregation. They served as the living tradition of the Order and edified the new novices and postulants by their holy lives until their blessed deaths.

In June 1830 Metten was officially declared a Benedictine Priory.[8] The two venerable monastics started their holy work in great poverty. As small and insignificant as this planting may have appeared, there nevertheless was a lot of talk about it, partially in its favor, partially against it. One day, it was the summer of 1832, the conversation among the priests of Altötting also turned to Metten, when the young vicar, Sebastian Wimmer, commented that he might like to go there himself. However, when his superior immediately replied, "Well, then just go," Wimmer felt a little harshly treated, since it seemed to him that his superior must not appreciate him sufficiently, being so quickly ready to let him go. Yes, for a moment he even regretted this statement that he had not given a great deal of thought to. However, he soon regained his composure. Resolved not to take his words back again, he replied, "Then that's what I will do."

After seeking the counsel of his greatly valued teacher and fatherly mentor, Bishop Wittmann, and obtaining his agreement, he applied for admission at Metten with the following reference, and was accepted without any hesitation.

Reference

This is to certify that during his year long tenure as priest at the pilgrimage shrine of Altötting, Fr. Sebastian Wimmer has distinguished

---

[6] [original footnote] Fr. Ildephons Nebauer was known as an author. He wrote: 1) *Tentamen Physicum et Mathematicum,* Straubing 1785; 2) The four books of the *Imitation of Christ,* in Latin hexameter and in German verse. Regensburg, 1822, II Edition 1849; 3) *The Sacrifice of Reconciliation on Golgatha* (a drama) Straubing, 1827; 4) "Necrology of Fr. Placidus Scharl, O.S.B. of Andechs," Munich 1814. See Linder, *The Writers of the Benedictine Order in Bavaria,* 1880. I, p. 301.

[7] [original footnote] See Lindner: *The Writers of the Benedictine Order in Bavaria,* 1880. II, p.47.

[8] The two old monks returned in the spring, regular common prayer in choir began on 28 May, several novices were invested on 31 May, but the official opening of the monastery as a priory occurred solemnly on 1 June 1830 under the hand of Bishop Sailer, with many ecclesiastical and governmental officials in attendance. See Michael Kaufmann, *Säkularisation, Desolation und Restauration in der Benediktinerabtei Metten,* 1803-1840 (Metten, 1993) 296-302; Kaufmann, *Chronik* (2016) 415-418.

Altötting

himself by untiring diligence in his studies and in all his professional dealings, as well as having earned the full respect of his superiors through his truly priestly conduct, so that in every regard he deserves the grade of "excellent."

Joseph Albrecht
Director of the Pilgrimage Priests' College

The above reference also is confirmed in its entirety by the royal parish office and the spiritual supervisory office.

Altötting, August 26, 1832
Stenfelder

In September 1832, the following five very respected priests entered the novitiate at Metten:

1) Herr Leonhard Scherr, with the name in religion, Fr. Gregor. In 1838, he was elected prior and, two years later, Abbot of Metten, which office he carried out in a manner that brought many blessings, until he was elevated to the Archbishop's Chair of Munich-Freising in 1856.

2) Herr Anton Leiß, Fr. Rupert in the Order. When the aged Prior Ildephons Nebauer Nebauer resigned his office due to his great age, Fr. Rupert took his place on January 11, 1837. As Prior, he made all possible efforts to improve the temporal affairs of

his monastery along with the spiritual ones. However, he was destined to develop his activities for the benefit of his Order at another place. Already on October 1, 1838, the king invested Fr. Rupert as Prior of the newly founded monastery at Scheyern. The buildings as well as the land of this Abbey had changed owners five times between the time of dissolution in 1803 and the restoration by King Ludwig in 1838. Named Abbot, Fr. Rupert proved to be a man of piety and simplicity as well as of learning. Under him, the monastic life blossomed internally and the temporal affairs outwardly until he was called to his eternal reward in 1872.

3) Herr Sebastian Wimmer, Fr. Bonifaz in the Order.

Metten Abbey

4) Herr Wolfgang Sulzbeck, with the monastic name Fr. Xaver. In October 1835, Fr. Xaver, along with Fr. Boniface and three other monastics from Metten were sent to Augsburg to help out at the newly established St. Stephan Abbey. When King Ludwig reestablished the Weltenburg Monastery along the Danube in 1842, Fr. Xaver Sulzbeck was named Prior of the same. Weltenburg is revered as the oldest monastic foundation in Bavaria, inasmuch as its founding dates back to St. Rupert and Duke Thassilo I. However, Fr. Xaver resigned his office in 1849 and was sent to help out at St. Boniface Abbey in Munich the following year, where he took the position of first pastoral vicar.[9]

---

[9][original footnote] Fr. Xaver Sulzbeck is also known as an author. He wrote: *The Life of St. Corbinian*, 1843; *The Life of St. Wolfgang*, 1844; *The Life of St. Gotthard*, 1863; *The Life of St. Otto*, 1865; Dramas, 1861.

5) Herr Joseph Bacherl, in the Order, Fr. Pius, died in 1844 as Capitular of Metten. All these priests professed their solemn vows on 27 December 1833.[10]

---

[10]The records of the archives at Metten give more precision to this data. See Wilhelm Fink, *Das Profeßbuch der Abtei* (Munich: Kommissionsverlag R. Oldenbourg, 1926) 62-64; 65-66. This is the first volume in the series of the *Entwicklungsgeschichte* of the abbey. See also Michael Kaufmann, *Säkularisation*, 312-315. Rupert Leiß made profession on 2 July 1833; Bonifaz Wimmer, Gregor Scherr, and Franz Xaver Sulzbeck made profession on 29 December 1833; Pius Bacherl on 16 February 1834. The date of their entrance into the novitiate would have been a year earlier, in each case; their monastic names were conferred at the end of the novitiate year, on the occasion of their making profession. In English their monastic names were: Rupert, Boniface, Gregory, Francis Xavier, and Pius.

CHAPTER THREE
Father Boniface develops great activity in Bavaria.
His plan is to found a monastery in America.

Secretary of State Wallerstein, who had all the power in his hands in Bavaria at that time, wanted to found a monastery based on his ideas, to which all other Benedictine monasteries of Bavaria were to be subject. For this purpose, he selected the Abbey of St. Stephan in Augsburg which was to be newly founded. "Here the Order is to take over the lyceum and the gymnasium and also make themselves available for other tasks. The former Free Abbey of Ottobeuren is to be reorganized as a priory, and along with Metten, is to come under the control of St. Stephan." This was the plan of the statesman, and by royal decree of December 20, 1834, the endowment of 50,000 florins which the king had promised for the founding of Metten, was not sent there, but rather to St. Stephan. Father Barnabas Huber was named Abbot by the king (he made profession on November 13, 1794, at Ottobeuren).

The monks were borrowed, at least temporarily, from the following monasteries: five from Metten, one from Altenburg, three from Einsiedeln, one from Emmaus, two from Gottweig, two from Kremsmünster, one from Lambach, one from St. Lambrecht, one from Marienberg, three from Melk, one from Michaelbeuren, one from Muri, one from the Scottish monastery in Vienna, and three from Seitenstetten. This was the reason why Father Boniface Wimmer and his four confreres from Metten were also transferred to the new St. Stephan Abbey in October 1835. The Secretary called the fathers of Augsburg "the cheerful Benedictines." When he had been in Metten on a previous occasion, he had uttered (the fortunately non-prophetic words), "Metten, you won't amount to anything." This was reported by a witness who heard him with his own ears. In Munich, he commented, "The Benedictines of Metten are too pious; the king does not want any long faces." Soon novices applied in Augsburg, so that the monastery could do without outside help in a few years. Metten won its independence from Augsburg again after one year, and mainly through the untiring work of Father Boniface, who spared no effort on behalf of this cause by writing to many prominent individuals who had influence with the king, asking

St. Stephan Abbey in Augsburg

them to put in a good word on behalf of Metten.

After returning from Augsburg, Father Boniface became the pastor at Stephans-posching. Then in 1839, we find him to be the procurator at the new Abbey of Schey-ern; and the following year he and five confreres were transferred to the so-called Holland Institute[1] in Munich where he functioned with great success as a professor and a prefect until his departure to America.

At Metten, Father Boniface had received the living tradition of the Benedictine Order as a precious inheritance from the venerable seniors, Father Roman Raith and Father Ildephons Nebauer. In the process of re-organizing anew the Abbeys of St. Stephan in Augsburg and of Scheyen, he additionally learned the practical aspects of how monastic life could be renewed and spread. Through his active participation in the memorable events of the restoration of these monasteries, he gained a most valuable education which would prepare him for his future calling. The experience he gained from these foundations would be most useful to him in the implementation of the great undertaking for which Divine Providence had chosen him.

The rule of bureaucracy had reached its peak among the states of the European continent by then; and a reaction was already approaching. The police state was as oppressive of the political freedom of the citizens as of the Catholic Church. This explained why overpopulation was not the only reason for the ever increasing inclination toward immigration to overseas countries; rather it was even more the irresistible attraction of freedom, which the United States offered to all those who wanted to establish a new home for themselves in its far-flung regions. At the same time, a strong

---

[1] [Original footnote] This institute received its name from the Benedictine, Father Holland from the Abbey at Neresheim, which he restored after the secularization.

Scheyern Abbey

calling to mission work arose among the clergy, most likely as a result of the extensive immigration, so that the immigrants in foreign countries would not be deprived of pastoral care. While these thousands and millions of immigrants found a new home for themselves in America, they, at the same time, not only contributed to the growth and strength of the free country, but also helped mightily with the founding of new churches, new schools, and new dioceses, and then engaged with lively participation in the apostolic work of the missionaries, in order to spread the true faith in the new country. Thus, one of the reasons for the thriving growth and quick proliferation of the Catholic Church was the oppressive and controlling attitude they had suffered at the hands of the bureaucracy in the old country.

This is well expressed in Weber's song, "The Thirteen Linden Trees":

> *All the giants are but dwarfs,*
> *All the lords but poor servants;*
> *Though they want evil,*
> *they must support the good;*
> *They must serve order,*

even though they carry on wildly;
for the good is everlasting,
and victory must be God's.[2]

Only many years later did Father Boniface meet missionaries in Rome from Brazil, Africa and Australia, who had received the call to their apostolic work from Divine Providence at the same time he did in 1846. In that same year of 1846, Capuchins had journeyed to Brazil, to the German colony Isabella, in the Espiritu Santo Province, under the leadership of Father Wendelin, a native Tirolean, who earlier had been engaged in priestly ministry in Bavaria for some time.[3] In the same year, the Very Rev. Dr. Knoblecher founded a mission in Khartoum in Africa, while at the same time, two Benedictines, Dr. Benedict Serra and Dr. Rudesind Salvado from the famous Cava Abbey in Southern Italy, sailed around the foothills of the Cape of Good Hope, in order to labor in Australia for the conversion of the natives. Sixty miles from Perth, they founded New Nursia Abbey.

Dr. Salzbacher, Chancellor at the Cathedral of Vienna and board member of the Leopoldine Foundation, whose purpose is the support of foreign missions, undertook a tour through North America in the year 1842. After his return, he published the observations he had made about the conditions of the Catholic Germans in the United States. In his report, which appeared in print in Vienna in 1845, he expressed the wish, on page 349, that Benedictines would also establish a settlement in North America. It was repeatedly pointed out in the mission annals, as well as in several journals, that at the present time the emigration from Germany to America was

---

[2] Friedrich Wilhelm Weber (1813-1894) wrote an epic poem entitled *Dreizehnlinden*. Published in 1878 by Verlag Ferdinand Schöningh in Paderborn, it consists of 25 cantos of four line trochees. The story is set in the time of Louis the Pious, son of Charlemagne, from the spring of 822 to the summer 833, and describes the conflict between Franks and Saxons, pagans and Christians. While the story is fictional, it utilizes some historical names; and the monastery *Dreizehnlinden* [Thirteen Lime Trees] is likely a literary rendition of the history abbey of Corvey on the Weser River. The poem employs inter-textual alliteration rather than line-ending rhymes. The poem was translated into English by Maximilian A. Mügge (1878- ?), and published as *Corvey Abbey* ("*Dreizehnlinden*") (St. Louis, Mo.: B. Herder Book Co., 1923); but Mügge employed what popularly was called "Lockslely Hall couplets" (see the introductory note to *Corvey Abbey,* page ix). The quotation here is from XVII,4, vii. However, the translation of this and other passages will not be that of Mügge, which at times takes great liberties in order to fit it into rhyming couplets, but rather a more literal rendition by Maria von Mickwitz, with some very minor polishing by Warren Murrman. Oswald Moosmüller probably used this poem in his history of Fr. Boniface Wimmer and the founding of Saint Vincent, because in the poem the history of the monastery of Dreizehnlinden (the various monks, their communal prayer, the civilizing labor) is shown to have been an important part of the Christianization of the peoples of Northern Europe.

[3] The Brazilian states in the south of the country attracted European immigration in the second half of the nineteenth century with the promise of free land. The first Germany colony in the small province (1859: state) of Espirito Santo, which was located along the Atlantic Coast east of Minas Gerais and north of Rio de Janeiro, was established in 1844 at Santa Isabel (now Domingos Martins) by families from the Hünsrück district (southeast of Trier) and more arrived from Pomerania in the 1850's. Later large numbers arrived from Italy. But the vast majority of later German immigrants would settle in other southern Brazilian states, especially Santa Catarina and Rio Grande do Sul.

taking on ever greater dimensions, and that the lack of German priests was becoming ever more noticeable.

These reports had attracted the full attention of Father Boniface. With growing desire, he sought to acquaint himself with all new reports from the mission countries. Whatever about this topic he caught sight of, he read with intense interest, until a serious inclination toward the mission life was stirred in his lively mind. While Father Boniface now found himself in this state of mind, in his spare time he already started to make plans in his thoughts about mission work, though for the time being, he considered these only as castles in the air. However, behold, just about this time—it was shortly before Easter 1845 – he was surprised by the visit of a man, who could, like none other, strengthen his interest in the mission life. Not only that, but with lively imagination and a strange, attractive persuasiveness, he explained his plan in greatest detail and with the conviction that it could actually be carried out. And he did this with an ease that charmed Father Boniface and filled him with total confidence in this man.

This man was the Reverend Peter Heinrich (Henry) Lemke, born in 1796 in Mecklenburg, and between 1834-1837 was assistant to the famous missionary, Prince D. A. Gallitzin, founder and pastor of the little town of Gallitzin-Loretto in Cambria County, Pennsylvania. Around 1830, a wooden church was built about 15 miles from Loretto, under the leadership of Prince Gallitzin, and dedicated to St. Joseph. For several years, they both took care of it as a filial parish, but then Prince Gallitzin suggested to his assistant that he establish himself there full-time so that he might be able to better care for the settlers scattered among the surrounding woods of the Allegheny Mountains. Accordingly, Father Lemke acquired 400 acres of woodland, about three miles from St. Joseph's Church and erected for himself a log house at the source of the Susquehanna River. This property Father Lemke offered to Father Boniface for carrying out his plans. Through this conversation Father Boniface became rather familiar with the situation in America, especially with that in the wooded region of the Allegheny Mountains, where Father Lemke had established his home.

The next thing was for him to develop his plan of operation in greater detail, put it on paper, and publish an article in the *Augsburger Postzeitung* on November 8, 1845. "Every Catholic," he writes,[4] "who cherishes his faith must take a deep interest in missionary labors. But religion as well as patriotism demands that every German Catholic should take a special interest in the missions of America. To us it cannot be a matter of indifference how our countrymen are situated in America. I, for my part, have not been able to read the various and generally sad reports on the desolate

---

[4]The following lengthy excerpts from Fr. Boniface's newspaper article are rendered partly in dependence on the very good translation provided in Jerome Oetgen's *Mission to America*, Appendix 2, 491-497. It was printed in Colman J. Barry, *Worship and Work: Saint John's Abbey and University 1856-1992*, 3rd. ed. (Collegeville, Minn.: Liturgical Press, 1993) 479-85; and John Tracy Ellis, ed., *Documents of American Catholic History*, 3 vols. (Wilmington, Del.: Michael Glazier, 1987), I:279-88. However the translation provided here is also in some places more dependent on the text provided by Fr. Oswald.

condition of Germans beyond the ocean without deep compassion and a desire to do something to alleviate their pitiable condition. Thus I have given much thought to the question of how they might be practically assisted. It is not difficult to understand what should be done—more German-speaking priests should be found laboring for the spiritual welfare of our countrymen in America. The only question is how to get a sufficient number of German-speaking missionary priests and, then, which priests would be most suitable for the mission work? The answer to the second question will also give the solution for the first. I cannot agree with Dr. Salzbacher when he says that the spiritual needs of our countrymen can be provided by perambulating missionaries, who go about like the Wandering Jew from grove to grove, from hut to hut; for unless such a missionary be a saint not much of the spiritual man would remain in him, and even then by such transient visits not much lasting good could be accomplished. The missionary, more than any other priest, stands in need of spiritual renewal from time to time, consolation and advice in trials and difficulties. He must, therefore, have some place where he can find such assistance: this may be given by his bishop but he will find it more securely in a religious community—in the midst of his confreres.

"He should also have a home to receive him in his old age or when he is other-wise incapacitated for missionary labors; he should have no worldly cares, otherwise he might neglect or even forget his own and others' spiritual welfare. All this can be had only in a religious community. For this reason, therefore, religious are better adapted to missionary work than diocesan priests. In a community the experiences of the individual become common property; all have a common interest, stand to-gether and have the same object in view. A vacancy caused by death or otherwise can be filled more readily; and having fewer temporal cares, they can devote themselves more exclusively to the spiritual interests of themselves and others. This will only be the case when the religious priest is equipped with the necessary means of the clerical state, true spirit of the Order, and sufficient income for his needs."

Father Boniface goes on to explain that he does not intend to speak about missions to the Indians, nor about parishes in towns or in the country, nor about established congregations, which already have churches, schools, and priests; he only has in mind German settlers who have established themselves there only in recent times, far away from towns, scattered in remote areas. The entire hope for the future rests on the formation of an American clergy. Even though until now many priests and much financial support have come from Germany, one must not expect that for the distant future. He continues to write, "But even supposing that everything remains as it is, we cannot hope to have [a sufficient] supply of priests as long as we have no means of securing a native clergy for the United States of America. For the number of those who are educated at Altötting or elsewhere in Germany is not in proportion to the continually increasing emigration to America, not to speak of the natural increase of Germans in America itself."

Father Boniface points out further how once upon a time the conversion of England, Germany, Denmark, Sweden, Norway, Hungary and Poland was, to a large extent, carried out by the Benedictine Order, and in such a manner that it lasted for centuries. This success, however, can be credited to the fact that the missionaries erected monasteries that stood like outposts and fortresses, where the contemplative and the active life were beneficially combined, where scientific studies, education of the youth, manual labor, and farming were engaged in, and from where a priestly ministry was carried out in all directions. What once was done in the Middle Ages might now be done again, and in no country more easily and better than in America, where there still were huge expanses of uninhabited land.

"Were one to acquire a sizeable piece of land at a very minimal cost in the interior of the country, far from cities, and to erect a Benedictine monastery on it, it would soon become the center of a German colony. The new settlers would consider it advantageous to establish themselves near such an institution..."

"Such a monastery would from the very start be of great advantage to German settlers, as to those who would live near it... In a short time a large German population would be found near the monastery, much as in the Middle Ages, villages, towns, and cities sprang up near Benedictine abbeys. Then the monks could expect a large number of children for their school, and in the course of time, as the number of priests increases, a college with a good Latin course could be opened. They would not be dependent upon the tuition fee of the students for their support, which they could draw from the farm and the missions (though these would not be a source of much income in the beginning). Thus they could devote their energies to the education of the poorer classes of boys who could pay little or nothing, and since these boys would daily come in contact with priests and other monks, it could scarcely be otherwise but that many of them would develop a desire of becoming priests or even religious. I am well aware that to many readers these hopes and expectations will appear too sanguine...

"Is it any wonder that he should show no inclination for the priesthood when he sees a priest scarcely once a year; when divine services are held in churches which resemble hovels rather than churches, without [splendor and solemnity], when the priest has to divest himself of his priestly dignity, often travels on horse-back, in disguise, looking more like a [traveling soldier] than a priest, when the boy sees nothing in the life of a priest but sacrifice, labors, and fatigue?

"But all this would be quite different if the boys would come in daily contact with priests, if they received instructions from them, if the priest could appear to advantage, better dressed and better housed than the ordinary settler, if young men could learn from observation to realize and appreciate the advantages of a community life, if they could learn to understand that while the life of a priest requires self-denial and sacrifice, his hopes of a great reward are also well grounded. Yes, I do not doubt but that hundreds, especially of the lower classes, would prefer to spend their lives in well regulated monasteries in suitable and reasonable occupations, than to gain a meager livelihood by incessant hard labor in forest regions. Let us remember that here in Bavaria from the year 740 to the year 788 not [fewer] than 40 Benedictine monasteries were founded and the communities were composed almost entirely of natives from the free classes, who had enjoyed the advantages of freedom in the world and could have chosen the married state without any difficulty or hindrance. Why should we not reasonably expect the same results in the United States where the conditions are so similar?

"But such a monastery in North America would not draw its recruits exclusively from the surrounding country, but also from the great number of boys, who either during the voyage or soon after their arrival in America lose their parents and thereby become helpless and forsaken. An institution, in which such unfortunate children could find a home, would undoubtedly be a great blessing for that country. And where could this be done more easily than in Benedictine monasteries as described above, in which young boys could not only attend school, but also do light work on the farm or in the workshops and according to their talents and vocation become priests or at least educated Christians and [capable farmers]? Surely, many of these would gladly join the community as brothers or priests, and thus repay the monastery for the trouble of educating them.

"In this way a numerous religious clergy could soon be secured, and then some [missionaries] might be sent out to visit those Catholics who scarcely ever see a priest; occasionally at least they might preach the word of God and bring the consolations of religion even to those who live at a great distance from the monastery; small congregations could be established, and the seminary could soon furnish a goodly number of secular clergy.

"But where could the Benedictines be found to establish such a monastery [or even several] in North America, and where are the necessary means for such an undertaking? The writer is informed that there are several Fathers in the Benedictine Order in Bavaria who would gladly go upon such a mission, and with regard to Brothers there would be no difficulty whatever; within [the past] few years not less than 200 good men have applied for admission into one of our monasteries. It is a well-known fact that of those who are studying for the priesthood many are joining the Redemptorist Order simply because it offers them the hope of becoming missionaries in America.

"The necessary funds could easily be supplied by the Ludwig Missionsverein. Bavaria annually pays 100,000 florins into the treasury of this Society. Would it be unfair to devote one tenth of this sum to the establishment of monasteries in America, especially since just now hundreds of our own nationality are seeking homes in the United States, and consequently the money contributed would be used to further the interests of Germans in general and our countrymen in particular?...

"Let us, therefore, no longer build air castles for our countrymen in America. Let us provide for their religious interests; then their domestic affairs will take care of themselves. Benedictine monasteries of the old style are the best means of checking the downward tendencies of our countrymen in social, political, and religious matters... If every Religious Order develops a healthy activity within its sphere, the result will be doubly sure and great. North America will no longer depend upon Europe for its spiritual welfare, and the day may come when America will repay us just as England, converted by the Benedictines, repaid the continent of Europe."

U.I.O.G.D.[5]

---

[5]Abbreviation for the Latin phrase *ut in omnibus glorificetur Deus:* that God may be glorified in all things.

CHAPTER FOUR
The proposal of Father Boniface generates interest.
His plan is to be carried out. His candidates.
The journey to America. Temptation to give up the plan.
Arrival in Carrolltown.

This article in the *Augsburger Postzeitung* was much read and much discussed. The proposal seemed as simple and modest as it was practical and timely. The members of the Central Directory of the Ludwig Mission Association considered the matter and could not refuse their approval to the proposed plan. When even King Ludwig expressed interest in it, people started to inquire about the person who submitted the article. Father Boniface, when asked if he would be willing to implement his own plan, answered in the affirmative, provided that his Superior, the Abbot of Metten, would give his consent. As might be expected, the latter was by no means inclined to do so, but eventually could not refuse his assent, when he saw how much interest many influential men showed in the matter, including the papal nuncio in Munich Monsignor Morichini, the Auxiliary Bishop Count Reisach, Court Chaplain Joseph F. Müller the business manager of the Mission Society, and the highly respected Professor Joseph Görres. The choice of the region where the settlement was to be established was soon made, because it was decided to accept the offer of Father Lemke. Thus, Father Boniface immediately approached the Very Rev. Michael O'Connor, DD, Bishop of Pittsburgh, who gladly granted him acceptance into his diocese.[1] At the same time, five students of the academic high school, who felt a calling to monastic and missionary life, applied.

Today, we can hardly imagine what an isolated little country Bavaria was at the time, how little interaction it had with the outside world, so that Father Boniface's undertaking appeared to be a very daring venture that some viewed with suspicion. The above-mentioned students themselves may not have felt quite firm in their resolve, as is evident from a letter they had jointly addressed to Father Boniface on

---

[1]Michael O'Connor was born in Queenstown (Cobh) Ireland on 27 September 1810. He was ordained a priest in June 1833 in Rome where he attained a doctorate in theology in July 1833. He came to America in November 1838, taught seminarians in Philadelphia, was assigned as pastor in Pittsburgh in June 1841, and through the efforts of Bishop Francis Kenrick was selected as the first bishop of the newly erected Diocese of Pittsburgh in August 1843. See Henry A. Szarnicki, *Michael O'Connor: First Catholic Bishop of Pittsburgh... 1843-1860* (Pittsburgh, PA: Wolfson Publishing Co., Inc.) 17-35.

February 16, 1846. Only the firmly resolute language in which he replied the very next day relieved them of any further doubts. Only one of them withdrew. This letter of Father Boniface is unique and too well suited to characterize this man who was called like Aaron, that we would deprive our readers of it.[2]

> B. & D.
> Munich, February 19, 1846
>
> My Dear Friends!
>
> In reply to your communication regarding our proposed mission to America I wish to submit the following. If I rightly understand the tenor of your letter, you wish to inform me that, as matters now stand, you are not satisfied with the mere prospect of becoming Benedictines and missionaries in America, but that you are anxious to know whether I intend to take you with me at once, or leave you in the Institute until you complete your regular course of studies, or send you to one of our monasteries to become acquainted with the *Holy Rule*. You also intimate that unless you first live here under the same *Rule*, you might later regret the step which you are planning to take. I can even see the beginning of wavering in your resolution to follow me. I do not find fault with you for submitting these questions, and in response I wish to send you the following reflections for your serious consideration:
>
> 1. You must above all be determined to become priests and good priests.
>
> 2. You must be determined to become religious not only to be united to Christ more closely and follow Him more faithfully, but, if necessary, do more for Him, to suffer for Him, and not by any means to go with the intention of becoming priests more easily or, still less, to escape temporal cares.
>
> 3. The vocation calling to the priesthood in itself is a great grace, and that to the [monastic] religious life a greater one, because it is a state of perfection, and that to the missionary life still greater, because it is an apostolic vocation.

---

[2]The letter appears in *Boniface Wimmer: Letters of an American Abbot*, Jerome Oetgen, ed. (Latrobe, Pennsylvania: Saint Vincent Archabbey Publications, 2008) 26-30. But this version is a bit fuller.

4. We should consider it a great privilege that God deigns to use us as instruments in founding an institution which, if the foundation is well laid, will confer untold benefits on the people of the United States. If you consider this well, you will not put yourself forward without vocations. But if you feel the call within you, you will not allow yourselves to be deterred by obstacles from following this impulse, because the greater the sacrifice, the greater the reward. We will be able to say to Our Lord with Peter, *Ecce nos reliquimos omnia* ("Behold, we have given up everything and followed you. What will there be for us?") Undoubtedly he will give us the same answer that he gave to Peter, recorded in the Gospel of St. Matthew, chapter 19, verse 28.[3]

If these are your sentiments, you will never have cause to regret having followed me when you are in America. The main reason is not that you are in quest of beautiful surroundings, a comfortable house, or a life of ease, but that you are seeking the opportunity to carry the cross of self-denial after the crucified Jesus, to save or regain souls that otherwise would be lost and for which His blood would have been shed in vain.

What I know about America I have learned only from hearsay or from what I have read about it. I must be prepared to meet all possible emergencies. I am giving up a comfortable and honorable position and cannot reasonably expect another. I am leaving behind relatives who are poor and therefore stand in need to me. I am parting from kind superiors and confreres who honor me and only reluctantly consent that I go. I am renouncing a position in which everything is well ordered to enter upon an entirely new state of life in which everything has to be started anew and be put in order.

I do this because I feel an inner compulsion and imperative, although I take upon myself difficulties, cares, and hardships. My heaviest burden, however, will be that I must carry out my plans with men whose willingness, confidence, and vocation have first to be tested.

You see, therefore, that I have no advantage over you. I am willing

---

[3] Verses 28 and 29 read as follows: "Jesus said to them, "Amen, I say to you that you who have followed me, in the new age, when the Son of Man is seated on his throne of glory, will yourselves sit on twelve thrones, judging the twelve tribes of Israel. And everyone who has given up houses or brothers or sisters or father or mother or children or lands for the sake of my name will receive a hundred times more, and will inherit eternal life." Citations from the Bible in English are taken from *The New American Bible, Revised Edition.*

to take you along because I am confident that you will gladly share my joys and sorrows in the service of God and of our neighbor. If you join me, you must be animated by the same confidence in me. If you cannot have this confidence in my integrity, my honesty, my zeal, my experience, and my determination, do not go with me. Under such conditions you would not obey, and I could not keep you. We must all be animated by a mutual love and confidence in one another. Perhaps next to confidence in God, these qualities will often be the only means to console and support us in our difficulties and hardships. Through harmony small things grow; through dissension great things are destroyed.

To that end you should consider it a privilege to be allowed to take part in a work like this. I will be glad to have good and zealous helpers. But you must not imagine that you are doing me a favor by going with me. The reception into a religious Order is something that must always be sought and asked for, no matter how welcome an applicant may be to a community. For this reason, do not go with me to please me, but on the contrary, consider yourselves fortunate and honored if you are found worthy to take part in such an undertaking. God is able to raise up children of Abraham from stones. He made Paul out of Saul. If my undertaking is from Him, He will send me co-laborers, wherever they may come from. I am sure of this. Therefore I will not persuade or entice you to go and thus render you unhappy if you have no vocation. You will never have cause to cast this up to me. I do not know the future. I show you only the cross. If you take it upon your shoulders, very well. But do not complain afterwards when from time to time you feel its weight. Jesus said to his apostles, "I have told it all to you beforehand," [Mk 13:23] and "Behold, I am sending you like lambs among wolves" [Lk 10:3]. He said it to us also, and I say it to you: If you are frightened when you hear their howling and see their gnashing teeth, then stay at home. If with the grace of God you have not the courage to do and suffer these things for Him, to go wherever obedience requires, to allow yourselves to be used as willing tools, then do not enter the monastery and by no means go with me to America. It is true that in America men are free to profess whatever religion they please. Non-Catholics are more numerous, powerful, and wealthy than are the Catholics. We cannot tell how long they will respect the laws. It is possible that they may persecute us and put us to death. I can vouch for nothing. I am prepared for everything. Whoever wishes to follow me must also be prepared.

As you desire to go with me, it will not be necessary to complete your course of studies if you wish to go with me right away. In America no one will ask you whether you have completed your entire course of studies. However, if you wish to finish it, it must be done by July, and I hope to arrange this for you. The preparations for it will have to be made here in your current circumstances... E. would therefore have to leave his classes at Easter and study with others. The school subjects would suffice. If you do not want to accompany me right away, you could finish up after vacation time in November or December, in order to be able to go on to the university. There can be no thought about entering into [the priory at] Weltenburg, etc., for then the danger of your changing your mind would be great, or else your intention and calling must be so weak.[4]

I would not advise you to enter a monastery here to make your novitiate before you leave. You would soon become accustomed to many things that you will not find in America, and this would result in unpleasant comparisons. I know of a religious community that receives no one who belonged for even an hour to another community. Whether it would be better for you to accompany me or to remain and continue your studies is a difficult question to answer. Although I have given the matter much thought, I am unable to say which is preferable. If you wish to accompany me at once, I will take you along without much ado. But your decision must be made soon because I will have to make arrangements accordingly, as two may have some difficulty getting released from army service. You will have time to become acquainted with the *Holy Rule* before you leave. As soon as the copies I ordered arrive, we can begin instructions without delay. It will not take long to read it and you need not fear it, for it is very moderate. You must also get the consent of your parents and guardians. Only after a written statement of this is on hand will I be able to arrange matters with the government, and I shall do so before Easter.

Each one will take along what he possesses. Whatever may be left

---

[4]This sentence is very difficult to decipher; but the gist appears to be an attempt to dissuade a candidate from "trying out" monastic life first in Bavaria, as becomes clearer in the following paragraph.

after the fare to America has been paid will be his until he makes his religious profession. After that it will belong to the community. However, if one has poor relatives, he may leave it to them, according to the *Holy Rule*. He who has little will take little. Let each one endeavor to get as much as may be required to secure an outfit, namely, the necessary books, a habit, clothing, etc. The money that I have will be sufficient for a time if we work a little. Work in the fields and other hard work will naturally devolve upon the lay brothers, but at times we may be obliged to lend a helping hand. The housework, apportioned according to each one's physical condition and with regard to the fact that they are preparing for the sacred ministry, will fall to the lot of the clerics. When I begin to explain the *Rule*, I will inform you of the order of the day, insofar as it may be determined at present. The details can be arranged only after our arrival. We will have everything that can reasonably be expected: a house, clothing, food and drink (at least good fresh water). We will have time for prayer, meditation, and study, for practicing in teaching and preaching, and for other useful occupations so necessary to ward off the evils that result from idleness.

If to all this everyone adds good will and cherishes a kind regard for his brothers, then our little monastery will be a veritable paradise. Even if suffering, sickness, poverty, or persecution should occasionally be our lot, as they are not wanting in any place, still they will be like pepper and salt to season the monotony of our daily routine. They will remind us that there is nothing perfect here below and that we must carry the cross of affliction because the road to heaven is narrow and thorny. Just let there be no Judas among us. Let no temporal considerations motivate us. Let not ambition be our goal. Do not render my life nor yours miserable through such aims. If you feel that you are weak, it is no disgrace to stay at home; but to come along without being animated by pure and holy intentions would be acting the part of Judas.

From this you know my opinions in the matter. Consider well whether you are satisfied with what I have said. May God guide you in your decision. I will not entice you, nor will I tempt you to go; but I will take you along if you desire to follow me.

P. Boniface

These five students thus would become the first candidates for the priesthood which Divine Providence brought to Father Boniface for the establishment of a monastery in America.[5]

In addition to these, another fifteen upstanding young men joined him, some tradesmen, some farmers, who planned to enter the monastery as lay brothers. One may boldly assert that not one of these could have even remotely anticipated the importance of the undertaking, nor the extent of the spiritual as well as temporal benefits which would arise for themselves as well as for so many others. Just as the merit of the individual should truly not be measured by his success but by his intention, so must the individual in a community never alone take credit for success reached or fruits won. Here the saying, "*singula quae non prosunt unita juvant*," applies not only to things, but also to persons; for what the individual may not be able to accomplish, joint efforts can.

Cum pera et baculo, i.e., with just pouch and staff, Father Boniface and his companions could not travel to America; therefore, the friends and supporters of the undertaking hurried to make contributions. Some brought books, others church vestments, etc. The aged Bishop Ziegler, O.S.B., of Linz gave 500 Gulden and promised to give more later. The Ludwig-Mission Society gave 6,000 Gulden for starters, other benefactors contributed smaller sums.

Finally, the immediate preparations for the journey began with a spiritual retreat. The day of departure from Munich was July 25, 1846. They traveled by way of Augsburg, Ulm, Stuttgart, Mannheim and Mainz to Rotterdam, where they shipped out on the three-master "Iowa." While still on the ship, Father Boniface started to write a letter to the Very Rev. Bishop M. O'Connor of Pittsburgh, announcing his arrival and, in reference to his earlier letter, again asking for acceptance into the diocese. This letter was mailed only the day after his departure from New York,[6] and the Bishop replied by return mail with the following kind letter:[7]

> Pittsburgh, September 25, 1846
> Most esteemed in Christ!
>
> Your letter, which you began to write on the ship on September 5, and took to the post office on the 21st, I received today. I don't know how it happened that you did not see Father Lemke, who traveled to New York to meet you. With only a few words I would like to tell you that

---

[5] In fact, only four of them would make the decision to accompany him.

[6] Fr. Boniface and his companions disembarked in New York on 15 September. They left New York by train, possibly as soon as 19 September, and traveled over Philadelphia where he may have mailed his letter, and on to Harrisburg and Hollidaysburg, arriving at St. Joseph's in Cambria County on 30 September 1846, after a long journey by train, canal boat, and on foot. See Oetgen, *Mission to America,* 59-60.

[7] Archives, Saint Vincent Archabbey [ASVA], M. O'Connor to B. Wimmer, no. 1. The letters of Bishop O'Connor to Fr. Boniface in this collection are in Latin.

your arrival is a very welcome event, and that it will be my greatest joy when you will establish a monastery of the great Benedictine Order at a suitable location in this diocese. You do not need to worry about the stipulations I spelled out for you in response to the letter you previously wrote to me.[8] All of them, or rather the only one that needed to be met, you have already met, and I am certain that nothing will stand in the way of arranging everything in such a manner that it will be agreeable for you and will benefit religion. I am glad that you have announced your intention of coming to Pittsburgh. The most suitable time will be next week, when we are holding a diocesan synod. On the first Sunday of October, we will dedicate the new church of the Redemptorist Fathers with great solemnity. I receive you with greatest joy and thank God that he has granted our diocese this new proof of his goodness. I am sure that before this letter reaches you, Father Lemke will be with you and will explain everything. I write these lines in haste, in the few free moments between the spiritual exercises I participate in with the clergy of the diocese.

Commending myself to your prayers, I remain

Your humble servant in Christ,
M. O'Connor
Bishop of Pittsburgh

After a good ocean voyage, Father Boniface and his companions had arrived safely in New York on September 16. There he visited with the Redemptorist Father Rumpler on Third Street, the aged Vicar General Raffeiner in Williamsburg, and the Benedictine pioneer, Father Balleis in Newark. These gentlemen knew the land and the people, and therefore, he could hope to receive good advice from them.

"If you want to hear words of wisdom, you must ask gray-haired men."

---

[8]The earlier letter of Fr. Boniface to Bishop O'Connor has not been found. Nor has the response of the bishop which was sent to him in Bavaria. Nor has the letter of 5 September 1846 been found. From the contents of this present letter from Bishop O'Connor, it is clear that the bishop's earlier response included permission to found a monastery in the diocese of Pittsburgh. The stipulation which the bishop found to have been "already met" was presumably written permission from Fr. Boniface's abbot that he might come to labor in the American missions and to establish a monastery of the Benedictine Order. It may have been a copy or similar to the document from Abbot Gregory Scherr that was supplied by Fr. Boniface on 26 February 1846 to the Mission Society; see *Boniface Wimmer: Letters of an American Abbot*, ed. Jerome Oetgen (Latrobe, Pennsylvania: Saint Vincent Archabbey Publications, 2008) 32.

But, how disappointed he was! What kind of advice was he given! They all declared unanimously: to found a monastery with such people—that would never work. He might as well give up his plans now. With a few awkward students and a bunch of poor tradesmen and farmers, one could never establish a monastery or a seminary in America; that was a quixotic undertaking! He should not get involved with Father Lemke; all he was looking for was someone to buy his land. They advised him, therefore, to dismiss the brothers; he himself should take over a German parish, and the students he might try to place in some diocesan seminary.

They mentioned several examples of educational institutions and seminaries which had been established by bishops, priests, and religious in various locations in the United States, but which had not been able to sustain the struggle for their existence over time. In New York City itself, two Jesuit priests, Kohlman and F. Fenwick, along with scholastics Michael White, Jakob Redmond, Adam Marschall, and Jakob Wallace, had established an institution of higher learning in the year 1809, which they moved to the corner of 5th Avenue and 15th Street in the year 1811. However, only two years later, in the year 1813, they were forced to give up the project. Later, when the Bishop of New York, Very Rev. H.J. Dubois, D.D., made several attempts to establish an educational institution in the city, for which he had summoned school brothers from Ireland, he also saw these plans also fail in a short time. However, this did not deter him from acquiring a beautiful property in Nyack, along the Hudson River, in order to found an educational institution there. With great solemnity the cornerstone for it was laid on May 29, 1833, and as the building was rising in impressive style, he petitioned the legislature for rights of incorporation. However, he was very disappointed when he was refused this favor. The reason for this prejudice was the fact that the Protestant preachers of the area had intensely incited public opinion against this Catholic institution. Undeterred by this, the bishop pursued his plans; however, it was not long before the day when the sad news was reported that his seminary at Nyack had accidently fallen victim to a fire. Thereupon be made a third attempt in Brooklyn. However, here he found the conditions for obtaining the necessary property unacceptable. Finally, he built his college at La Fargeville, in the northern part of his diocese, and seemingly with good success. However, due to the great distance, he had to give this up also.

Several other similar attempts, especially in poorer dioceses such as Charleston, were also mentioned. In spite of such discouraging revelations about such experiences of others, Father Boniface believed that he still had another support upon which he could cast the anchor of his hope. If, he said to himself, his plan for a seminary should not succeed, he and his lay brothers would lead an ascetic life in the wilderness, as Trappists do. He was told that this too had already been tried. Even Trappists had started settlements which they later abandoned, and, in fact, one of these had been

at the very location of Father Lemke at Carrolltown, where he would see their abandoned log cabin for himself in a few days.

Similar undertakings with lay brothers had been tried here, also. In the year
1813, Bishop Flaget of Bardstown in Kentucky developed a plan to get several young
professionals from different trades together, who would be willing to live a communal
life and dedicate themselves to God through religious vows. Each one might take on
apprentices. Some might want to work together, without getting in each other's way,
while others might have their separate workshops. However, all of them should be
within the enclosure or fenced-in area, which would then serve as the cloister. They
should have specific hours when they would gather for prayer, spiritual reading, etc.
For thirteen years, the good bishop had nurtured this plan, until he saw a way to put
it into practice. In the spring of 1826, he was finally able to establish the Brotherhood of St. Thomas. He modeled his group after the Brothers of Christian Doctrine
of France, and his intention was that, as soon as their number would have increased
sufficiently, he would select some of them, who might seem particularly suited for
this, to assist his missionary priests as catechists and in the management of their
temporal affairs.

The brothers professed simple vows for three years and were under the direction
of the Very Reverend M. Derigaud. The following year, the bishop moved this community to Casey County to a farm he owned. Here the brothers, eight in number,
erected a building for their monastery, which they called Monte Casino, after the
famous Benedictine Abbey in Italy. Most of the brothers practiced a trade, and the
original plan of the bishop seemed to achieve its purpose completely by all appear-
ances. However, the ways of Providence are inscrutable. It was not long until the
Superior of the House, the Very Reverend M. Derigaud, was called from this life. As
a result, the bishop had great difficulty finding a suitable successor to this self-sacrificing priest. Finally, he found no other solution than to call the Brothers to Nazareth
(in Kentucky) so that they would there elect a Prior from among themselves. However, it became evident that all these good plans had a short duration. The election of
the Prior had taken place; however, they were still lacking a suitable priest to lead the
Brothers, and the result of this was that after only three years, the whole Brotherhood
was dissolved.

Such talk from the mouths of experienced priests almost caused Father Boniface to waiver in the confidence with which he was moving toward the realization
of his plans. Finally he countered, "Now that I have come this far, I want to at least
make an attempt to see if it is possible after all." Once he had, as it were, shaken off
all objections and doubts, he hurried to escape the hubbub of the big city. On the
way to the train station, he met Father Lemke, who inspired him with new courage
and cheered him up with his inexhaustible good humor. Under his caring guidance,

they finally started on the journey to their new destination full of longing and happy anticipation. On September 19, they left the Metropolis of the West, took the train to Columbus in Pennsylvania, and then rode on a canal boat as far as Hollidaysburg. The rest of the way to Carrolltown they covered on foot. Already on the way there, the closer they came to their longed-for destination, they noticed many large rocks that seemed to fairly cover the ground here and there. They also saw numerous gigantic dead trees, standing ominously in the fields. Then, when they reached the place itself on the evening of September 30 and they finally could say, "we are here"," a low, plain looking slab hut was pointed out to them as the chapel, and a poor looking log house as their living quarters; and they could see with their own eyes that they had not come into a "land flowing with milk and honey." Carrolltown was only in its beginnings. The place was generally still known as "St. Joseph," and it was called this after the log church that was located three miles farther in a northwesterly direction at what was named Hart's Sleeping Place.

Carrolltown is located twelve miles northeast of Loretto, which was the establishment of the missionary Prince Demetrius Gallitzin,[9] on one of the ridges of the Allegheny Mountains, near the watershed of the Susquehanna and Allegheny Rivers.

Father Lemke had actually enclosed one of the main sources of the Susquehanna by building his spring house, his kitchen, his dining room, etc. right on top of it. About half a mile from this building, along the northern slope of the so called "Old

Meeting of Father Lemke with Prince Gallitzin

[9] [original footnote] After Father Gallitzin was hurt in a fall from a horse, he used to ride through woods and fields in a low sled, pulled by two strong horses, even in the summer. The etching in the book shows Father Lemke meeting the princely missionary for the first time in the woods.

Loretto Road," a colony of Trappists had settled at the beginning of this century. However, they did not stay long. The above-mentioned St. Joseph's Church was built around 1830, under the direction of Father Gallitzin, who pastored it as a branch of his parish. In 1834 he encouraged his assistant, Father Lemke, to acquire some land near this church and to settle there, in order to take care of the Catholic settlers of that area, as he himself had done in Loretto until then.

One of the oldest settlers of that area and co-founder of the parish was a man named Johann Luther, whose life could have provided interesting material for a novel. He was born to Protestant parents in Thuringia, and was, at least Father Lemke so asserted, a descendant of Martin Luther himself. As many others, he was hired out to England by the Grand Duke of Hesse, along with the rest of the mercenary troops, and then taken to America in 1776 to suppress the struggle for independence. After the surprise attack at Trenton, when Luther had come to understand the real situation, he wanted to choose freedom for himself also, and took off toward Pennsylvania in great haste. Pursued by English loyalists, in fear of his life everywhere, he fled into the lonely forests of the Allegheny Mountains. After many adventures, a Catholic girl saved his life when he was in extreme danger. She later became his wife, and he himself joined the Catholic Church with the assistance of Prince Gallitzin. One of his great grandchildren now wears the habit of St. Benedict at St. Vincent.[10]

Fr. Boniface wrote his first letter following arrival in New York to Court Chaplain Müller. However, several other priests from New York also wrote to [Fr. Müller] at the same time, in order to call his attention to several points which they considered important and useful in regard to the undertaking. They explained to him how quickly someone who had money and wanted to buy land here could find himself among "friends" who were hoping to gain profit for themselves from this. Because of this, Father Müller hurried to give Father Boniface his well- intentioned advice, by writing the following:[11]

> Munich, 5 October 1846
> [postmark N.Y. Dec 21]
> Reverend Friend!
>
> Today is the burial day of our old Lord Archbishop, who died during a Confirmation trip in Mühldorf at 8 o'clock in the morning on 1 October...[12] Meanwhile several letters have arrived from America in regard

---

[10] This was Fr. Aloysius Luther. He was born on 26 April 1871 and made monastic profession on 11 July 1893; he was ordained to the priesthood on 2 July 1898 and died on 2 May 1952.

[11] These are excerpts from the Court Chaplain's letter, ASVA, J.F. Müller to B. Wimmer, no. 2.

[12] Lothar Anselm von Gebsattel, 1761-1846. He became the first archbishop of Munich and Freising in 1821. He was very involved in the struggle over the religious education of baptized children in marriages of mixed religion; he held the view that all the children of such marriages should be in the Catholic Church and be raised Catholic.

to your mission. They all warn me not to let you go to St. Joseph, unless you want to lead a merely ascetical life. The ground is not supposed to be worthwhile for farming and America is said to have a surplus of good land. I however think that this little place would be in keeping with your intention. You want to establish schools for the education of the clergy and to seek perfection. Even if the ground does not give rich yields, it can certainly feed industrious hands and that is sufficient.

Since your departure several individuals have applied. I would like some information in this regard, whether you still can use some people, and with what characteristics and skills...

Be clever and cautious in all things. Europe and America are watching you. Just as is the case everywhere, a good thing has its peace[13] and its supporters. If one has not overlooked anything, then one's conscience is peaceful.

Greet all of your people for me in a most heartfelt way. Join both a Christian and edifying life to a true trust in God. May God be with you all! Do not forget at the altar your entirely devoted friend,

Jos. Ferd. Müller, Court Chaplain

---

[13]The expected word here might be "friends," and indeed in German Freunde and Friede are close; but the word the Hofkaplan wrote in the original document is surely Friede or "peace." It could be an example of a simple slip of the pen, when the conscious attention of the mind has galloped ahead and left the writing to the automatic but distracted action of the hand.

CHAPTER FIVE
Father Boniface visits the Most Rev. Bishop of Pittsburgh.
He sees Saint Vincent for the first time.
He leaves Carrolltown. The start of monastic life.

Father Boniface, whose cradle had stood in the so called "Dark Soil" region, the most fertile wheat country in Bavaria, contemplated the harsh, rocky, and mountainous countryside around Carrolltown with a heavy heart. This was not how he had imagined America when Father Lemke had described his new homeland, his creation, and his parish to him in Munich a year before with persuasive words, and described the success of his activities of many years in detail. Father Boniface now found himself in Carrolltown and looked for the "town," or at least the "village" of which Father Lemke had presented himself in Munich as being the founder. That half a dozen wooden huts earned the title of "town" so easily for themselves in America, was something he was not familiar with. He came to believe in general that, in this country, considerable misuse was being made with the concepts behind words such as "church," "house," and "town." Perhaps, of course, the people, like surveyors or architects, were able to imagine grand plans from a few lines, or that, like philosophers, they postulated the existence of hidden powers and possible capabilities *in potentia*.

Father Boniface then set out for Pittsburgh to pay his respects to the Most Reverend Bishop and to present his references to him. While the bishop expressed his appreciation for Father Boniface's plan, he at the same time suggested to him that Carrolltown, in his opinion, was not at all suited as a place for a monastery and a boys' seminary. The bishop said he himself would make him a far better offer, since he had a place that was just cut out for that kind of an institution. This place was closer to the city, only forty miles away, and much closer to transportation. In fact, a railroad line which would connect Philadelphia with Pittsburgh was already in the process of being built, and was located quite close to this place. In short, they agreed to make the journey to this place, that is, Saint Vincent, the very next day.

Already his first glimpse of the area convinced Father Boniface that here the land was more fertile and the climate milder than in the Allegheny Mountains where Carrolltown was located. Moreover, a parish already existed here, with sixty families, half of which spoke the German language, though the majority of them had been born in America. Here Father Boniface found a fine looking church, built of bricks, 87 feet in length and 57 ½ feet in width, a two-story rectory, 40 feet square, along with several farm buildings. This church comes with two pieces of property. On one of these, 315 acres in size, the above buildings are located. The other one, 150 acres in size, is seven miles away from the first. Father Boniface had to agree completely with the bishop that this place had many more advantages for the establishment of a monastery and a seminary than St. Joseph's and Father Lemke's place in Cambria County. He took leave of the bishop with many thanks, hurried back to Carrolltown, and related to his companions what he had seen and what a promising offer he had received.

On October 11, a parish meeting was held at Saint Vincent, and the following letter to Father Boniface was generated, expressing the group's wishes:[1]

> St. Vincent, Pennsylvania
> October 11, 1846
> Reverend Boniface Wimmer:
>
> Having learned that it is your intention to establish a monastery of the Benedictine Order in this country, the members of which devote themselves to the care of souls and to the education of youth, and feeling convinced that you cannot find in Pennsylvania a place better suited for these purposes than the farm attached to St. Vincent's Church, we the undersigned do earnestly request you to come here and establish here the monastery above alluded to.
>
> In our own name and in the name of the other members of this parish, every man of whom, if he had time, we feel assured, would join with us in the sentiments we now express, we beg leave to assure you that we shall be always ready to do everything in our power to aid you in your benevolent undertakings, and support you in the discharge of your arduous mission. This farm has been given for the support of the pastor of the church for the time being. Trustees were appointed to preserve the property for the purpose for which it was granted, but being in your hands it could be used for this purpose in the most effectual manner. When worthy clergymen are living here attending this congregation and this farm is neither destroyed nor damaged, the people neither have nor claim any right to interfere with it. No one at the present mo-

---

[1] The text appears in Oetgen, *Mission,* as Appendix 4, 502-503.

ment would be inclined to give the least trouble or annoyance but on the contrary all would be delighted at your coming amongst us. Lest, however, anything of the kind should be anticipated in the future, we pledge ourselves to do everything in our power to make your position independent, so that when the above objects are secured you may feel certain that no one shall even have it in his power to give you the least annoyance.

Here are listed the names of the [four trustees and 54 other] heads of households and members of Saint Vincent Parish.

Following the reception of this letter, the decision was quickly made. Early on the morning of October 16, Father Boniface and his group of brothers were on their way through the extensive forests, along with their baggage, which consisted of 44 trunks. Even though the distance between Carrolltown and St. Vincent is only 56 miles, the journey nevertheless took two days and required an outlay of two hundred dollars. The entire group traveled on foot, with the exception of two sick brothers, who followed, riding on the baggage wagons.

The most memorable day in the history of St. Vincent is October 24, 1846, for on this day the cornerstone of the spiritual foundation of the monastery was laid, by Father Boniface giving the habit to his companions. On this day also, common prayer in choir was begun, which since then has continued regularly at set hours and, it is hoped, will continue without interruption for centuries. Father Boniface was happy now, for with his mind's eye he could see his ideal, the monasteries of the golden age of monasticism in the Middle Ages, the imitation of which he had as the goal of his life's work.

The words of Weber could be applied to him:[2]

> "And since new days are built upon the rubble of old ones,
> A clear eye can perceive the future by looking back."

However, worldly people, whose ideals are shaped by the prevailing zeitgeist, contemplated his efforts only with a pitying smile. In their eyes, his undertaking was nothing but an attempt to establish a poorhouse or an orphan asylum, which any well-populated city would be able to establish much more easily and with all modern conveniences. But to establish a monastery after the manner of the medieval ones, that they considered a thing of the past, something that was obsolete. [In their eyes] it was a totally out-of-date concept, an establishment that was no longer something that belonged in our times.

---

[2] Weber, *Dreizehnlinden*, XVII, 3, ii.

It is true, customs change with time, and in many instances, this can be progress. However, in his essence man remains the same, his needs the same in all times:[3]

> "Humans are the children of all times, of all climes, whether they live under birch bushes or palm trees."

The passions, the temptations, the dangers with which humans have to struggle, always remain the same. However, the high ideals for which we must strive also remain the same. Whoever questions whether monastic life is still relevant, needs to understand that the purpose of monastic life is nothing other than the striving to imitate the poor, humble, dedicated and charitable life of Christ as perfectly as possible. Not everyone is called to monastic life, for:[4]

> "It is not for everyone to entomb oneself alive, mutely in a bleak monastic cell detached from the tumult of the world, the wicked one."

St. Benedict did not establish his Order as an asylum for individuals who are tired of life, but rather as a school for living, as he explains in the Prologue to his *Rule,* where he says: "Therefore we intend to establish a school for the Lord's service." [5] This thought is also expressed well by Weber:[6]

> "He who led you out of the world into the silence of the monastic cell, wanted to show you the right way into the world, the desolate."

Two days after the investiture, Father Boniface wrote the following report about his experiences to date to his most important patron, Court Chaplain Müller, in Munich:[7]

> St. Vincent, Pennsylvania
> October 26, 1846
>
> Reverend Court Chaplain:
> When you see the name of the place where this letter is written, and the date, you will probably say, "Why is he not at St. Joseph's?" We changed our residence and are now 50 miles southwest of that first colony in one of the most beautiful and salubrious spots in America

---

[3] Weber, *Dreizehnlinden*, XVII, 3, iv.
[4] Weber, *Dreizehnlinden*, XXII, xxix.
[5] RB, Prol. 45.
[6] Weber, *Dreizehnlinden*, XVII, 1, vi.
[7] The letter is contained in Wimmer: *Letters* (2008), 49-52.

for a Benedictine monastery. The most reverend bishop offered me two farms of 315 and 150 acres.[8] They are the foundation of Father Brouwers, a pious missionary who lived here towards the end of the last century and donated them for the support of the pastor to minister to the Catholics who are scattered over the whole county. The bishop also wishes me to start a seminary as soon as possible to educate young men to the priesthood. At present there is no such institution in the country,[9] but such a school is most necessary for the Church in the United States. Boys of the wealthier classes usually study for secular professions. For this reason, almost all the secular clergy are of foreign birth: Irish, German, French. The whole diocese of Pittsburg has only one native-born American priest, and he, although of German descent, understands little of the language of his ancestors. Other dioceses are in a similar condition. Therefore, priests are not only too few for the number of people, but, being foreigners, often do not have the confidence of their parishioners. Moreover, they themselves come to understand the mind of the people only gradually, especially if in mixed populations they speak only one language.

The Irish and German Catholics usually live close together, and when the pastor, even if he resides among them, speaks only one language, one part of the congregation seldom hears a sermon or is without spiritual assistance in the confessional and when sick. What is still worse, almost all the schools are controlled by non-Catholics. Therefore, missionary seminaries, not in Europe, but here in America, will be the only means of solving the problem. Our people are so well convinced of this that no other method is ever mentioned. Such institutions must be established on American soil. Likewise, everybody concedes that only a religious order can maintain such seminaries for poor boys because such institutions must have a sufficient and assured income. Lay brothers by their work can provide this support. Unfortunately, endowments are so far non-existent. Thus, only an order that has lay brothers can hope to succeed at present. A mendicant order cannot carry out such a plan because it possesses no property. Therefore, the situation that confronts us calls for an older order that in addition to its priests also has lay brothers. This is the Benedictine Order with its

---

[8]The German text adds that there is also a "large, beautiful church" and another large building, both of brick.

[9]Footnote 59 in Wimmer: *Letters*, 50, points out that Fr. Boniface here means that there is no Catholic seminary exclusively for German-speaking students.

varied membership. Here our Order has all the opportunities to rise to new life. I defended this theory in Bavaria, and now I am glad to find it confirmed here by experience.

How far this Benedictine foundation corresponds to those ideals, only the future can tell. Everything is dependent upon the blessing of God who can give both the inspiration and the fulfillment. Anyone who considers the meager means with which the start had to be made, may be somewhat concerned, and, as for me, my friends and acquaintances cannot be more so than I. However, they may also have good hope, for, as history teaches, everything that God does, tends to begin small and slowly, proceeds gradually, and often succeeds contrary to human plans and expectations. Also, we must remember that God can raise children of Abraham from stones.

This is the basis of my hope and confidence. The foundation is laid, the beginning made, the temporal support given—not only for me and my companions but also for others who are willing to work with us. What we need most now are good priests, or such who soon can become priests and who have a true vocation for religious life. I do not doubt that Lord will send them because He knows best what is most necessary here.

Although our community is not yet fully organized, we are keeping the following order as well as we can. We rise at 3:45 o'clock to meet in the parish church where at 4:00 o'clock, I say Matins and Lauds with the four students in the choir loft while the brothers recite one-third of the Rosary and other prayers in the sanctuary in front of the high altar. At 5:00 o'clock, when the sign is given, meditation begins and lasts an hour. After that, I say conventual Mass. This is followed by a frugal breakfast for the brothers while we [Wimmer and the clerical students] recite Prime, during which the *Martyrology* and a chapter from the *Holy Rule* are read. The rest of the morning, the brothers work and the students attend classes or study, with a short interruption at 9:00 o'clock, when we recite the Minor Hours.

At 10:45 o'clock, all are called again to the church for adoration of the Blessed Sacrament and particular examination of conscience. At 11:00 o'clock, we take dinner, after which the students have a short recreation and the brothers receive instruction in the religious life. At 1:00 o'clock, the brothers recite the second part of the Rosary and then work until 5:00 o'clock. During that time, the students have classes or lectures, which are interrupted by the recitation of Vespers at 3:00 pm. All attend spiritual reading or the explanation of the *Holy Rule* from 5:00 to 6:00 o'clock, when the brothers recite the third part of the Rosary and we say Compline. Finally, common night prayers and general examination of conscience conclude the day. At 9:00 o'clock all retire... [letter incomplete][10]

At 9:00 o'clock everyone goes to bed; i.e. on the straw sack—for the feathers still have to be grown. Thus our days pass, one after the other, alternating beautifully between work and prayer, and although the days are longer here in winter than in Bavaria, they are still too short for us, because we have work in abundance. Primarily most of the work is preparatory, especially construction of workshops so that the carpenters, smiths, and locksmiths can begin their activities. In the spring we will then have to proceed with building to make room for a number of brothers, whom I expect to come from Bavaria, and for pupils. Some of the existing farm buildings also need to be renovated or new ones built.

We would welcome additional experienced carpenters, masons, and joiners, who would also have to do some other work if circumstances required, and who have a calling to the monastic life. They would, however, also need to be able to get along without Bavarian beer, since we have nothing to drink here but good, fresh, and healthy water. With this news about our experiences so far, I would also like to express my sincere gratitude to all the generous benefactors who have supported me and my companions in any way, and to assure them that our remembrance of them will always be very precious to us, and that we pray for them daily.

Praised be Jesus Christ!
Father Boniface Wimmer
Superior of the Benedictine Mission

---

[10]Thus ends the translated letter in Wimmer, *Letters*. But the letter continues in Moosmüller's book, 67, rendered here in our translation.

This letter, written so simply and naturally, characterizes the right man at the right place. At the same time, it reveals that the hand of Providence has already been at work. Someone who set about with such determination and such modest demands, in order to establish a monastery, could not be lacking blessings from above. The Court Chaplain, who can rightfully be called a co-founder of St. Vincent, hurried to express his complete satisfaction with this report by replying as follows:[11]

Munich, November 25, 1846

Reverend, most esteemed friend, beloved son![12]

I was overjoyed at your letter of the 26th and, with me, all those who wish you well.[13] Even more, it pleased me to learn from you that you did not take on Lemke's lands but rather took possession of the land offered by your bishop.... [14]

Our new Archbishop is actively[15] involved in the mission society and is quite well-disposed towards you....

I will probably send you a count as a new member, namely Pastor Marogna,[16] until now in Breitenthal, who resigned his parish and is becoming a missionary. He is a pious and upright priest. His brother is envoy in Turin....

Be so good, as to make out a warrant of reception either to me or to the Director Fr. Lacence,[17] so that things will go more quickly. Now I

[11]The translation of the text of the complete letter can be found in ASVA, J.F. Müller to B. Wimmer, 3.

[12]In a number of his early letters, Fr. Müller addresses Fr. Boniface as "son."

[13]The text of the largest part of the letter can be found in Wimmer: *Letters* (2008), 49-52.

[14] This represents a change from the view he expressed in his previous letter of 5 October. The change may have come about due to the bishop's intervention. It also indicates the good working relationship between the two men, one which would develop further in the future; for while the Court Chaplain made strong recommendations and at times expressed disagreement, he also acknowledged and supported Fr. Boniface's need to make decisions in the actual situation.

[15]This word is an estimated translation of an unclear word (schützig?) in the German. The new archbishop was Karl August Graf von Reisach, who had been bishop in Eichstätt and became archbishop in Munich in 1846. As archbishop and, accordingly, also president of the Ludwig Missionsverein, 1846-1855, he was a major benefactor of the Benedictine mission in the United States.

[16]Charles de Marogna was born in Villa Lagarina, Tyrol, on 17 September 1803. He was ordained to the priesthood on 30 March 1826. He made profession as a Benedictine monk at Saint Vincent on 21 August 1853. For a time he was prior at Saint Vincent and later at the foundation in Minnesota that became St. John's. He died on 27 March 1869.

[17][original footnote] R.P. Plazidus Lacense, O.S.B. was born on 26 April 1802 in Regensburg, was ordained priest on 1 May 1825, and made profession at Metten on 26 May 1839. For many years he served as Director of the Hollandeum [Royal Academic] Institute in Munich.

am no longer worried in your regard. You are out of danger. The Lord guides everything for the best. The Holy Spirit once again has shown the way....

On the feast day of Saint Francis Xavier our Archbishop is preaching and the Nuntius is celebrant at the high Mass. Your bishop is valued by him because he was his student (at the Propaganda in Rome)....

Jos. Ferd. Müller, Court Chaplain

Father Boniface was well aware that he would have to serve a kind of novitiate for the bishop of Pittsburgh, for it was a mark of wisdom that the bishop should exercise caution in regard to a foreign priest who had just recently come to the country. Even though the references Father Boniface had brought along from the Archbishop of Munich, the Abbot of Metten, and the Bishop of Regensburg highly recommended him, he nevertheless could not just give him a position as a pastor right away,[18] nor were the positive references proof that Father Boniface actually had the ability to carry out an undertaking like the projected one, successfully. Only a few years earlier, a priest with six well-disposed young men had opened an educational institution at the same place in St. Vincent. Even though these had an advantage over Father Boniface and his companions in that English was their mother tongue, their undertaking foundered. What was more reasonable, then, than that the bishop considered it his duty to observe the further progress patiently, so that what had already happened once would not be repeated due to excessive haste.

The property on which Father Boniface lived with his companions and where he planned to establish his monastery, he could not acquire through purchase, but only by being canonically installed as pastor of St. Vincent; however, to install a priest in this manner in a mission country like the United States was not considered opportune. Accordingly, as a precaution, and to prove his sincere agreement with the undertaking, the most reverend bishop issued the following document on November 5, wherein he appoints him as pastor *pro tempore:* [19]

I have named the most reverend Father Boniface Wimmer, of the Order of St. Benedict, pastor of the church of St. Vincent, near Youngstown, in this Diocese. As pastor, he has a legal right to the property of approximately 500 acres, which, it seems to me, should be more than sufficient for the support of 50 monks, if it is properly farmed. This farm is the property of whoever is the current pastor. However, I am willing to arrange matters in such a manner that the Superior of the Benedic-

---

[18] [original footnote] Provided that the necessary permission from the Holy See was given.
[19] This letter does not appear in *An American Abbot,* except for two brief quotes from it (p.75)

tine monastery that is to be established there is to be the pastor forever and to leave to him the complete and uncontested right to the use of this property. By giving the pastor the use of this property, no further obligation can is imposed other than that he, himself, or through a vicar, will take care of priestly ministry for the benefit of the people of the surrounding area. As soon as the Benedictine priests are willing to take over this parish forever, I will grant them such right, so that no one could contest it, either before a secular or an ecclesiastical court. I would also be pleased if they would establish other monasteries in this Diocese, where they themselves would live a monastic life, as well as devote themselves to the education of young people for the secular or clerical state, and for priestly ministry.

Given at St. Vincent near Youngstown in the state of Pennsylvania on

November 5, A.D. 1846.
+Michael O'Connor
Bishop of Pittsburgh

Although this document was valid only *pro tempore*, Father Boniface was very grateful for it, for under the circumstances, he could not expect more. For this reason, he hurried to report this happy news to his untiring benefactor in Munich. The Court Chaplain replied in his fatherly manner:[20]

Munich, December 23, 1846

I received your two letters and see from them how God has guided everything for the best. You have settled in St. Vincent. Fine, but there is one thing which I ask you, *do not forget the Germans.* You went to America to protect, teach, raise them, etc. That was also our intent.... Therefore if you wish to count on continuing support, I must impress upon you, that you "do not neglect the Germans."[21]

[Pray often for your Reverence's most devoted and warmest friend,] [22]
Jos. Ferd. Müller, Court Chaplain

---

[20]This is an excerpt from a letter, which can be found in full in ASVA, J.F. Müller to B. Wimmer, 4.

[21]He underlined this thought above. Here it is in quotation marks; perhaps it is a quote from King Ludwig.

[22]The words in brackets have been copied from the original text and added here to indicate something of the warm relationship between the two men.

The court chaplain never wrote long letters, but what he wrote was clear and unambiguous. He was happy, on the one hand, about the advantages that the property at St. Vincent offered over that of Father Lemke's—a milder climate, better ground, and even more in that there were an existing church and other buildings. On the other hand, he was concerned that the true purpose of the mission—to care for the German immigrants by raising priests from among their own sons—might be put on the back burner because half the congregation did not speak German and the other half only Pennsylvania Dutch. Father Boniface and his companions had recovered from the hardships of their lengthy journey, had set themselves up in the limited living space available at St. Vincent for

Joseph Ferdinand Müller

the time being, and were starting to feel at home. They appreciated this place all the more because they had felt so disappointed in their expectations upon their arrival in Carrolltown. All of them now experienced their "first fervor," and in spite of their poverty, they felt fortunate and looked full of hope toward a promising future. After they had spent three months here, Father Boniface painted the following picture about their activities for the Augsburger *Sion*. The letter is dated February 1, 1847:[23]

> "You have probably received my first letter in which I announced my fortunate arrival at St. Vincent. Soon it will be four months that we have been living and working here, laboring, building, praying. While blacksmith and locksmith pound the anvil so that the sound rings out far and wide, 4 - 6 men cut down trees in the woods when the weather is favorable or split shingles under a safe roof, when it is storming and blustery outside. The hand of the saddler has already produced four new harnesses for the horses and two riding saddles, although he has a lot of work besides, repairing shoes and boots, which are gradually falling apart. The tailor has not yet finished all the habits and their accessories, because he is simultaneously also the binder or the cooper and besides must at times work with the hoe or the saw. Usually every-

---

[23]The *Sion* was a religious periodical published in Augsburg: Karl Kollmann, 1832-1872. Fr. Boniface's letter was printed in *Sion* 16 (17 Feb 1847) 193-197.

one works at his own trade, but at my order, everyone needs to help out anywhere where something needs done. This is necessary, but is always done willingly. One brother hauls coal, firewood, or timber or takes manure to the fields with four horses (I should have ten), while another brother looks after the cattle, the sheep and the pigs.

Two brothers are busy with preparations for the building of a saw mill, two are in the kitchen. The baker is quite busy trying to keep us in bread because it is our main staple, and the oven is very small. At the same time, he takes care of the laundry, but he does get a helper for that. My four seminarians are quite busy with intellectual activities; however, when the weather is good and circumstances require it, they also have to do physical work. Thus the cleaning of the church every Saturday is their responsibility. They also usually have to clean the house, take care of the sacristy, the sanctuary lamp, and whatever else falls to the task of the sacristan. My humble self directs all of it, but this is not difficult because all are willing to listen, stand together and support each other like brothers, enjoy working and do not like to be idle. However, as active as the hands are at work, everyone nevertheless immediately puts his tools down when the bell calls them to the church in order there to review the hours of the day that have passed, to improve what is necessary to improve, to reinforce what was good, or to offer Jesus Christ in the most Blessed Sacrament the adoration, honor and love that he so completely deserves!

We have motivation enough for this, for in all of the beautiful little countryside of Westmoreland, there is no church beside ours where the most Blessed Sacrament is reserved, and besides, no one comes to our church all week long except for me and my brothers. At times, it seems quite burdensome to go to the church seven times a day (the first time at four o'clock in the morning and the last time at half past seven in the evening), when it storms or snows severely, or when it rains in buckets, or when the melting snow makes every step toward the church muddy, or when the cutting North American wind chills you to the bone. However, I have never given in to the temptation not to go, because it hurts too much to see the most Blessed Sacrament, that is, Jesus Christ in it, to be so abandoned. Actually, it is a major consolation for me that it has, in a way, fallen to me and my brothers to remedy this sad situation and to make up for the lukewarmness of the Catholics and the unbelief of the Protestants. O, may it be granted to me to increase the number of those who will worship Jesus Christ and to make this church the center from which the Catholic faith and pious living will spread in all directions! There is much hope that this can happen.

The Protestants are divided into an amazing number of sects, which has given the better ones among them and those who are thinkers a distaste for any religious community, and they prefer either to attend no church at all or a Catholic one. The desire to become acquainted with our faith and doctrines is quite strong among many. Recently, a number of invitations were extended to my very reverend confrere, Father Michael,[24] to preach to some English Protestants. He did this on three different occasions (for which they sent the horse to carry him the 18 miles to them) and generated much serious interest. I also have been invited by German Protestants on the other side of the mountains, seven hours from here, to preach to them; but, unfortunately, I have not yet been able to fulfill my promise, partly because of the bad weather and partly because of pressing business. Why, recently one even came to my house to argue with me about faith issues which he then did with zeal and, in his way, with much skill! A few of his good friends were to be witnesses. When I had calmly knocked his weapons out of his hands and gotten him to the point where he didn't know anything more to say, he took leave (he is a native Bavarian from the area near Ansbach) and promised to be back when his son would be home from the university and could accompany him – he is studying to become a Lutheran pastor. I have shown myself in my habit in every place from where I was able to return home the same day.

I did attract some attention by this, but insult or mockery has not been directed at me. I hope the Protestants will in time get accustomed to seeing a monk, as they have learned to see and tolerate Catholics, for according to reports of the older people, no Catholic could identify himself publicly as such, as recently as fifty years ago. Now it is different. Occasionally our people do get a Protestant barb, but they know how to parry and give as good as they get.

Everyone recognizes that in this matter also, prayer will need to ac-

---

[24]This was Fr. Michael Gallagher, who stayed on as assistant pastor to help with the English-speaking parishioners.

complish most of it, for knowledge is not what is lacking, but desire. Where the truth is to be found, many are well aware and most have an idea; but pride, assimilated prejudices and indifference prevent them from seeking it. Yesterday the doctor of Derry, a little town two hours away from here, sent us a person who up to now was an unbeliever. He wanted us to pray for him because he wanted to be baptized and die a Catholic, for he was very ill. Ever since his family had become Catholic four years earlier, he had felt considerable inclination toward our church; even so, he delayed his baptism until today. However, many Catholics also live without church and priest because they are too far away from both, are too much among Protestants, and the priest does not know about them.

My parish covers a whole county of 42,000 inhabitants scattered over 19 towns and many individual farms. How long it takes for the shepherd to get to know his sheep! Those farthest away need eight to nine hours to get to church. Only when there will be more churches and smaller parishes will real ministry be possible. However, the people are mighty glad that there now is worship every Sunday, whereas only a few years ago it did not occur more often than every other week. Yet, priests are lacking, self-sacrificing priests, who would come here only in order to win souls. There would be plenty of work for them everywhere and they would reap the richest reward in most blessed success.

Yes, priests are what is lacking most here. However, at least I am no longer the only Benedictine here. The Most Blessed Virgin brought me a confrere on December 8, the Feast of her Immaculate Conception. It is the Irish priest Michael Gallagher, who had served the local parish for two years before my arrival. He generously relinquished it to make the establishment of the monastery possible and remained only to help out with the English-speaking Catholics. He at first quietly watched our activities, then participated in choir and all the other religious exercises, and on that day, after we had together implored God for light, he requested the habit after Mass, which I gave to him with joy.

My most reverend confrere, Father Nicolaus Baleis from St. Peter (Abbey) in Salzburg, also has voluntarily put himself under my obedience. However, his position at Newark is too important for me to call him away from there. Instead of getting help from him, I rather need to send help to him. I counted for certain on Father Gruber and waited for him with longing. However, he allowed the most reverend vicar general Raffeiner of New York to lure him away and went to Albany on January 3, where he took over the ministry to the Catholic Germans. Better now than later! (The Vicar General actually might have wanted to see me lured away, too, to get discouraged and give up my undertaking, had he been able.) A few days after I received this news, a valiant layman surprised me with his fortunate and unexpected arrival. It was the teacher A. Pühler from Zorneding, who had cheerfully overcome all obstacles to his departure that presented themselves, and arrived here safely after a good journey of 50 days (December 1 to January 20). He was incredibly welcome to me because, until then, I had had to do without celebrating ecclesiastical and Order feast days in choir due to lack of an organist. It seems the merciful Mother of Our Lord brought him to us. Since February 2 to 9 are days of indulgence here, I used this celebration for an eight-day long devotion in honor of the most Blessed Virgin to ask for her protection for our young monastery, and already the third day brought us the joy of receiving such a dear confrere! I also accepted a man from the Upper Palatinate, who has already been here five months, and two poor boys, so that we are now 25 in total. As yet, none of the brothers has run off, though that had repeatedly been prophesied to me. Rather, as far as I know, they are all well content, and I with them. May God be content with all of us!

We do suffer a good deal from winter. There is nothing nastier than an American winter. Up until close to Christmas the weather is rather mild. However, then it gets ferociously cold. At times, there is pouring rain, then east and north winds bring loads of snow, which the southern sun licks off a few days later. Thus, the weather is always changing and so suddenly at that, that it is not rare for two extremes to occur within one hour. The consequences are colds, catarrh, rheumatism, toothaches. For this reason, I am much obliged to Dr. Benedict Buchner, who introduced me to the knowledge of homoeopathic medicine and equipped me amply with a pharmacy of these medications. This has made it possible for me to help not only myself and my brothers, but also many other people.

Will I take in yet more brothers? I would indeed be very happy to accept a cartwright, as well as a cabinet maker and a competent bricklayer who would be knowledgeable enough to draw up a building plan and work from it. I would also be happy to have a carpenter, if he would have an inclination to the monastic life and would be content with what we have. Actually, I could use many more, such as a Benedictine or two from Metten or another Bavarian monastery; or priests who would take monastic life seriously, or good and well-versed theologians or philosophers who have obtained their degrees. If I would get the means to set things up properly, in such a manner as a large farming operation requires, I could support 50 men here, both priests and brothers; and if there should be more, they could easily be placed elsewhere. Anyone who might desire admission should contact Court Chaplain Müller in Munich (at Maxburg), in order to get more information. However, no one should imagine that there are mountains of gold here.

America is not Germany, and there is only one Bavaria. Many of the Bavarian immigrants who live out in the country have only water to drink, which is often not even good. If they knew that at home, most of them would have no reason to emigrate. I have already met many who are not doing well. It is a hard struggle for them and they barely make ends meet. As is the case everywhere, the fortunate are but few.

Father Boniface Wimmer

CHAPTER SIX

History of the Parish of St. Vincent. A loyal friend.
Worries and tribulations of Fr. Boniface. Fr. Petrus Lechner
of Scheyern comes to St. Vincent with eighteen brothers.

Fr. Boniface was about to make the parish of St. Vincent in Western Pennsylvania the foundation of his monastery. Therefore it will be of interest to learn when and how this parish, its church, and its property had their beginning, especially since it was the oldest parish in the Diocese of Pittsburgh.

The seeds of the establishment of the parish of St. Vincent date back to the year 1787. That year, and the next, six Catholic families moved from German settlements near Philadelphia in order to settle west of the Allegheny Mountains, in Westmoreland County, not far from Greensburg. In March of 1789 they bought a piece of ground in Greensburg in order to build a church on it and to establish a cemetery. Soon afterward several other families from Goschenhoppen, which is located 45 miles west of Philadelphia, joined them. The latter had been promised that a priest would visit them from time to time and would give them the opportunity to receive the holy sacraments. This promise was kept. Before that year was ended, as Heinrich Kuhn,[1] an eye witness, reported to us personally, the Rev. Johann B. Cause came and celebrated the holy Mass at the house of Johann Probst in the month of June.

In the fall of the year 1789 the Rev. Theodor Brouwers, Ord. Min., arrived in the area. This priest was born in Holland, entered the Order of St. Francis Minor, and worked as a missionary in the West Indies. No further details about his earlier life are known. His health was poor and he died after only one year here, on Oct. 30, 1790. When Fr. Brouwers landed in Philadelphia, probably in the month of July of the year 1789, he went to live with Fr. Peter Helbronn, pastor of St. Mary's Church. Attempts were made to persuade him to stay in the city, but to no avail, because Fr. Brouwers had in the meantime made a plan for himself, which he wanted to carry out before the end of his life. His intention was to go to the Far West —that is how all land west of the Allegheny Mountains was called at the time—in order to establish a church for poor settlers who did not have one. After he heard about the Catholic settlers in Westmoreland County, he bought a piece of land, comprised of 162 acres, prior to

---

[1]This would be Henry Kuhn III, who was at that time yet a young boy.

leaving Philadelphia; it was known as "O'Neil's Victory," located seven miles from St. Vincent, along the Loyalhanna Creek.

As already noted, he came to Greensburg soon after this and lived at Christian Ruffner's until he would build a house and a chapel on his own place. Accompanied by Heinrich Kuhn he went to look at his piece of land in order to choose a suitable site on which to erect the buildings. Mr. H. Kuhn[2] felt that the location was too remote for access for many of the Catholic settlers. So Fr. Brouwers abandoned his plans, and was soon persuaded to buy another piece of property, which was located more centrally in the parish. This place, then called "Sportmans Hall," belonged to Joseph Hunter of Harrisburg. The parcel of 313 acres had a sales price of 475 pounds sterling. On this piece of ground there was only a small cabin around which a few acres had been cleared. The rest was woods. The purchase was made on April 16, 1799, in the presence of William Mapher and Joseph Cook.

Right afterwards Fr. Brouwers had a house built there, one and a half stories high and 17 ft. square. However, the health of this good missionary was already so poor that he often fainted during Holy Mass on Sundays the following summer, since he had to fast until noon. It was evident that the days of his life were numbered. For this reason he made his will, in which he directed that this property which he had purchased was to belong in perpetuity to whoever was his legitimate successor as Catholic priest of the parish. In the year 1834 Fr. Stillinger built a beautiful brick church on the property which Fr. Brouwers had procured. It was built on the same spot on which the log chapel [built in 1810] originally stood, and measured 87 ft. long and 51.5 ft. wide. It was blessed on July 19, 1835, the feast of St. Vincent de

Sportsman's Hall

---

[2]This would be Henry Kuhn II, who died in 1808 and is buried in Saint Vincent Cemetery.

Paul, by the Most Very Reverend Bishop Kenrick, D.D., of Philadelphia, assisted by the Rev. Peter Lemke and James Stillinger. This is now also the church of the present St. Vincent Abbey. The Diocese of Pittsburgh was only established eight years later.

> "A faithful friend is a sturdy shelter; he who finds one finds a treasure.
> A faithful friend is beyond price, no sum can balance his worth" (Sirach
> 6: 14-15).[3]

The truth of these words was also proven in the young monastic community of St. Vincent. If it is true that "all beginnings are difficult," it was all the more so for Fr. Boniface and his brothers, since they had to lay the ground work for a great endeavor far from their homeland, in a strange country, not knowing the language, burdened by poverty and obstacles. The soul of the whole undertaking was Fr. Boniface. He was the leader; everyone looked to him, and he was well aware how important it was for him to keep up his courage and energy. From time to time, and though his heart also grew heavy, the arrival of a friendly little letter from his most loyal friend, Court Chaplain Müller, was like soothing and healing balm on the wound. He often wrote every week, or at least a few times a month, and his letters contained wise counsel, like a father's to his son. Besides that, some substantial help in the form of a check was enclosed. An example of the above is the little letter of May 4:[4]

> Munich, May 4, 1847
> My Reverend Friend!
>
> ...At the last meeting [of the Mission Verein] 4500 fl were allocated to you for this year. You can count on that. In August I sent you a bill of exchange for 100 pounds sterling as journey money....
> Now continue on in your zeal and caution; and I will not tire doing everything possible for you.
>
> Jos. Ferd. Müller, Court Chaplain

In several letters Fr. Boniface had expressed the wish that a few priests from the monasteries of Metten, Scheyern, or St. Stephan in Augsburg, might come to help out at St. Vincent, at least for a few years. Since none of the respective abbots of these monasteries had so far taken any steps in that direction, the Court Chaplain did not rest content with his repeated urgent petitions in writing. Instead, he decided to intensify his untiring efforts by getting on the road and traveling in person from one monastery to the other in April 1847, in order to accomplish his goal.

---

[3]Translations throughout this text are according to *The New American Bible* (Nashville: Catholic Bible Press, 1986.

[4]The full text of the letter can be found in ASVA, J.F. Müller to B. Wimmer, letter 7.

He presented his case to the abbots and their conventuals, suggesting that it was not only honorable and meritorious, but also appropriate that they should send at least one or two priests to help out the good Fr. Boniface for a couple of years. Indeed, the abbots had to confess that the zeal and solicitousness with which the Court Chaplain concerned himself for the foundation of a Benedictine monastery in America almost put them to shame, and that they should consider it a duty, rather than a mere act of charity, to support the enterprising Fr. Boniface. At the same time the abbots explained that they were not entitled to give orders in this regard, but could merely make a proposal to their capitulars. In case one or another of the priests would volunteer for the mission, they would grant him permission to go to America.[5]

How fortunate the Court Chaplain felt, when his zeal for this good cause was finally rewarded by each of the three abbots agreeing to offer help for "his St. Vincent," as he liked to call it. Scheyern wanted to be the first, and right away, since "quick help is double help." The other two monasteries felt they needed to delay their help until the following year.

Since the Court Chaplain considered it particularly important that the priest who would be sent would function as professor of theology for the clerics, as well as a novice master, the community of Scheyern decided that Fr. Peter Lechner would be the best suited man for these offices. Fr. Peter, whole-heartedly devoted to being a monk, agreed, since a gentle wish from his Superior already was a command for him. He was born March 7, 1805, at Pfaffenhofen. In the year 1829 he attained a doctorate in theology, and on November 1, 1839 he made his solemn profession at Scheyern. He combined in himself all the traits of a scholar and an ascetic, which one could only wish for in a professor, a novice master, and a prior for the young yet-to-be-formed monastic community of St. Vincent. He is also well-known as an author, as more than thirty works have been published as fruits of his studies.

A few weeks after this, Fr. Peter and his eighteen travel companions, the brother-candidates, started to prepare for the journey and their future calling by participating in a spiritual retreat. On June 3 they boarded the sailing vessel "Cumberland" in Bremerhaven. As soon as the journey started, Fr. Peter, a practical ascetic, introduced the brothers to the daily schedule, as it is customarily followed in monasteries. At certain hours, morning, noon, and evening, they prayed the rosary aloud together. He also instructed them in daily meditations. On Sundays he preached to all their fellow passengers, as well as the ship's crew. Altogether there were 400 persons on the Cumberland, some of which had very mixed reactions in regard to religion. Nevertheless no one on the ship could refuse to respect the humble and learned monk. Their journey was repeatedly delayed due to unfavorable winds, so that they reached the Azores only on June 28. When they beheld a Catholic church among the steep

---

[5]Fr. Oswald paints a rather benign portrayal of the situation, since the Bavarian abbots were hard-pressed to address adequately their own man-power needs and were reluctant to grant permission for this venture. That they indeed would provide some help was an act of generous, greatly needed assistance .

cliffs on the southern island of Santa Maria, they felt as though it was the loveliest sight they had ever laid eyes on. The following day they passed the larger island, San Miguel. Finally, on the afternoon of July 19, their eyes espied the wooded hills of Newfoundland in the gray distance. After they had passed Grace Island in the St. Lawrence River on the 27th of the month, they landed at Quebec on July 30. Here they boarded a steamboat, which brought them to Montreal. From there they continued their journey across Lake Champlain, then by canal to Troy. A steamboat on the Hudson River brought them from there to New York, which they reached on August 7. They traveled by train as far as Harrisburg, where they boarded a canal boat which took them to Blairsville. The rest of the 16 miles to St. Vincent they covered on foot. They finally arrived there in the evening of August 17, exhausted but happy.

There was joy in the house, great joy, because brothers had come to brothers. Everyone went to the church right away, the ones to give thanks to the Lord for their safe journey, the others for the help they were receiving. Fr. Boniface named Fr. Peter prior, and transferred almost all responsibility for the spiritual education of his young monastic community to him. However, he did not in the least dictate to him regarding this task, but left everything to his judgment. Fr. Peter, for his part, proved himself to be completely worthy of the trust placed in him. He was in the right place, being that theology and ascetics were his main preoccupations. Accordingly, he kept very close watch over the studies of the clerics.

Along with the arrival of his new confreres Fr. Boniface received a significant amount of financial support, which increased the confidence in his undertaking in various quarters, since it became evident that he must have powerful friends across the "great waters." On October 9 the second investiture took place, with two clerics and fourteen lay brothers receiving the habit.

In the meantime Court Chaplain Müller waited with concern for a letter announcing the safe arrival of his esteemed friend, Fr. Peter, and the brothers. Finally he could not wait any longer and so wrote to Fr. Boniface on August 22:[6]

> Munich, August 22, 1847
> Most reverend friend:
>
> I have been waiting for ever for notice that Fr. Prior Lechner and his companions have arrived safe and sound, but up to now I have waited in vain. And I must send on my bills of exchange that I promised you by the end of August, without having heard about the fate of these good people. You are receiving enclosed 2 bills of exchange, the one for 120 pounds, the other for 80, which I bought for the sum of 2428 fl. The

---

[6]The full text of the letter can be found at ASVA, J.F. Müller to B. Wimmer, letter 11.

other half you will receive at the latest by the beginning of December, so that you can arrange your promises of payment accordingly. If I am able to send you money earlier, this certainly will happen....

We have begun with God and with his help and grace we will also reach the goal that we have laid out....

Jos. Ferd. Müller

Just as a contractor has to make sure to build a solid and safe foundation above all else, so Fr. Boniface considered it to be his duty to secure for his Order the title to the land on which he wanted to build his monastery. He had already been informed that the property did not belong to his bishop, so he would not have been able to obtain the desired title from him. Fr. Theodor Brouwers had purchased the property, and had deeded it in his will to whoever would be his legitimate successor as pastor of St. Vincent. Soon after Fr. Brouwers' death the parish became entangled in an unpleasant legal proceeding regarding this land. Later, the legislature of the State of Pennsylvania, in response to a petition, handed the management of the two properties deeded by Fr. Brouwers, Sportsmans Hall and O'Neil's Victory, to a committee of five men, who were to be elected yearly for this purpose by the Catholic parish of Westmoreland County. These men were to manage these properties according to the rules and laws of their church and to use them for the benefit and purpose that had been listed and designated by the testator in his will. This act of the legislature was signed on March 7, 1821 A.D., by the Governor, Joseph Heister, the Speaker of the House of Representatives, John Gilmore, as well as by the Speaker of the Senate, William Marks, Jr., and was thus given force of law.

The worries and apprehension that haunted Fr. Boniface during the first few years of his residence in America can only be appreciated when we consider the unpleasant experience he had had since his ordination in a European police state, whose government oppressed the Church like a sinister nightmare. As soon as Fr. Boniface had made the decision to emigrate to America, he made plans for his undertaking in such a manner as would be most suitable for a country whose government left the churches to the churches, following the practical motto, "Help yourself," and where the government did not pay a salary to either bishops or priests, but where they were also not required to serve as census marshals or provide lists of recruits. Now, however, when Fr. Boniface had chosen the place for his foundation, now that he already stood at the threshold of the building of his monastery, he was himself forced to adjust to a situation very different from what he had expected. As inviting as the area at St. Vincent seemed, he nevertheless felt it as a heavy burden should it be impossible for him to receive an unencumbered title to the property, and that it would be necessary for him and his monastery to remain under the governance of the trustees. Additionally, he was concerned about the conditions which the diocesan bishop might impose on the monastery. The beautiful images of a free and independent monastery foundation gradually started to lose their vivid colors in his mind. He was hearing some things about the trustees of the St. Vincent parish from the past that were by no means very encouraging, and the only thing that let him hope for a better future was the thought that their unpleasant past experiences would finally make them tired of conflict.

Fr. Boniface corresponded frequently with the reverend bishop in order to seek his counsel regarding his plans. Bishop O'Connor and Fr. Boniface were in complete agreement regarding the final goal, that is, the establishment of a monastery and a seminary for boys. However, their opinions diverged regarding the execution of the plan. Fr. Boniface had designed his plans in Germany, before his departure to America, before he really knew the land, the people, and the language. He had imagined that he would settle in the middle of a vast forest, far from any city and any traffic, on the outer reaches of civilization, as it were, where he would not expect any help from anyone other than his friends in Bavaria, where he and his brothers would support themselves by the work of their hands. Here he wanted, like the Benedictines of the Middle Ages, to create a model operation of farming and animal husbandry, which would enable him not only to sustain a large monastic family, but also a school for boys, without having to depend on the tuition of the students for the support of his institutions. He had made it his mission to primarily take care of Germans, and to assure the education of boys from German families.

At first glance one can see that this plan of Fr. Boniface was born of a reaction in his mind, a disgust against the government control of the Church in his old homeland, and from a yearning for the priceless freedom of America, for which no effort or hardship would be too much to expend. This idea alone, and even more its implementation, are worthy of a strong spirit; for only a noble, self-sacrificing personality could take it upon himself to leave his homeland, his prestigious and secure position, friends and colleagues who loved and appreciated him. And why? In order to go to a faraway and foreign country and to lead a life full of the greatest hardships and privations, in order to undertake the foundation of a monastery under circumstances that seemed quixotic and risky even to those who were enthusiastic supporters of the Benedictine Order and the missions.

Bishop O'Connor, intimately acquainted with the conditions in the country, respected the generous intentions of Fr. Boniface. Right from the beginning he had set him on the best track toward the achievement of his goal by transferring to him the church and the property at St. Vincent. Little by little he also tried to persuade him to use means that were readily available and very suited for implementing his plans more speedily. Above all the bishop wished that Fr. Boniface would also accept boys who spoke English, because this would mean that his young priests, clerics, and novices would have the best opportunity to learn the English language right in their own home. Also, by accepting such boys from the Diocese of Pittsburgh, the monastery would be making itself useful to a wider area and in that manner earn the good will of the priests and of the people. Finally, it would provide additional income for the monastery, even if it were not a lot. The bishop declared that he did not by any means wish that the boys he would send to St. Vincent for and from the Diocese of Pittsburgh would become a burden; rather he was willing to pay a moderate tuition for them.

On April 14, 1847, Bishop O'Connor wrote a letter to Fr. Boniface with the offer to send him several students along with an English-speaking priest, who would serve as a professor. He presented all the details clearly, so that Fr. Boniface might be able to see that he would benefit from this arrangement also. The latter, however, was not convinced that his original plan was not the better one. The yearning for preserving his independence as much as possible had taken root too deeply in his heart for him to be able to make a decision to accept responsibilities that he could not fulfill by his own or his monastery's resources, i.e., without outside help. With this in mind he responded to the above letter from the bishop.

In order to get a clear idea of the dilemma in which Fr. Boniface found himself, and because of which any progress in his undertaking was impeded for the time being, we will briefly summarize the concerns about his position which continually preoccupied him:

1) If he were to die, his brothers would have to leave St. Vincent immediately, and in case they had made any improvements or built any buildings, they would not be able to claim any compensation.

2) It was in the bishop's power to send Fr. Boniface away at anytime, not only from the St. Vincent parish, but also from the diocese. In each of these instances the brothers would be left homeless and on their own, and all the labor and money invested in the buildings they erected would be lost to them and to the Order.

3) On the other hand, if he had purchased some unencumbered piece of property elsewhere, the Order and his brothers would be able to keep it for their home if anything were to happen to him. And they would be able to enjoy the use whatever improvements or construction they would have made on that property.

4) He was upset by the awareness that he himself was not able to fulfill his duties as a priest toward the English-speaking members of his parish.

5) He realized that under the existing circumstances it would be very risky to establish a seminary which he would be able to manage only with outside help.

Fr. Boniface presented his concerns to the reverend bishop in numerous letters and sought his counsel. The latter made a real effort to bring about a satisfactory agreement, as can be gleaned from the following letter:[7]

Pittsburgh, May 13, 1847

Very reverend B. Wimmer, O.S.B.!

It seems to me that you are of the opinion that I have demanded much more from you than I actually have done. However, I hoped that all concerns would have been resolved by way of the conversation with Mr. M...so, in order to remove all doubts, I am offering two basic conditions from which I have had no intention to deviate, nor plan to in the future:

1. In regard to the parish ministry, I do not want to require anything more of you than that for which the previous priest of St. Vincent had been responsible, and that comes naturally with this ministry.

2. I do not want to deprive you and yours of any funds that you are planning to use for the education of the [German] boys. All I request of you is that among the boys whose education you have made your task, you will promise also to include a few who someday will consecrate their energies to this diocese. It seems to me that there is nothing intimidating about these two requests, nor must you say that I am imposing severe conditions on you.

As far as the mission is concerned, you are offering me more that I have asked for. I did not demand that you support a diocesan priest, neither a German nor an English one, unless it were for the purpose of ministering to the English-speaking parishioners who live within the boundaries of the St. Vincent parish, until such time as the Benedictines would be able to take care of this. I would not obligate you to pastor anyone, be they German or English who lives outside of the above-named district...

Far be it from me to impose an unfair burden on anyone, even if he were to agree to it...

+ M. O'Connor

[7]Letter of M. O'Connor to B. Wimmer, ASVA, letter 14; see also *Chronicon* I, 91-100.

Fr. Boniface now also informed the bishop of what Court Chaplain Miller had written to him, namely that a Benedictine priest, along with eighteen men who wanted to become brothers, was on his way to America in order to join him. On June 26, 1847, the bishop replied to express his joy that Fr. Boniface would be getting such significant help for his growing monastery in the very near future.[8] In this letter the bishop also stressed to Fr. Boniface that one should not have a school for boys in conjunction with a monastery that was home to a theological seminary. Since Fr. Boniface had been planning to found both of these types of institutions, he would advise him to establish each in a separate location, and he made him a very good offer of a very suitable location. In making this well-intentioned offer the bishop cited the experience of others,[9] though he could also have referred to the practice of the Bavarian Benedictine Congregation, as noted in their statutes in Chapter 2, paragraph 3.

---

[8] M. O'Connor to B. Wimmer, letter 18, in ASVA; see also *Chronicon I*, 108-111.

[9] [original footnote] vgl. *Sketches of the Life, Times, and Character of the Rt. Rev. Benedict Joseph Flaget, First Bishop of Louisville*. By M.J. Spalding, D.D., Bishop of Louisville, 1852, pages 300-307.

CHAPTER SEVEN
Fr. Boniface decides to give up the parish at St. Vincent.
He visits St. Mary's Colony in Elk County.

After Fr. Boniface had already been at St. Vincent with his brothers for eleven months, he had to admit to himself that he had really not advanced the main cause of his undertaking by even one step. He had to admit to himself he had not yet found the place of which he could say, "It is good for us to be here; let us set up our tent here."[1] There was no lack of strong arms; there was no lack of skilled hands. Thirty lay brothers yearned to hear his word telling them to start building the monastery. But, how could he start to build his monastery on a piece of ground that neither he nor his Order owned, nor had any assurance of owning? According to ecclesiastical, as well as secular, law the property belonging to the church at St. Vincent was allotted only to whoever was the pastor of the parish at any given time. Fr. Boniface's assignment as pastor was, however, for the time being, subject to revocation. If he were to lose his position, which might be a possibility at any time, he would not have any Benedictine who could be his successor.

The reverend Bishop of Pittsburgh did give him his promise to "recognize as pastor of the parish whoever was the superior of the Benedictine monastery that was to be built at the church of St. Vincent, and to install him as such as soon as he would be notified of his legitimate appointment or election, provided there were no canonical impediments." However, Fr. Boniface asked himself, when would all this take place? Would not a second and maybe even a third year pass by without any results, like the first one? Should he abandon his plans now that he seemed so close to their realization? Now that so many eyes were on him? Now that so many helpers and so much in the way of means were at his disposal? No, he said to himself; things will need to be different. America was a large country, and there were other places. By the end of October 1847 he had made his decision to abandon St. Vincent and to look for another location. Consequently, he informed the reverend Bishop O'Connor of this decision in a respectful but resolute written statement.

---

[1] The saying alludes to what was said by Saint Peter on the Mount of Transfiguration (see Mt 17:4).

The difficulties that were frustrating his plans stirred a strong desire in Fr. Boniface to get better acquainted with the land of the state of Pennsylvania, and only with the "land," for he had firmly made up his mind never to establish a house of his Order in a large city. He was especially eager to see the German colony of St. Mary's in Elk County, which is located approximately 120 miles north of St. Vincent. Already more than two years earlier he had read some very interesting news about this settlement, written in the mission annals by Fr. Alexander Czwitskowitsch, C. SS. R.[2] Thus Fr. Boniface had developed the highest respect for this priest even before he had met him. He saw in him a hero who sacrificed himself for the welfare of his fellow men, who had buried himself in the dense forest, as it were, where he had to do without all the comforts of civilization, in order to create a home for the poor immigrants, where they could find a church and a school, where they could live quietly and peacefully like in a Christian oasis. He wanted to meet this Fr. Alexander; in him he saw a model of himself, and from him he wanted to learn. Fr. Boniface had already recognized the realization of some of his plans, at least to some extent, in Fr. Alexander's report of October 20, 1844, when he read the following:

"The progress (of the colony) is extraordinary; I never imagined that it would be so quick and beautiful. The settlement is growing day by day. There are already 50 families here, over 200 souls. Every week new people move in. Over a hundred families have joined together and will arrive by next spring. All are of the best character and class, so that no one dares to join who does not want to choose for himself and his descendants a Catholic life, a Catholic education, based on Catholic principles...The saw mill is in operation, but because of the continuing arrival of new settlers it can barely meet their needs, because new houses have to be built all the time. I myself am currently involved in building a frame church and a school. Here I can do as much with a hundred dollars as I could do with a thousand in the cities, and thus I can fulfill what I have had in mind for a long time, but was not able to carry out. God's Providence directs everything for the best. Since all the inhabitants are Catholics, a Catholic way of life is implanted from childhood, which makes it easier to find young men who want to join the ranks of the clergy and to become worthy native-born priests. Finally the parish is becoming independent through the support of the settlement, which is absolutely necessary for apostolic effectiveness. Shortly we will no longer need to support ourselves with begging but be able to assist all who need help, for free, according to our *Rule*; that is what the future promises, as things stand. The benefits that arise for

---

[2] The text was in *Annalen des Glaubens,* vol. 12 (20 October 1844) 377-382. It was a German translation of a letter in French written from Baltimore, 12 October 1843, printed in the *Annales de la Propagation de la Foi* (from Lyon). Fr. Alexander was described there as the superior general of the Redemptorist missionaries in America.

the Catholic Church from this settlement are great and invaluable, the true extent of which only our descendants will be able to assess fully. As for me, God has let me experience their hardships; others will have the benefits without the hardships."

At the request of the bishop, Fr. Boniface had agreed in the summer of 1847 to celebrate mass for the Catholics of the little town of Indiana once a month. Since this place is located along the road between St. Vincent and St. Mary's, about 90 miles from the latter, he decided to travel to St. Mary's in October following his regular visit to Indiana. He made the journey on horseback since the road was just about impassable for a carriage at this time of year. Heavy rains had hollowed the road out in some places; in other places branches, whole tree trunks, and tree roots covered it. Never in his life had Fr. Boniface seen a more impassable trail. In some places he had to ride through potholes filled with water and mud two to three feet deep. For nine miles the road wound through a dense pine forest with not a settlement in sight. On the third day after leaving Indiana he finally saw the "town" he had heard so much about. He stopped at a house whose residents were from Tirschenreut, and asked for directions to the church and the rectory. The people sent a boy to be his guide, since there was still a fairly lengthy stretch of woods in the middle of the so-called town, which blocked any view of what lay beyond. Having arrived at the little monastery, the Redemptorist fathers welcomed him with great joy. A few hundred steps from the church was the convent of the Sisters of Notre Dame, who were in charge of the school. Here he was surprised to find Miss von Pronath among the Sisters, a daughter of the re-founder of the abbey at Metten, as was mentioned above.

The original layout of the town covered a very large area; the streets were all named after saints; each settler received a farm, which might often be several miles distant from the church, along with a lot in town, on which he was obliged to build a house. A certain percentage of the income gained from the sale of the land was designated for the building and support of the church and the school. All this sounds very nice, but it did not remain that way for ever, for some of these arrangements, as well as the layout of the town itself, suffered considerable changes over time.

If it is true that one most values that which has been won with great effort, one can understand how precious their new home was to the first settlers, the pioneers of St. Mary's, who had paved the way for the rest. During the first years several of the settlers fell on such hard times that they not only had to prepare their bread from oat and bean flour, but actually resorted to plants growing in the wild to satisfy their hunger. Some who had already paid for their lots and built their houses on them preferred to give it all up and to leave the settlement, in order to look for work in a town. Others were prevented from doing so only because they could not come up with the means for the journey. Among the first settlers of St. Mary's there also were some men of considerable wealth. These made the greatest efforts, at considerable cost, to transform the wilderness they found into a model community, as if by magic. They had the mighty trees of the forest removed, stump and roots, built comfortable roads, created beautiful gardens, built greenhouses for flowers and rare plants, and planted tree-lined avenues. However, they found that their efforts were not crowned with the hoped for success, and they eventually also moved away, impoverished financially and disappointed in their calculations.

The secret of success in any undertaking is usually found in perseverance. Thus it becomes evident how important it was for the success and the prospering of this settlement that Fr. Alexander kept the spirits of the settlers up. He was not only their spiritual leader, but he also took the keenest interest in the temporal welfare of his parishioners, by always being ready to offer counsel or a helping hand. He had the intention of opening a house of studies here for the young members of his Order. Supported by his confreres he undertook step by step improvements. He joined two creeks, Silver and Elk, into a canal, and thus directed sufficient water to the place where he had established a saw mill. He had whole stretches of forest cleared, thus providing the poor settlers both income and bread. He encouraged them and raised their hopes for a better future.

Everything Fr. Boniface saw and heard at St. Marys he took in. He was like a man who wakes up from a dream and sees that that which he has dreamt about has turned into reality; in this way, and exactly in this way, he had envisioned his own establishment in America, as he developed his first plan when he was still in Munich. Fr. Alexander told him, among other things, that the land grant association owned 58,000 acres and that they had recently entered a contract with the School Brothers from Lothringen for deeding 1,000 acres east of St. Marys to them, with the sole condition that they would establish a settlement there.

Mr. Garner, the land agent and surveyor of the association, conducted Fr. Boniface on a tour around the area and showed him a piece of land nine miles to the north which, he assured him, the company would gladly give him without charge, on condition that he would establish a monastery there. This piece of land was a valley enclosed by mountains on three sides and open only to the south, with a small crystal clear stream running through it. It did look rather frightful, but Fr. Boniface envisioned that it might actually get to look quite inviting in time and be very suitable for a quiet monastery, once his brothers had cleaned it up and cleared some of the dense woods. It seemed to him that this was the kind of place that suited his taste. For this reason he planned to get in touch about it as soon as possible with the Messrs. Benzinger and Eschbach, the owners of the land, who lived in Baltimore. To his reverend friend in Munich he wrote that if only he had two more priests of his Order, he would already start up the next spring.

CHAPTER EIGHT
The Most Reverend Bishop tries to calm
Father Boniface's misgivings.
Report on the community of St. Vincent in December 1847.

One can imagine that Bishop O'Connor was upset about the letter in which Father Boniface informed him about his decision to give up St. Vincent and to leave. It had already been for a full year that he had indulged in the pleasant hope that he would in the very near future see the building of a monastery and the start of a seminary on the hill of St. Vincent. And now all these beautiful and promising plans were to come to naught because of some difficulties that Father Boniface allowed to scare him away, even though in his [the Bishop's] eyes, they were nothing but minor vexations. The threatened departure of Father Boniface he considered a serious loss for the diocese and wanted to make at least one more vigorous attempt to prevent it. For that reason, he took up his pen and expressed his thoughts about the whole situation in a Latin letter addressed to Father Boniface. In those days, they still carried on their correspondence with each other in the Latin language.

Pittsburgh, November 2, 1847[1]

Beloved in Christ!

Since it appears that your decision to leave St. Vincent is so firm that it is almost impossible to persuade you to do anything else, it may not be worthwhile to discuss any of the points that you raise in your letter. However, I do want to say a few things.

In regard to the security of the title to the property which you can obtain there, [I can tell you that] the monastery you would build in that place [St. Vincent] would enjoy the same rights as it would on any piece of property that you would buy yourself. The same right would also pass on to your successor. Whatever other people might say, you can rest

---

[1]M. O'Connor to B.Wimmer, letter 22, ASVA.

assured that this is really how things stand. Since I have already explained the circumstances to you several times, it is not necessary to repeat what has already been said.

As far as the burdens[2] are concerned that go with the St. Vincent parish, you are by now well acquainted with them. I am sure you are not the kind of person who would find them to be a reason for giving up the most suitable place in favor of purchasing a less favorable one, which you would then, to boot, have to first fix up with much difficulty and hard labor. Were you to choose wooded land, you would probably be spending as much money in a single year for clearing it as would be enough to pay off the indebtedness that still encumbers the St. Vincent Church. Were you to buy a developed property, you might well pay as much as twice the amount of that debt. Besides, there would not be a church there, nor probably any of the other buildings you already have at St. Vincent. You could have the English-speaking parishioners be pastored by a diocesan priest who could live in the monastery or outside of it, how ever you would prefer. You could also have your monks pastor them, as soon as that would be possible ... The undertaking you are engaged in is definitely worthy of all praise. It will be of great benefit for religion, and I will be most grateful for such a blessing. As Bishop, I owe gratitude to everyone who starts anything that will be of benefit to the Catholics of this diocese. Proof of my gratitude and my desire to support good things I have shown in your case by relinquishing the place and the property to you which are, after all, of considerable value.

You did acknowledge that the location itself is the most suitable for the establishment of a monastery and a seminary. At the same time, the difficulties that concern you seem to me only imaginary ones, or at best, very minor ones. So, I cannot help but say that you would be acting totally unwisely if you were to subject yourself to the expense, the work, and the loss of time that would be required until you could get another place into the same shape in which St. Vincent already was when you came ... However, if you feel impelled by circumstances which are not known to me, I do not want to put any obstacles in your way.

---

[2] This is a direct translation; judging from the information a few sentences later, this may have been a way of saying "debts."

I give you my fullest permission to establish a monastery within the borders of this diocese among the colony of St. Marys, or near Indiana, or at any other place that you would consider more suitable. I place no other stipulation but that you pray for me. I have confidence that the monastery, wherever you will establish it, will serve everyone's edification and promote our holy religion in the best possible way. I just regret that you will lose money and labor by wanting to flee from imagined problems, and in the end you will not have the kind of institution that would be as well suited to your purposes as St. Vincent could be.

I remain your servant in Christ,
+M. O'Connor
Bishop of Pittsburgh

The reasons set forth in this letter had to weigh heavily in favor of St. Vincent. Right after his return from St. Marys, Father Boniface entered into correspondence with the main leaders and property owners of the colony, Messrs. Eschbach and Benzinger of Baltimore. A referral from the bishop also put him in touch with Mr. Keating, the owner of a large tract of land in both McKean and Potter Counties.

After calmly considering everything he had now seen and heard, the thought of keeping St. Vincent grew ever stronger in his mind. On a piece of woodland which he hoped the above gentlemen would donate to him, he would establish only a branch, which, however, would in reality be more in line with his original ideal. These thoughts he communicated to the bishop, who was most pleased with this news, because he realized from it that the temptation [to leave St. Vincent] was finally overcome. Let us hear his reply to Father Boniface:

Pittsburgh, December 30, 1847[3]

Dearest in Christ!

The day before yesterday I received your letter ... I am happy that everything is now settled and that you are content in your mind. On my part, I also hope that there will be no roadblocks in the future that would delay the progress of your undertaking, and I ask you to candidly let me know at any time if I can be of any help to you. I wish, and very much so, that the boys' school can soon be opened, but I do not want it to happen before you can do it without detriment to discipline or

[3]M. O'Connor to B. Wimmer, ASVA, letter 24.

great hardship. If you would wish to have the document (regarding the transfer of the parish) in another form, I will prepare one ...

Wishing you every good fortune in the new year and commending myself to your prayers, I remain etc., etc.

Postscript:

I do not believe that Mr. Keating intends to attach any conditions to the donation of land he intends to make. He would only expect that a religious institution would be erected on it in the near future. He did not write anything other than the letter I forwarded to you. It is known, however, what gentlemen like him want, and I have talked to him more than once about the establishment of such an institution on property he owns. I don't doubt that he would be willing to let you choose a piece of land, at least in an area where he himself would want to purchase additional land. He has many thousands of acres in the counties of McKean and Potter. Some of this land he owns, of a large part he is only the manager for a French company, which received these properties from the American government as compensation for help during the War of Independence, if I remember correctly. Those two counties belonged to them almost in their entirety. I do not know how much of this is still left that has not been sold. However, it should certainly be several thousand acres. He made a donation for the high school in Smethport, the main town of McKean County, and donated much additional land for other public institutions. I do not doubt that he will make a significant donation of land to you for the establishment of a monastery, partly from piety, and partly due to his love of Benedictines under whom he had received his education at Douay, partly also, or maybe mainly, due to self-interest. Such a donation might help him to sell his remaining property more quickly and for a better price, which would surely be the case after the establishment of such an institution. I hardly know what advice I should give you. The town of Smethport, which is located in the middle of his land, is about a day's journey (about 30 miles) from St. Marys. You could travel there yourself to see it. If I could do anything, not just by giving my permission for the establishment, but perhaps also as a mediator in the negotiations with Mr. Keating, I would always be willing to do so. If you would like to

take a look at the area, he would be happy to give you a letter for his
manager, who resides there, and undoubtedly would escort you and
show you all the places you would like to see."

As long as Father Boniface was not able to make up his mind as to whether
he wanted to stay at St. Vincent, he was also not able to let his brothers make their
professions or to start with the actual construction of the monastery. In these difficult
circumstances, the help of Father Peter Lechner was most welcome for him. The latter
dedicated himself with all his energies to the internal management of the monastery,
directing the studies of the clerics, instructing the brothers in ascetic life, making
sure they were faithful in their spiritual exercises, and inspiring everyone by being
an exemplary role model. Father Boniface, on the other hand, did not want to upset
anyone by any premature information about his inner struggles, and sought relief for
his mind by taking care of the smaller, outlying mission stations such as Salzburg,
Indiana, and Greensburg. In December 1847, he wrote a detailed report about his
own house as well as the mission in general to the Augsburg *Sion*.[4] Some of what he
wrote follows:

"After a long silence, I am finally getting around again to sending you
some news. Though it may not be of interest to the general public, it
might at least be welcome by the friends and relatives who support us
in our work. On October 24, it was already one year that I have been
here with my companions in order to found a monastery based on the
Rule of St. Benedict. A firm foundation for this was obtained, when the
Most Reverend Bishop, Dr. Michael O'Connor of Pittsburgh, issued
a document on December 6, 1847, to the effect that the church and
the property that belong to it, with all the rights and authority attached
thereto, were transferred to our Order forever. I and every one of my
legitimate successors are to be the pastors of the parish and enjoy the
undisturbed possession and use of the church and all that is attached
to it. Since the church and the property attached to it have been incorporated by the state, i.e., recognized by secular government also
as property donated to the Church for the use by Catholics, neither
can be sold nor touched in any way. Thus, perpetual possession of
this property is assured as certainly as any legislation anywhere can
assure it. Since, in addition, the episcopal declaration has transferred
the right to the property to the Order forever (a transfer that will be
reinforced by the hoped-for confirmation by the Holy See), the mon-

---

[4] The Report to the *Sion* is dated 1 Feb. 1848; it appeared in the edition of 17 Feb. 1848, vol. 16,
193-197.

astery founded here has obtained everything it needs in regard to its temporal requirements, and everything it possibly could expect and attain, given local circumstances.

We now are three priests, three clerics, three scholastics, and one organist (who also is a teacher), which equals ten. Then there are 24 lay brothers. Several of the brothers have more than one trade, such as weaving, binding, tanning, spinning, knitting, etc., and engage in these activities as needed. By the way, everyone has to allow himself to be used for every kind of work, when necessary. This applies even to the students, especially when hay or grain needs to be harvested and when corn needs planted. It makes the dear bread taste better to them when they have had to help earn it by the sweat of their brows. That is what they do in their vacation. Everyone is busy and needs to be busy. The benefit is that we are all healthy and only rarely need outside help for our establishment, only the use of wagons and plows. So much now for our monastery, or rather the people who make up the monastic community, since the monastery building itself must first be built. What has so far been serving as its residences are only three houses, spread fairly far apart.

Pastoral ministry we practice in the two counties, Westmoreland and Indiana, with the exception of a limited region that lies between the two, surrounding the town of Blairsville. In that district, the vicar general of the diocese, Father Stillinger, ministers. He is of German descent, born in America. These counties have a combined length of approximately 90 miles and a width of about 40 miles. Westmoreland County has about 42,000 inhabitants, Indiana around 16,000. Here, the English population predominates; there, the German. Catholics constitute not much more than 20%. Among the Protestants, the Presbyterians of the old and of the new school, are the majority. In addition, there are Methodists, Baptists, Dunkers, Simonists (Anabaptists), all in a colorful array. Very many families live without church, without worship, without a preacher. The Catholics have five churches, of which ours is the original one [mother church] and the oldest one in all of Western Pennsylvania, founded by a Franciscan from Holland by the name of Brouwers. However, it exists in its present appearance only since 1837. Before that, it was a very small chapel, and even earlier, worship was conducted in the old house in whose venerable *rudera*[5] some of my brothers now live. It is very roomy, but not solidly built . . .

It is a great consolation for me that I have gotten my valued confrere, Father Peter Lechner, as a teacher for my students and for the brothers. He is an excellent model of a true monastic for all of us. May the dear Lord reward Scheyern Monastery and its venerable abbot for sending me this support.[6] It is a further consolation for me that I can proclaim the Word of God at least monthly to the Catholics of Indiana, who formerly did not belong to our district, administer the Holy Sacraments to them, and preserve and strengthen both young and old in the Catholic faith. However, it is a terribly painful feeling to know that there are so many in need of help, and to be able to help only so few of them and so rarely! And the loss of even one soul does very noticeable damage to the church here. For example, there are two extended families with very many members living in the Salzburg area, whose ancestors were Catholic but who all now have fallen away to the Sects, because there was no one there who took care of them.

I have also found several Catholic families who now have no religion at all, and whose children are not even baptized. But they are also the ones who live farthest away from the church, among many Protestants. How much care I have already put into talking to them, visiting them, instructing them! And how little it helps that I usually can come back only after several weeks! And the children, often between seven and eleven, will, if they are not won for the church, create again as many Protestant or totally godless families in another twenty years. Hundreds of their children have been lost to the church in this way; and unfortunately, many more are still perishing, many of them because they themselves are too indifferent; many because they have been ensnared by the heresies all around them; many, finally, because they often have not had any opportunity in years to maintain their relationship with the Church. They themselves do remain Catholics, but see their children succumb to heresy. Thus, tremendous damage results for the Church from the dearth of priests; and at the same time, it loses out on a great gain that is no less important, for many Protestants could be won over, if only the care of our own would leave us enough time to think of the outsiders! Oh, confreres, Oh, priests in Bavaria, in

---

[5]This word apparently refers to the ruined or at least shabby condition of the building.
[6]Abbot Rupert Leiß had been a fellow novice with Fr. Boniface at Metten.

Germany, woe to you if you don't help! Our common fatherland sends us thousands of brother Germans across the ocean every year, and the Church [sends] barely one priest for 10,000! Don't say, "We have enough work at home, those who want to have priests, should stay [at home]!" This is not how love talks, not the love for our brothers, not the love for our holy Mother, the Catholic Church ...

I cannot let this opportunity pass without expressing my and my confreres' deepest gratitude to the most revered members of the Central Committee of the Ludwig Mission Society for their gracious support. This alone has made it possible for me to build our establishment on such a firm foundation that one can hope that, with God's grace, it will endure for a very long time and always be a strong support for our German brothers in the countryside of Western Pennsylvania, both in national and religious respects. In addition, it can be hoped that it will eventually become the mother of many other, similar institutions – which actually could start now already, except for the dearth of priests. I also would like to assure all members of the Ludwig Mission Society that we consider them our allies and our benefactors, we pray in common for them daily, and we use their gifts, when it comes to ourselves, only for the barest necessities, and conscientiously for the purpose for which they were offered, namely the preservation and propagation of the true faith. May they, too, remember us, and especially me, in their prayers, that we may all live, work, and die in the true spirit of the Order.

Father Boniface Wimmer

CHAPTER NINE
Fr. Boniface turns to Rome in the year 1848.
The first building. Report about Fr. Lemke's place.

One year and three months had passed since Fr. Boniface had settled at Saint Vincent with his brothers. The buildings they found upon their arrival made for very crowded living quarters for so many persons even at the start. The need for a new building that would provide more room became even more urgent when the brotherhood was increased by 18 men with the arrival of Fr. Peter Lechner and his companions.[1] Industrious hands and knowledgeable supervisors would have been quite good at meeting this need, and Fr. Boniface would never have hesitated to get the job going had he not felt held back from such an undertaking due to the dilemma in which he found himself. As noted earlier, the question kept coming up as to how sure he could be that the property, as well as the buildings to be constructed on it, would remain in the possession of his religious community. The answer was always the same. Only whoever was the current pastor of Saint Vincent had the rights to the property. Fr. Boniface himself, however, was the pastor of the parish only by way of a call that was subject to being rescinded. Were he to give up on his position as pastor or were he to lose it, his whole community would have to reach for their traveler's staff.

After serious deliberation Fr. Boniface believed he had finally found the means by which he would be able to reach his goal, at least partially, under the given circumstances. He was going to try to obtain a document from his bishop in which his position and his prospects would be described in detail, and then he would have this paper ratified in Rome. The most reverend Bishop O'Connor met his wishes in this matter also in a most obliging manner, with the following letter:[2]

> Michael O'Connor, Bishop of Pittsburgh by the mercy of God and the grace of the Apostolic See, our greeting in the Lord to all whom this concerns,

---

[1] In August 1847.

[2] M. O'Connor to B. Wimmer, ASVA, letter 25, 15 February 1848.

Since Fr. Boniface Wimmer, of the order of St. Benedict, from the Monastery of Metten in Bavaria, came to this country supplied with the appropriate authority, in order to found a monastery of the Benedictine Order, in which also boys, especially of German descent, were to be formed for the priestly profession, and requested our permission to establish it in our diocese, we have responded to this petition, permitted him to do so, and assigned to him the property of the church of St. Vincent in Westmoreland County, where he can canonically establish the monastery. Besides that, we have granted him that whoever the Superior of the monastery is, would always be the pastor of said church of St. Vincent, and we promise that he would be assigned to that position as soon as his election or appointment has been made known to us and we did not know of any canonical impediment. Since with this office he takes on all the rights and obligations associated with it (among which is the right to the two properties which Fr. Theodore Brouwers left to the priest of the above church in his will), he or one of his confreres whom he might appoint for the ministry there, with our permission, shall be subject to us and our successors in all matters that pertain to the parish ministry, and shall obligate himself to give an accounting to us, as do other priests in the rest of the diocese.

In confirmation of this we have signed this letter and affirmed it with our seal.

Pittsburgh, February 15, 1848

+Michael

(L. S.) Bishop of Pittsburgh

The next month, Fr. Boniface turned to the Holy See in Rome with a petition for obtaining the permission of the higher ecclesiastical authority for the following:

1. That he might establish a monastery at St. Vincent based on the rules of the Order;

2. That this monastery would enjoy all the rights and privileges which monasteries in general are given, without any exceptions;

3. That the parish of St. Vincent, in its present size, be incorporated into the Order of St. Benedict, that is, into the monastery that is located at the church of St. Vincent, in perpetuity;

4. That the legitimate superiors of this monastery, whatever title they may have, be simultaneously the pastors of the St. Vincent Parish, with the right to designate

one of their confreres as vicar;

5. That they be given both the management and the use of the yield of the two properties which belong to this church and which are designated for the support of its pastor;

6. That he, with the permission of the most reverend bishops, might be permitted to found and establish monasteries of the Order of St. Benedict also in other places in the United States.

Just at that time the Most Reverend Bishop Martin Henni of Milwaukee was about to travel to Rome. Fr. Boniface did not want to pass up this good opportunity, so he requested the Bishop not only to take the important petition along but also to put in a good word for it with the proper authority. And this is what actually happened. The pro-secretary of the Sacred Congregation for the Propagation of the Faith. Monsignor Alexander Barnabo, submitted the above petition to the Holy Father Pius IX during an audience on July 23, 1848. After serious deliberation on the document, he concurred and gave the Most Reverend Bishops of Pittsburgh the relevant authority to carry out what had been requested. That was all well and good, but how long did Fr. Boniface have to wait until he received notification of this?

Who does not know about the year 1848? The storms which threatened European governments that year and the next like heavy thunder clouds caused much confusion and brought many undertakings to a standstill. Fr. Boniface and his brothers were also to feel an effect of this, for, as will be noted below, this document, being expected with such longing, did not reach his hands before 1850.

He did not have reason to doubt that his petition would be granted; actually he could presume it. Without this presupposition, however, his situation would indeed have been a precarious one. In good faith, therefore, he proceeded to think seriously about building his monastery. First of all, he had a brick kiln constructed and other building material brought in. Once everything that was necessary was brought to the place, the cornerstone for the monastery building was laid and blessed on the Feast of St. Michael, September 29, 1848.[3] This day brought new life to Fr. Boniface's community. He himself felt his spirits totally lifted up by his happy expectations for the future, for as he turned the first spade for the foundation, it was as if he could already picture the completed building in his mind. He now believed himself to be standing at the threshold of the realization of the goal he long had yearned for.

> "With intelligence and patient cheer, they built with plumb and balance, with square and saw and hammer, ax and trowel day by day, until their diligence succeeded to firmly found cell and monastery..."[4]

---

[3]This date of course also marks the patronal feast of the monastery at Metten.
[4]Weber, *Dreizehnlinden*, II, 10-11.

This building was to be three stories high, sixty feet long, and forty feet wide. To this day, this building is still in use; the first floor is the refectory, the second, the chapter [meeting] room, and the third, a study hall. In a letter from December 21, 1848, Fr. Boniface describes the above building to his untiring benefactor, Court Chaplain Müller, and also mentions taking over the parish at Carrolltown and the purchase of the remainder of Fr. Lemke's land. He goes into detail, as well, about his agricultural plans, some of which, however, did not work out, such as the one about the raising of sheep. During the following severe winter, they all died due to the lack of feed.

The closest post office for St. Vincent at the time was in the small town of Youngstown. That is why the following letter is dated from there.

Youngstown, Westmoreland, December 21, 1848

Most reverend, most revered Sir!
Beloved Father!

You have recently once again earned this title many times over by what you have been doing for me and mine. I can see my indebtedness toward you growing ever greater and feel my poverty most in that I cannot return the favors, though I know that you do not expect that, nor even think of it, since it is only the love of God and neighbor, and your joyful devotion to a beautiful and noble cause that inspire and motivate you. Please accept at least my sincere thanks, and those of my confreres, at the end of this year, for all the good you have done for us in the course of this year. Along with our thanks, please also be assured of our daily communal prayer. God will add other and better rewards!

Also rewarding should be the fact that we have not been working in vain, that, though slowly and with much effort and with a thousand inconveniences, the first Benedictine monastery is rising up, securely and on a good foundation or at least it seems that way, and preparations for a second one have begun.

I hope you have received my letter in which I reported to you how I have repeatedly had dealings with Fr. Lemke and have bought his property, how everything fell into place so mysteriously, that I was easily able to do so, and almost had to, and how not only our effectiveness was broadened by this, but that it will also improve our subsistence, at least in time.

On December 6, 1848, exactly one year after our staying here was assured by a written document, I traveled to Cambria County with two priests and four brothers in order to take over the German parish there and to establish a little monastery after I had been formally authorized to do so by the bishop. I had not scheduled that day ahead of time, did not even think of it being possible before the New Year. However, I suddenly heard that Mr. Stauber, the former missionary, was recalled and obliged to be at another post. And so I had to get traveling as quickly as possible. I only realized on the journey that this was the same date on which the foundation for the first monastery was laid, and now it was already bringing a second one ...

Since I have to pay a 300 dollar installment to Fr. Lemke every year, until the 2000 dollars I owe him are paid off, I have to make sure to derive some use from the farm already this year. I will do this by means of animal husbandry, since we receive only ¼ of the winter harvest (¾ goes to the man who was Fr. Lemke's farmer until now.) For this reason, I bought 120 sheep in Indiana and sent them there and also intended to buy all of the farmer's animals for 200 dollars.

As for St. Vincent, we have just come to the point where we will have the roof completed by next week if the weather is favorable. Then our house will be 90' long and 40' wide, and three stories high.[5] All of next year must be spent on building a good and large barn with extensive stables. We will be lucky if we can complete it; but we will profit greatly from it, because then I will be able to keep a great many more animals. Right now I have 53 head of cattle, 350 sheep, over 100 pigs, 12 draft horses, and two colts. All of this is paid for except for some 40 dollars for the sheep, which I need to pay for only nine months from now. As you can see, I am making good purchases with your beautiful pieces of gold. Everything related to the farming operation, wagons, plows, threshing machines, harnesses, saddles, etc., etc., is in the best condition. At the same time we are always looking for improvements in fields and woods and meadows. Without a substantial number of livestock we cannot support ourselves. If we have any luck with the sheep, we will have not only nourishment, but also clothing, grease,

---

[5] The first part of the building, 60 feet long, was extended by an addition of 30 feet.

and a net income of 200 - 300 dollars yearly, to boot, depending on the price of wool. Please forgive me for writing so much and so often about farming. It is of greatest importance for me, for if I can feed and clothe 70 persons from our farming operation and from the income of the parish, a great deal has been accomplished.

I recently also bought 400 acres of woodland on the Ridge, seven miles from the house, at 1 ½ dollars an acre. It is wild, rocky land and only useable for pasture, but covered with beautiful trees – oak, chestnut, black locust, hickories.[6]

If I will really receive what you believe you can promise me, it will be just enough for these purchases and for the buildings ...

On the Feast of St. Andrew [30 November], we again had several scholastics and lay brothers who made simple profession, after the importance of this step had been laid upon their hearts during the preceding retreat.

---

[6]The timber was necessary for the planned constructions at Saint Vincent.

CHAPTER TEN
Fr. Thaddeus Bruner and Fr. Adalbert Pluns, Ph.D., come from Metten to help out. First Profession.

onari in magnis pulchrum—the very striving for greatness is beautiful. In his letters to his friends Fr. Boniface usually described various plans. His closest friend, the Court Chaplain, however, often made an effort to hold him back, reminding him to exercise caution. Though he agreed with the latest plan that Fr. Boniface reported to him, his intention to take on Lemke's place, his response to the proposals regarding St. Mary's and Indiana was a clear warning—"take it slowly; first put the house at St. Vincent on solid footing." However, Fr. Boniface had chosen for himself the motto, "Forward." The details he wanted to leave to others.

Crowded quarters, an unfinished house, whose rough walls remained without plaster even on the inside for several years, etc.—such deficiencies should not disconcert a great mind, in his opinion. In just the same way he had not been deterred from having the first profession ceremony on October 24, 1846, for fourteen lay brothers, though he had only six habits at his disposal.

In several letters to the abbot of Metten he had tried to describe extensively how much good could be accomplished for the salvation of abandoned souls in the mission district entrusted to him if a few energetic priests would come to work with him.

After Scheyern had set a good example, St. Stephan Abbey of Augsburg came through also and sent their Fr. Andreas Zucktrigel[1] to help out at St. Vincent for three years.[2] At Metten, as well, preparations were made at the end of the 1847/48 school year to offer support to the energetic confrere across the ocean. Fr. Thaddeus Bruner, Fr. Adalbert Pluns, and brother candidate Gammelbert Daschner[3] were to help out at Fr. Boniface's foundation. They arrived at St. Vincent at the end of October 1848.

Fr. Thaddeus was born November 9, 1821 at Wörgl in Tyrol, made profession

---

[1][original footnote] He later was the prior of Oelberg Monastery [Oehlenberg] near Strassburg.

[2]In fact Fr. Andreas helped out from October 1847 until January 1853. Upon his return to Europe, he entered the Trappist monastery of Oehlenberg. More extensive information on Fr. Andreas can be found in Warren Murrman, "A Bavarian Missionary Monk in the 'Land of Freedom': Fr. Andreas Zucktrigel, O.S.B." in *ABR* 62:2 (June 2011) 202-216 and its sequel in *ABR* 64:2 (June 2013) 154-177.

[3]Br. Gammelbert Daschner (1817 – 1870).

at the Abbey of Metten on April 11, 1847, and was ordained a priest the same year. Fr. Thaddeus possessed all the desirable characteristics of a missionary: he was young, very energetic, learned, and a skillful speaker. At St. Vincent he became the first prefect and professor at the seminary as it was starting up. Later he served in parish ministry at several of the missions: at St. Mary's in Elk County, at Carrolltown, and other places. The church at Cooper Settlement was built under his leadership.[4]

Fr. Adalbert Pluns was born on January 17, 1790, at Stintenburg, Prussia, of Protestant parents. He received an education in the sciences, earned a doctor of philosophy degree, and made a name for himself as a man of letters. After spending several years in England, France, and Italy, he devoted his activities to the stage and was given charge of a theater in Berlin. Now that he seemed to have reached the pinnacle of his material good fortune, he suddenly suffered some heavy blows of misfortune, or so he believed at that time. In reality, these were nothing other than rays of grace with which the hand of the Lord touched him. He lost his not insignificant wealth in a fire; and what would be more natural than that this taught him to pray? Through prayer, moreover, he attained the grace of the true faith. With his whole soul he became a child of the holy Catholic Church. As soon as he had freed himself from all earthly fetters and family matters, he made the decision to leave everything, take up his cross, and follow Christ. In order to put this decision into action he knocked at the gate of the monastery at Metten, and it was readily opened to him.

After he had completed his novitiate and taken simple vows as a lay brother, he found at Metten a great field for the use of his extensive knowledge. His departure for American brought about universal regret among the students.[5]

An occurrence as happy as it is important to be noted occurred on April 15, 1849. On that day the first members of the young monastic family were secured for the Order by means of their solemn vows and consecrated to God. In the presence of an assembly of many people, who had never witnessed a sacred rite of this sort, Frs. Benedict, Placidus, and Celestine pronounced their vows in a loud voice before their spiritual father, promising stability in the Order, conversion of morals, and obedience, according to the *Rule* of St. Benedict.[6] From now on they were to be dead to the world, living for the Lord alone. As a reminder of the interior act of the will, they lay prostrate before the altar, a large black pall with a while cross was spread over them, and burning candles were placed at the four corners. Even the church bell tolled as for a funeral.

---

[4]The current address of St. Severin Church is Drifting, Clearfield County; it is a mission from St. Mary of the Assumption in Frenchville and is part of the Diocese of Erie. While a newer construction is now used, the original log church is still standing. In Fr. Thaddeus' day, it was tended from St. Benedict's Church in Carrolltown, which is now located in the Altoona-Johnstown Diocese.

[5]The gifted Frater Adalbert (1790 - ?) taught for a few years in the school at Saint Vincent but found the living conditions in the mission monastery too rigorous at his age and he left the community.

[6]Benedict Haindl (1815 – 1887), Placid Döttl (1818 – 1852), Celestine Englbrecht (1824 – 1904).

A profession ceremony,
a vow to bind oneself for life
to the observance of the evangelical counsels,
does not detract from true freedom,
but actually secures it all the more,

because freedom is the beautiful state
of submitting to God's will,
without hesitation, with joy,
renouncing one's own will.

And then on April 20, 1849, these three newly professed monks were ordained to the priesthood.

In a letter to a student of theology in Munich, who had inquired about acceptance at St. Vincent, Fr. Boniface expressed his sadness about the prevailing lack of priests in the United States, and the great losses to the Catholic Church.[7]

St. Vincent near Youngstown, Westmoreland County,
June 5, 1849

Honorable Sir!

I was very happy and surprised when I met the deliverer of your dear letter and her companions in Baltimore on May 14, one day before I got ready for the trip home from the Council [of Baltimore]. They were all well and proceeding toward their destination full of trust and in good spirits, though cholera had recently tried to get in their way all along the Ohio and the Mississippi. The most reverend bishop of Dubuque showed them the favor of permitting them to travel under his protection as far as St. Louis. Your earlier letter I received only after I came home, because you had mailed it from New York.

I see from it that you and several of your friends are considering becoming Benedictines and one day to labor alongside myself and my confreres for the Holy Church. That makes me extremely happy, and you will never regret it once you will have put your intentions into action.

It makes me extremely happy, I say. In the beginning my mission seemed somewhat quixotic, even to my best friends, and when they

---

[7] The letter was published in *Sion* 18 (1850) 135-140. It was obviously intended for the eyes of many others, as a recruiting tool.

contemplated the difficulties of the undertaking itself, and even more, those of my personality, they almost had to come to such an opinion. I was well acquainted with both, but looked beyond that at the needs of the American Church and the infinite goodness of God, who is strong in those who are weak, and pursued my honest intentions and my inner compulsion with as much awareness as I had of my unworthiness and my deficiencies. I did find difficulties that had to come my way, but so far I have also always found the necessary means to overcome them, through the wonderful assistance of Divine Providence. Before three years had passed, I was already able to found three settlements of our Order in this country, which in time have to become enormously important for the American Church, if God's blessing reigns over them and the spirit of St. Benedict within them. Your letter strengthens my hope because it offers the prospect of an increase in numbers and strength and good will among the monastic community; and, therefore, I say that it gives me very great joy.

You will also never regret working here, and doing so as a Benedictine. Here the fate of the world will be decided, as well as the destiny of the Church, and quickly, at that. In decades things get done here which elsewhere did not happen in centuries. I believe the entire Christian Church history, in all its phases, will repeat itself here in one century, albeit in a new way and under very different conditions. We win or lose everything, depending on whether we appear on the battleground in time or too late. Just as Germany did not receive anything from America because it did not send any settlers at the time of the discovery and colonization, so the Church would be excluded or die in the bud if she would not send missionaries, or assure that the ones now working here would be continually replaced and increased and empowered to be equal to any foe. Only a person who has no eyes, or does not want to see with the ones he has, can fail to notice this.

So, priests, good energetic priests is what is needed here. Every year thousands are lost to the sects and even more to the Free Masons; and especially the young people are in danger. It is a fact that the Catholic faith has rarely been passed down as far as the third generation of a family in recent times, and it is estimated that there are six million apostates! In spite of the immense number of immigrants, there are only a little over a million of us Catholics because the young people are almost always lost; and the only reason is the lack of priests. If there were more priests, we could easily have as many converts.

Who, then, would not want to work here as a priest, when he could prevent so many losses and have hopes of so many conquests? However, a priest – alone, abandoned, stationed in isolation – what can he accomplish? He can work for the salvation of souls. But what about his own well-being? It may be many days' journey to the next priest who could give him counsel, hear his confession, give him consolation and encouragement! The bishops are at a loss about what to do in order to increase the number of young priests; they either do not have any seminaries, or no professors, or no students, or not enough of anything anywhere!

That is where the religious Orders must step into the breach. They always have been the ones who were mainly responsible for bringing about conversions and preserving them. For our Germans in the cities, it is currently the Redemptorist Order that has earned invaluable merits in this respect and that continues to do so.

Listen, you German young men, you German theologians and priests! Our German youths who want to become priests do not have a single institution where they could study, where they could receive priestly formation, in order to keep their German brothers in their Catholic faith. But, no! They do have one now, through only a single one, one where poor boys also can be formed for the priesthood, even very poor ones, who cannot even bring with them books or clothes. It is St. Vincent, where five Benedictines priests and thirty six Benedictine brothers have toiled in the sweat of their brows to start it, where this year thirteen boys have found education and maintenance, this poor little monastery built with the coins that both family heads and house servants contributed to the mission society.

With this, my dear young friend, I have outlined the road you can travel one day in the land of your hopes. Our Order has the task of serving the German Church in America, that is, for the time being, but not exclusively. It is understood, of course, that as Benedictines, it is our highest calling to live the Benedictine life. Education and ministry derive then only from that. Of course we need energetic men, but good

Benedictines even more than learned persons. It would certainly be very desirable if you and your friends would come over to us some day as well educated theologians. It would be no less desirable, though, if you would already come now and, full of good will and a good disposition, would join actively in building up the spiritual aspect of the monastery, and, by your zeal strengthen, enliven, and promote the zeal of the novices.

We rise at a quarter to four in the morning and go to bed at nine o'clock in the evening, do not eat any breakfast, have a frugal meal at eleven o'clock, but enough to satisfy our hunger. On Sundays, Mondays, Tuesdays, and Thursdays we eat meat, the other days, grain dishes; these we also have daily for our evening meal (at six o'clock), except for Sundays and holidays. Priests who travel outside the monastery or engage in mission work keep only the church fasts. During Lent we eat meat only on Sundays. The lay people are also bound by the church rules regarding abstinence, and they keep them conscientiously the whole first and last weeks of Lent and all Wednesdays, Fridays, and Saturdays of the period. Choir prayer is at 4, 6, 9, 12, 3, and half past 6 o'clock.

Come soon. Good thoughts must be put into action quickly. But, as God wills! Vocation requires sacrifice; and that is love!

Yours,
Boniface Wimmer

An Autography from King Ludwig

Even after his abdication, King Ludwig I of Bavaria continued his custom of annually donating a sizeable sum from his income for the support of foreign missions. However, for the distribution of this money he did not proceed only on the basis of the petitions he received. Rather, he consulted with Court Chaplain Müller who could provide the best advice because, due to his position as administrator of the Bavarian Mission Society, he was personally acquainted with overseas bishops, monastic superiors, and missionaries, had an extensive correspondence in regard to the missions, and published the mission *Annals*. It need not be mentioned here that Fr. Boniface and his young foundation were never forgotten on these occasions. This also explains why the latter never failed to send a report about his work to his noble benefactor from time to time. One such letter Fr. Boniface sent to King Ludwig on July 23, 1849, to which he received the following reply in the king's own hand:

Berchtesgaden, August 30, 1849

Rev. Superior,

With heartfelt joy I perceived the positive tone of your letter and the report that the German monasteries, both male and female, are thriving. I wish that you would express to all whom you have mentioned to me that I take a lively interest in their work which is bringing so many blessings. At the moment I cannot tell whether I will be able to grant any support, but maybe I may be able to do so soon. It is "maybe," however, since I am receiving as many requests for assistance now, as when I was still on the throne, though my income has been significantly reduced not only at the time when I laid down the crown but ever since then. How many a useful grant I would still have liked to make! You observe very correctly that in order for the Germans in North America to remain German, the formation of German priests is required; that school and religion classes continue to be taught in the German language is a necessary condition for the maintenance of a German presence. May God's blessing continue to rest on the work of the German Missions.

From one who knows to esteem you,
Ludwig

CHAPTER ELEVEN
Novitiate. Scholasticate.
The Educational Institution at St. Vincent.
Father Boniface describes his monastery in the year 1849.

U p to this point we have mostly followed the general plans of Father Boniface and looked at the external means by which he tried to bring them to fruition. Now we also want to take a look at the internal activities of his young monastery.

Here we find first of all a novitiate, that is, the institution for the formation of monks, an institution upon which depends the future weal or woe of the monastery. For from the novitiate must arise the young strength and vigor of the Order, which is needed to continue and perfect the labors of the founders and predecessors. A life of freely chosen poverty and unconditional obedience, as the monastic state requires, without a doubt presupposes a high degree of self-denial and therefore rightfully demands a long and serious period of testing of the will and of the strength of whoever strives toward the goal of higher godliness with joyful courage. The ascetics of old recommended that the novice master test the obedience and the humility of the novices by the way of severe discipline and humiliations. Father Boniface believed that at St. Vincent the lack of comforts, the meager and rugged daily life, and the hard labor more than made up for such practices.

In addition to the novitiate there is the scholasticate. This is an institution for men aspiring to be monastics who have not yet completed their classical studies. They receive the habit with a shorter scapular and no cowl. They recite Prime and Compline from the Divine Office in the choir chapel. They attend school together with the secular students of the college. In a way the institution of the scholasticate was already established by St. Benedict when he laid the foundation for his Order at Subiaco. The first scholastics whom history has recorded for us were St. Maurus and St. Placidus. The latter was entrusted to the care of St. Benedict when he was a boy of seven years, the former when he was twelve. In Chapter 59 of his *Rule* the holy founder of the Order speaks about the admission of the sons of nobility and of the poor, and in Chapter 30 he deals with the disciplining of the younger boys who live in the monastery.

The tradition of the Benedictine Order of later centuries continually calls attention to the institution of the scholasticate. Thus, for example, exterior and interior monastic schools were discussed at the Synod of Aachen in 817, where it was determined that only those who wanted to become monks would be accepted into the interior schools.

"Benedictine life is our first task", Father Boniface wrote to a theology student, "the next is the education of the youth."[1] The first task is of the very essence of monastic life; the formation of good monastics is the *sine qua non*. The second task always follows the first, as the history of the Benedictine Order shows. It is sufficient in this regard to point to Father Mabillion's treaties on monastic education in which he sets forth for the abbot of La Trappe that Benedictine monasteries were not established in order to become academies of [secular] learning, but rather to teach virtue. In fact, learning was to be propagated only to the extent that it served religious perfection.

At St. Vincent we find a Latin school as early as 1849 with thirteen students under the direction of Father Thaddeus Bruner. In 1852 the number of students had risen to thirty, and two years later the young institution had grown into a college of ninety students. The rapid blossoming encouraged the monks entrusted with the leadership of this institution to put their whole heart and soul into their work. They had frequent meetings among themselves in order to confer about the most appropriate means for handling discipline and to advance learning. When they at times turned to the superior of the house regarding such matters in order to have him decide in doubtful cases, Fr. Boniface was particularly fond of pointing them to the practices used at Metten and other places where he had experience, or he gave reply by way of applying a suitable proverb. Giving out detailed rules of conduct was not to his taste, since he wanted to give his young priests and clerics sufficient leeway to thoroughly develop their own talents. In order to justify his approach he liked to tell the following anecdote from the life of his unforgettable teacher, the blessed Bishop Wittmann.

Once, when he was still rector of the seminary at Regensburg, he came to the monastery of Benediktbeuren on a vacation trip. He spent some pleasant time there, but what interested him most, as noted in his diary, was that he had finally found a man through whom the hearts of young people seemed to be drawn to God. "This", he wrote, "is Father Wolfgang Vizthum, O.S.B.,[2] seminary rector of Benediktbeuren,[3] a man gaunt and pale, but full of openness and liveliness of spirit". Wittmann had already heard it from others, and now he was seeing for himself, how

---

[1] It would seem that Fr. Oswald is referring to some of the content of the letter in chapter 10.

[2] Father Wolfgang Vizhum, O.S.B., Ph.D., see the *Authors of the Benedictine Order in Bavaria*, by Aug. Lindner I. Reg. 1880. At the same time there lived in this monastery Fr. Sebastian Mall, Ph.D., laster professor of oriental languages at the University of Munich; Fr. Aloysius Buchner, Ph.D., later professor of theology in Munich, where Abbot Wimmer was one of their students, as mentioned above.

[3] The monastery church was dedicated by St. Boniface on October 22, 742.

the students of Father Wolfgang were distinguish-
ing themselves in fear of the Lord and virtuous
behavior as much as in their studies, and they
had to be held back more than urged on.
For these reasons he fervently longed
to discover the secret by which such
favorable success was being achieved.
He was convinced that this was possible only due to Father Wolfgang being
in possession of some system of unsur-
passed excellence. Therefore Wittmann
turned to the gracious Father with the
kind request to inform him of his method of
formation. However, how amazed he was when
Father Wolfgang swore to him that he did not

Bishop Wittman

possess any method. And when the good Father, puzzled by this question, replied
quite sincerely, "I don't do anything; this all comes about by itself," Wittmann was
a little disappointed for a fleeting moment. However, he immediately concluded for
himself that the first requirement for the formation of young people was humility.

For many years the same system that was used in most of the seminaries in
America was also used in the educational institution at St. Vincent, that is, clerics
who themselves were studying philosophy and theology had to take over [teaching]
several undergraduate classes. However true Cicero's saying may be that one learns
from teaching, this system nevertheless left something to be desired. In time this
need would be met in that only priests were used as teachers.

The beneficial influence which the environment and general daily routine at St.
Vincent exerted on the students is unmistakable. The awareness that here everyone
keeps to the same daily routines makes observing them easier for everyone. When
the students see that here everything is regulated by the lofty principles of religion,
that all keep great aspirations before their eyes, that only virtue, industriousness,
and piety are honored, that vice, in whatever form it may appear, is scorned, pun-
ished, and banned, it cannot fail that such an observation is of greatest value for the
youthful, still unspoiled minds of the students. How close his seminary was to Father Wimmer's heart, he expressed as early as the summer of 1849 in the following
letter to a friend in his homeland, in which he also remembers all the benefactors
who had so generously supported him in the founding of this seminary. From this
letter, as well as several other reports of his, it is evident that he always had had the
intention to invest all the support his noble benefactors gave him as a kind of in-

terest-bearing capital. He wanted to acquire land and property with it, the yield of which would provide the means of support for the institution in the future.[4]

Dearest Friend!

You want me to give you a history of our monastery. I would have complied with your wish already a long time ago, but modesty seemed to forbid me to write a history that in many ways is my history. Besides, the whole thing is also still in a state of becoming; and though its existence has been secured, it has, nevertheless, not yet reached the kind of maturity that would let it stand as something that has been completed.

In the meantime I will nevertheless attempt, as well as I am able, to pass between the "too much or too little", into which one can easily fall in writing such a tale, and to report what has so far been accomplished for our German compatriots here at our place, and to a large extent from mission money.

Our monastery, if I may already call it that, is located in Westmoreland County in western Pennsylvania, three miles west beyond the Alleghany Mountains, not far from the great highway [leading] from Philadelphia to Pittsburgh, and five hours from the canal on which every year thousands of Germans stream from Philadelphia or Baltimore to the West of the Union, and sixteen hours east of Pittsburgh. Its location is extraordinarily beautiful: on a hill, with a view toward the above-mentioned mountains, and the surrounding, equally hilly countryside. The climate is healthy and the soil fertile.

Our ministry extends over the entire county (with the exception of a small district along the canal), in which about 3,000 Catholics are scattered here and there among some 50,000 residents and who have only three churches. Almost the entire county of Indiana (with about 20,000 inhabitants) also belongs to our district, which measures 92 English miles in length and 51 in breadth. There are four churches but only a few Catholics.

In Cambria County our priests minister to the German Catholics on

---

[4]*Annalen* 17 (1849) 436-441. The letter to one of his [un-identified] friends in Munich seems to have been intended from the outset to be published; perhaps it was actually a "personal" report to a fictive person.

a regular basis as well, and they additionally help out in the districts along the borders of the neighboring counties. The two priests of our Order who minister in Cambria County live on an estate of 330 acres of land, of which only a third is being cultivated, however, and which also is part of the property of our Order.

A third place where a priest from our house presently serves, along with Reverend Balleis from St. Peter in Salzburg, is Newark, the capitol of New Jersey, only nine miles from New York [City].

At St. Vincent we currently have 5 priests, 3 clerics, and 36 lay brothers; at St. Joseph in Cambria County are 2 priests and 3 brothers; at Newark, 2 priests and 1 brother. Three of the priests belong to Bavarian monasteries and are here only to help out; the other six belong to the monastery [St. Vincent]. The purpose for which the monastery was founded was not only to take care of the spiritual needs of the Germans living in the county, but primarily to establish a seminary where poor, talented, and virtuous boys could be formed for the priesthood, in order to alleviate the dearth of priests. For this reason such a seminary was established as soon as possible and it currently serves a) beginners b) older students, who wish to become diocesan priests, and c) Order students

Now, who were the founders of this monastery? The instruments for this were I and my people. The means for it were supplied by the Ludwig-Mission Society, which contributed 6,000 florins for the travel costs and the very first setting-up expenses, and then 5,000 florins for each of the past 2 years. Without these moneys it neither would have been possible to begin the work nor to bring it to the point where it can now stand on its own, or almost on its own. Thus it is to members of this pious association, and especially to the most reverend Archbishop, Count von Reisach, and to the other most honorable members of the Central Committee that the honor and the credit belong for the foundation of a monastery for the formation of German clergy in the United States. If I were not fearful of offending his humility, I would have to make special mention of the Court Chaplain and administrator of the Ludwig-Mission Society, Joseph Ferdinand Müller. From the very beginning, and up to this hour, he has thought of me and my people with truly fatherly care at every opportunity, and he has spared no pains to be of invaluable service to us by his punctual, timely, and secure transmittal of the authorized funds, books, musical instruments, music and art supplies, as well as splendid altar linens and sacred vessels, etc, etc., a thousand helpful acts, for which only God can reward him sufficiently. Also written with glowing strokes in the register of benefactors of our monastery as supporters and co-founders are the most reverend Bishop Ziegler of Linz and Abbots Gregory of Metten and Rupert of Scheyern, as well as the recently resigned Prior of Weltenburg, Father Xavier Sulzbeck, and many private individuals.

In America it is especially the zealous Bishop Dr. Michael O'Connor of Pittsburgh, as learned as he is pious, who by his transfer of the church of St. Vincent to the Benedictine Order (December 6, 1847), facilitated our establishment of this first settlement at its beginning and who gave the new monastery its foundation. By his patronage and manifold demonstrations of good will, as well as his sincere interest in seeing the monastery thrive, he contributed significantly to its success and has earned the most heartfelt and warmest gratitude of the German members of his diocese and of all German Catholics, or rather, Catholic Germans.

The Lord, however, the Almighty One, the most active giver of all good things, who by his Holy Spirit brought about both the willing and the accomplishing in all who in some way participated in this endeavor, is the true builder; and to him alone belongs all honor for it, as it is also intended for his glory.

Boniface Wimmer.

CHAPTER TWELVE
A Fortunate turn of events.
Fr. Boniface travels to Germany.
Correspondence with King Ludwig.

Although Fr. Boniface lived with the strong confidence that the Holy See would grant his petition, which he had submitted already in March 1848, that is, a year and a half earlier, he nevertheless could not fight off some anxious feelings. Perhaps your petition will be rejected, the tempter whispered into his ear. But then he would console himself again with the thought that he had requested nothing other than authorization to accomplish a good work. So, persevere in patience, he said to himself; it will happen eventually. Then, when on gloomy days he looked back over all his striving and struggling, it seemed to him at times as though he always had to swim against the current.

In a letter to a friend he described in his characteristic way how he had held on to his original plan against all opposition, and what progress he had made in the past three years since his arrival in America, as well as what he was hoping for the future.[1]

St. Vincent, Westmoreland County
in Pennsylvania, Dec. 27, 1849

My Dearest Friend,

I don't know if you have already calmed down enough after your accomplishments—those momentous ones—that you achieved, in order to be willing to hear about our small matters...

You perhaps still remember that the purpose of my emigration was to found a monastery here (and, in time, several) in which the monks would not only lead a monastic life according to the *Rule* of St. Benedict, but would also educate talented boys for the priesthood, and

---

[1]The letter appeared in *Annalen* 18 (1850) 229-236 as written to a friend, identified only as Pastor A.M. in Pf, with a postscript, 236-239, containing a general appeal to diocesan priests who might have the desire to come to America.

not just those who were able to pay for the cost of their education from their own means, but poor ones, who would not be able to pay anything.

This is what I was striving for, and I still believe that I will be able to achieve it...

This idea was met with much approval in Bavaria already before I left, but also with an equal amount of opposition. When I arrived here, I received hardly more than sympathetic pity. From the first place where I thought of settling, I was driven away, partly by my own lack of trust in the success of my undertaking, and partly by the discouragement of some of my companions... Here at St. V. I also had to struggle with all kinds of difficulties, which, however, have all been overcome with the help of God.

Our membership now consists of 8 priests, 4 clerics, 3 candidates, and 40 brothers, for a total of 55 persons. Now, my dear man! Do you ask me as others ask, why such a crowd of brothers? Is that, you ask, your only accomplishment? Why so many? How do you feed them? Have a little patience. In America the religious Orders support themselves either a) by parish ministry, or b) by providing education, or c) by farming.

When I came to America I had no other way to reach my goal than this: to buy land, take in brothers, and have them construct buildings. Teachers had to be educated little by little; and since I was poor, I did it in order to take care so that we at least did not lack the most basic necessities. I did achieve that, not by my own strength, but by the help of God, and by the untiring activity and support of Court Chaplain J.F. Müller. Before I came, one priest could barely support himself adequately where now 80 persons can. The people of the parish do not contribute more than before, and, because of that, they cannot understand how I can manage, having all these men to take care of.

Some (those living at a distance) believe that I am extremely wealthy. Others, who occasionally partake of our monastic fare, look at me as a kind of magician that I am able to keep so many people here together, people "who could be earning money", serving them watery soups and boiled vegetables, while the poorest man around here drinks coffee, and eats meat and sandwiches.

You will perhaps think that I am a very lucky man. I certainly am a lucky man. My motto cannot be: *servus servorum Dei,* but I know, nevertheless, that I am, indeed, the servant of my servants, a man of toil and worry. When the brother rings the bell nine times at night to signal that everyone must go to bed, I often just start to think, what should be done tomorrow? Where can we get this or that? How shall we pay for this and that? How can we avoid this or the other? How can we improve this or that? So many questions to answer, so many requests to listen to or refuse, so many sad ones to console, so many ignorant ones to guide, erring ones to discipline, etc., and to present oneself trusting toward all, strong, and above reproach,—that, my dear man, is a task I would gladly leave to anyone else!

However, never lose courage, always hope for the best, and do not fear opposition and obstacles. Rather, overcome courageously, place child-like trust in God, and never lose sight of the firm, certain goal. That is what a man, a priest, a monastic must be able to do.

I truly do not write this to boast or to make a name for myself. I have sincerely regretted, and still do, that I am being talked about or that I am considered something special. And I am fully convinced that the next best Benedictine could have reached the same goal sooner and more surely, taking the same paths and using the same means. I have only become the instrument because it is the way of God to choose those who are weak, so that his action will be all the more visible. I write this only in order to admonish you and others, so that you do not remain cold and indifferent, and do nothing in despairing and disconsolate apathy, at a time when hell's agents are acting divisively and destructively everywhere.

Boniface Wimmer

On October 3, 1850 Fr. Boniface bought a piece of stony woodland on the ridge of a branch of the Alleghany Mountains, called the Chestnut Ridge, approximately 9 miles distant from St. Vincent. The purchase price was very high; but he was able to acquire two pieces of land of equal size bordering it for less than a fourth of the first piece. What expectations he had for this property at the time, what toil and expense would be expended on it, his own words will describe below.

On the first Sunday of Stptember of this year, Fr. Boniface decided to tundertake a trip to Germany. It was this same day that he had received the above mentioned document from the Most Reverend Bishop of Milwaukee, certifying his foundation by Rome. He communicated his intention to his abbot, Gregor Scherr of Metten, in the following letter:

Youngstown, Westmoreland County, PA
October 6, 1850

Most Reverend, Most esteemed Abbot!

After a year full of bitterness, suffering, and problems, during which life was made very trying for poor Fr. Boniface from inside and outside, and everything he had built up would almost have been ruined, if the Good Lord had not given him good friends, and calm prudence and steadfastness, everything has suddenly taken a turn for the better.

The state of my finances is not bad, my credit is better than ever, and three days ago I bought a farm property for 9,000 dollars, that is, 23,000 florins. It consists of 293 acres, equivalent to 300 Bavarian Tagwerk, and it borders my property.

This purchase and the wish to get several talented students, as well as several other wishes and reasons, have made me decide to go to Germany, as soon as the weather forces us to stop building. I hope to obtain enough money, by the grace of God and [generosity] of good people, to be able to make the first payment of 4,500 dollars on April 1 of next year. I hope for much, but I have never yet hoped in vain, because I firmly believe in the promise; "Ask, and you shall receive, seek and you shall find, knock and it shall be opened to you."

So, would you please arrange for lodging for your Fr. Boniface, either in the seniorate or in the carcerate,[2] where a stay for him might per- haps be fitting, provided that the steamer and the locomotive will bring me safely to Metten! As God wills! I will ask a Redemptorist, the pious Fr. Seelos, C.SS.R to give a retreat for myself and my people before I leave. Then I will allow the older brothers, who have persevered loyally in all storms and temptations, to make solemn vows, which they have

---

[2]This reference is not clear. *Carcer* in Latin is a jail. This may have been a humorous reference to a section of the monastery for the junior monks.

yearned to do for so long. I can do so now quite legitimately, since my position has been completely assured by the papal affirmation and authorization; our property has been guaranteed to us and is large enough for the support of numerous monastics; and the brothers have been tested over four years and have been found worthy.

The confirmation had been issued in Rome already on July 23, 1848, but due to the revolution its transmission was delayed. Bishop Henni brought it to us. It had been sent to him, and I received it from him just on the feastday of the Guardian Angels.[3] (Here he lists the six points of the petition, which are mainly aimed at having the Holy See recognize St. Vincent as a monastery founded according to the rules of Canon Law, and that the bishop's act of transferring the parish to this monastery be confirmed. Details about this matter were already mentioned earlier.)

The response to this petition was as follows:[4]

Granted by the holy Collegium held on July 23, 1848.

Pius, our Lord, and through Providence, Pope the ninth (of this name), announces after serious consideration of all the reports, through me, the undersigned prosecretary of the Congregation for the Propagation of the Faith, his consent to everything, and grants the necessary powers to the most reverend bishop of Pittsburgh, provided that no obstacles stand in the way. (L.S.)

Prepared without any kind of tax...

(Then Fr. Boniface continues in his letter to the Most Reverend Archbishop.)[5]

"I was just about to send another petition, prepared in spring... when this document arrived. You can scarcely image how pleasantly surprised I was, and what joy was felt all through the house and the parish...

---

[3] 2 October 1850.
[4] Copy in ASVA.
[5] Fr. Oswald makes a slip in referring to Scherr as Archbishop. He would become Archbishop of Munich only in 1856; at this time he was still the abbot of Metten.

We have a monastery now. The Lord has built it, and because he was the one who did, the human builders have not toiled in vain. He will also continue to build both inside and outside, and will eventually know and find a man who will improve and perfect what I in my inadequacy have either not started right or missed!

My stay in Germany will probably last three to four months. A long time and an anxious time! Though I am very much looking forward to seeing your Grace and all my confreres again, I have become so attached to my second country and my second homeland that it is harder for me to leave here than it once was to part from Munich. I am just worried that something might be needed while I am absent (perhaps because I overestimate my importance), though priests and brothers are encouraging me to make the journey, as they hope it will have good consequences. Unfortunately my Fr. Prior, Fr. Placidus Dötl, a dear man and excellent priest, whom I trust without reservation, has become very frail since Good Friday, so that I am very worried about him.[6]

I ask your Grace and all my confreres to remember me at the altar, so that I may arrive happily and safely at Metten, whole in body and soul, and that God's holy angels may guard and protect me and mine everywhere. I definitely hope to be in Munich before Christmas. With sincerest respect and devotion, and the request that you extend kind greetings to all my confreres, [I remain]

Your Reverence's and Grace's
Most humble [servant]
Fr. Boniface

Filled with hope, but at the same time with a heavy heart, Fr. Boniface took leave of his numerous monastic family, which honored him as their father and to whom they owed so much. Accompanied by their blessings and good wishes, he had a favorable ocean journey, and arrived safely in Bavaria in January 1851. Welcomed by everyone, he was not at all disappointed in his expectations. Twenty one candidates for the Order, seven of whom were clerics, joined themselves to him. When he paid a visit to King Ludwig, the latter promised him support in the amount of 10,000 gulden. On January 25 [1851] Fr. Boniface prepared a written report about his work for the king, and received the following reply:

---

[6]John Dötl was one of the four theological students who had accompanied Fr. Boniface to America in 1846. He received the monastic name Placidus. He was ordained a priest on 20 April 1849. Fr. Boniface's concern about his health was realistic, since Fr. Placid would die on 5 July 1852.

Father Superior Boniface Wimmer!

I have received your report of the 25th of this month, in which you express your thanks for my intended donation of 10,000 florins for the establishment of the first Benedictine Monastery in America, and in which you have given a description of the situation and beginnings of this first monastery, etc. By expressing my thanks to you for this, as well as your declared pious intention of celebrating a weekly holy mass for me, I want to reassure you that I take a lively interest in your undertaking and will receive any future reports about it with joy, if I have not already seen them in the *Annals* which I read. Kindly disposed toward you,

[I remain] Your well-affectioned
Ludwig
Munich, January 30, 1851.

The very next month, on February 27, the king had Court secretary Riedl write to Fr. Boniface in Metten that he was in possession of a new monstrance which he had bought several years previously on a special occasion in order to help an artificer out of some unfortunate circumstances. This monstrance was not exactly a masterpiece, but might nevertheless be suitable for a country church, and since the Catholic churches everywhere in America were still lacking in many things, he wanted to offer it to Fr. Boniface. Right after that, the king had a significant number of books with religious content registered and packed, in order to give then also as a present to Fr. Boniface. A special "gift deed" about this was prepared on March 27, 1851, reading, "for the newly established Benedictine monastery of St. Vincent in North America". This new evidence of the favorable inclination of his prominent patron encouraged Fr. Boniface to take advantage of the situation in order to at least give a try to placing a crown on his work. Since the king was about to depart for Rome the very next week, Fr. Boniface addressed a letter to him on April 18 in which he explained in detail what benefits would arise for the foundation at St. Vincent, if the monastery would be elevated to an abbey. The letter did not fail to have an effect, though at the same time the reply to it touches on an issue that even then threatened to become a Pandora's Box for St. Vincent. Let us hear the king's reply:

Rev. Superior, Fr. Boniface,

I have received your letter of April 18 of this year in Rome, in which you request that I approach His Papal Holiness about declaring the Benedictine monastery Mount St. Vincent an abbey. I have immediately had the royal Bavarian legate, Count von Spaur, take the necessary steps to approach Cardinal Prefect Franzoni about the matter. From him I have received the assurance that his Papal Holiness certainly would have no objections to elevate the St. Vincent monastery to an abbey, as soon as you would be able to receive an amicable agreement and approval of your intention to erect a brewery near the monastery from the bishop of your diocese as well as from several priests who are members of this diocese. By the way, further steps are even being taken in Rome to place the opposition of your bishop toward this establishment of a brewery in the proper light, stressing that in Bavaria and in Germany in general, the Benedictines owned breweries already in times past, and still own them, which increase the prosperity of a monastery and thereby also enable in part the work they can accomplish. Informing you of this, Rev. Superior, I assure you gladly of my esteem,

Your favorably disposed,
Ludwig
Munich, June 24, 1851

CHAPTER THIRTEEN
Homecoming to St. Vincent. Land and work on the Ridge. Report on St. Mary's, Carrolltown, and Indiana in the year 1851.

Enriched by many and significant presents, and sent off with many pious good wishes from many true and trusted old friends as well as new ones, Fr. Boniface left Munich on May 10, 1851. His traveling companions were twenty candidates for the Order with whom he boarded the steam ship "Washington" in Bremerhaven for the journey to New York. After a good sea journey they landed in the western metropolis at 5 o'clock in the evening on June 2. They quickly reached St. Vincent, where the young novices received their habits on the 18th of the same month. Seven of them were eventually ordained to the priesthood. Two of these are still among us, while the rest went to their eternal reward already many years ago. The first one to die was Fr. Ildephonse Johann Boeld, when he fell from a horse on the road between Loretto and Carrolltown on June 14, 1855. He was followed to a better life by Fr. Valentin Felder, who was run over and killed by the horse-drawn trolley on Canal Street in New York on May 28, 1857. Fr. Ulrich Spöttel met his death in Butler, Pennsylvania on July 28, 1859 due to a lung disease. Like a hero on the battlefield, Fr. Emmeram Michael Bliemel, chaplain for the Tenth Tennessee regiment in the War of Secession, met his death when a bomb exploded at Jonesborough near Atlanta on August 31, 1864. The fifth one of them, Fr. Roman Benedict Hell, died at St. Vincent of a painful stomach aliment on May 3, 1873.

Details about other events that occurred since his return Fr. Boniface describes himself in the following report to the administration of the Mission Society in Munich, dated November 7, 1851:[1]

"I left Munich on May 10 with a company of 26 persons, for whom I had taken on responsibility for the arrangements for the journey, of whom, however, only 21 really belonged to me. On the 16th we left Bremen on the steamship "Washington" for the return trip to America. The ocean crossing went very well and it was the fastest that the Wash-

---

[1]Published in the *Annals* 20 (1852) 388-397. This letter constitutes the bulk of chapter thirteen.

ington had ever made, for we reached New York at 5 o'clock in the evening on June 2, after 12 days and 22 hours. I and my companions reached our monastery at St. Vincent only on June 7, which was the Saturday before Pentecost, where we had been awaited with great longing and welcomed with much affection. How happy I was to see all my dear confreres again, and to be able to embrace and bless them. After we first thanked the Lord of Hosts who had safely guided us overseas and back again, I moved back into my modest little monastery, accompanied by resounding music, because our charges simply could not be dissuaded from offering us a sampling of their progress in music and by this to demonstrate their joy over my return and the arrival of so many new companions.

Now I took the oversight back into my own hands, which Fr. Subprior, Benedict Haindl, had in my absence carried out to my great satisfaction. Fr. Prior had unfortunately been ill the entire time and is only now recovering again.[2] I do not want to bother you with a description of the jobs that a superior at St. Vincent must carry out. May it suffice to mention that so much business waited for me that I did not even think of writing to my friends and benefactors in Germany for three months, in part because I could not find the time and in part because I first had to await the outcome.

The way the situation is here, it is not possible to stand still and to limit oneself to a certain area or place or number: we go forward, we must take hold of every opportunity and expand, even if we have not yet had time to complete a previous task. A house would not be all that difficult to manage, especially when everything is moving in a well ordered routine. However, on the one hand, our monastery is yearly growing so much in membership that I always have to look for new means of providing for everyone and keeping them occupied. On the other hand, there are religious as well as secular individuals here and there who pressure us to help where no one else is available or willing to offer help. So I have to buy or start something new every year, because every beginning is difficult and adds new worries and new work to the already existing ones.

Already during my absence my Fr. Subprior[2] bought a farm of 312 acres that had become available and which adjoins another piece of

---

[2]This would be Fr. Placid Döttl.

land of 425 acres that I had bought earlier. It cost only 3000 rheinish florins; but it is pretty neglected and will require much work to bring it up to par. For the past three months 10 brothers have been there to build a saw mill, since we did not yet have one up to now, and the lumber I need for the buildings took 1000 florins from us yearly. Every Monday morning they would leave the monastery and every Saturday evening they would come back. That is because the above mentioned 735 acres are located on the mountains, 7 miles from the monastery. The place where the saw mill was built is located in a terrible ravine through which a small creek, called the Sewickly, cascades, over two miles from the nearest house. Thus the first thing we did before the building [of the saw mill] began, was to build us a log cabin to live in. It measures only 14 feet square and was soon completed. Then we had to build a road so that we could get there with horses and wagons. That was no fun, but we, nevertheless, did manage to accomplish it in one week; of course, the Viennese would hardly want to take a pleasure trip on this road or visit this amusement park, but my brothers did manage to get in, first with a wagon drawn by two horses, then with one drawn by four. We killed a few rattle snakes that wanted to discourage us from staying... Swarms of mosquitoes that did not let us sleep at the beginning, we chased away with smoke...and so the building progressed quickly, in spite of the difficult terrain, and is now completed...[3]

Now a little about the colony of St. Mary's in Elk County.

It was known that this colony was founded principally by Fr. Alexander, C.S.S.R, but was given up two years ago, because it did not prosper as well as had been expected, and the Redemptorist fathers suffered very significant losses every year. After their departure I helped out with two priests for half a year,[4] until the most revered bishop found a diocesan priest to whom he could transfer the large parish. This was Rev. Schaffleitner, an Austrian from the Diocese of Linz, and a very worthy man. But he also did not stay longer than one year before he entered the Order of the Redemptorists. Thus there was no priest available again except for me and my confreres; therefore they turned to me once again.

St. Marystown is 115 miles from my monastery and therefore quite

---

[3] It is striking how Fr. Boniface includes himself in all this activity: we built the log cabin, the road, etc.
[4] From January through May 1850.

inconvenient for me to reach, first because of this distance, and then also because the roads are extremely bad in wet weather. The church and rectory had burned down in the past year, and it was not likely that the parish would be able to rebuild. Besides, we are only 9 priests; 2 of them are in Carrolltown, 2 others are not very healthy, and the more robust ones are needed for the ministry at home, as well as for teaching the Order candidates or the education of the boys in our seminary. It is easy to see that I could not feel a great deal of motivation to take over the colony, because it would cost me personnel, money, and sacrifice; and it threatened to rob me of a lot of time because more frequent trips would be required. However, the most reverend bishop wished it; the German compatriots wished it also; no help could be expected from elsewhere – and so I agreed to again send two priests to St. Marys, and this time with the promise of a permanent stay and formal transfer of the parish. I already had been to St. Marys three times in the past and therefore was fairly well acquainted with the place.

I made it a condition for the establishment of a monastery that a piece of ground of approximately 60 or 70 acres surrounding the church be added to round out the property... The landgrant society saw the reasonableness of my desire and granted what I demanded... In spite of this I incurred a cost of 2,500 to 3,000 dollars... The foundation for our future monastery in St. Marys consists of 734 acres of land, which formerly belonged to the Redemptorist fathers, 60-70 acres which the land-grant society added, and a nice saw mill...

During the winter the preparations necessary for the building of the church will have to be made, and as soon as spring arrives the actual building will have to start. Right now the whole congregation gathers for worship in the school building, where, of course, there is room for not even half of the parishioners, as they already number 1,300 persons. We have only 400 dollars toward the building expenses, which is little better than nothing, because a church for such a parish cannot be built for less than 7,000 dollars in this country. God will help!...

I now move with my description toward Indiana, by way of Brookville, 80 miles to the South. Four miles outside of this little town there are 300 acres of land which I bought recently, with a house, near the Catholic Church of this town... The farm costs 2,400 dollars, 1,500 of which have been paid; but the house costs 2,700 dollars of which only 1,300 have been paid. The rest for both places is to be paid off in yearly installments, along with interest...

Indiana is located right at the midpoint between St. Vincent and Carrolltown, and on the way to St. Mary's. It has 60 Catholic families and as yet no priest, because they are too poor to support one. Actually, there are several additional small Catholic settlements between Indiana and St. Mary's that are totally neglected. Therefore I could not help but be induced by the situation to buy some more property. In the course of the coming year I certainly hope to be able to station two priests and several brothers in that area.

Before returning to St. Vincent, I need to make a small detour to Hart's Sleeping Place, now called Carrolltown. I have had two priests there for the past 3 years, and recently added 6 brothers. I also bought 300 acres of land there for 3,000 dollars, of which 2,000 dollars have already been paid. However, this year another 700 acres have been added, which are located two miles from the place, in the direction of the Susquehanna River, and it will probably be the plot where the monastery will stand one day.

The two priests who are there, with whom the aged missionary Fr. Lemke resides, minister to the 260 families of the parish as well as to the Catholics in some parts of Clearfield and Indiana counties and at several other locations where the Germans do not have their own priest...

As for St. Vincent, there would be few people even in its immediate vicinity who, if asked, would know where it is, for it is neither a town nor a settlement, neither a village nor a castle. Rather, it is a fairly large hill upon which sits a nice church, which, however, unfortunately is not built very solidly. To the left of the church, in the direction of the nearby railroad, is a brick building, 130 feet long and 40 ft wide, 3 stories high. To the right there is a smaller house, also of brick, which is designated as a schoolhouse. Opposite the church, about 400 steps away, is a barn which is 126 feet long and 40 feet wide, and, according to American fashion, is 3 stories high on one side, and two on the other. It, too, is built of brick. Close by is a small log cabin, which was the residence of the first missionaries, and at the same time, the first church.

In the big, long house there reside 5 priests, an aged Irish missionary, and 16 clerical novices (of whom 3 will be ordained to the priesthood before the end of this month, after they make their profession). Then there are also 50 lay brothers, who work in the fields and meadows in spring, summer, and fall; and in winter they are busy with needle or awl, hammer or plane, etc., at different places in or around the house, except when the bell rings and they all quickly gather together. Additionally, there are 34 boys, some of whom are already sprouting beards, even though it has not been too long since they have started to decline *mensa* and conjugate *amo*. At other times there is singing and playing of various musical instruments, so that it gets rather noisy at times, and even our loyal Phylax,[5] who does not have a lot of musical talent, runs off howling, with his tail between his legs. However, when the more practiced and more talented ones get together, they can already execute some rather beautiful music pieces for church.

We are also very delighted to have a not insignificant library, which contains almost all the Latin Classics, several Greek ones, and very valuable historical works; and in the theology department, the old and the new literature is pretty well represented.

At the same time, Fr. Lucas,[6] the art teacher, has good supplies for his department, and he is quite taken up in bringing his students to a point where their accomplishments sometimes are really surprising. Due to the kindness and caring of Court Chaplin Joseph Ferdinand Müller in Munich we are well taken care of in this regard. Furthermore, we also have 300 oil paintings; of course there are no masterworks, but nevertheless a complete collection, consisting of portraits, landscapes, fruit and animal pieces, night scenes on canvas, wood, and tin. Additionally, we have many religious representations as well as [renditions of] individual saints, some of which also serve as altar pictures. Many of these paintings are unfortunately a little damaged; more or less all of them are in need of some restoration. Yet, they are a true treasure, for which I have to thank the kindness of our benefactor, Rev. Raiser in Munich. I received them only today and have been unpacking them,

---

[5]Already as a student in Munich, Fr. Boniface had had a dog with this name.
[6]This was Fr. Luke Wimmer (1825 – 1901), a nephew of Fr. Boniface. He professed vows on 8 April 1850 and was ordained a priest on 12 April of the same year.

along with 6 crates of books, a gift from the catechist, Mr. Brestlmeyer of Ried, for which we are very obliged to this kind donor. This was the rearguard of my baggage, which cost me 480 plus 64 plus 20 for a total of 564 dollars for transportation and customs charges.

This is all for my school. That is what is closest to my heart, and I do not spare any expense in order to offer my students every opportunity to learn, first what is necessary, but then also that which is useful and pleasant, to the extent that it contributes to the ennobling of the person. However, I cannot expect that they will all become priests. Some of them I have to take on from time to time to prepare them for holy confession and communion; but at least many will become priests, and, since they are learning both English and German, they will be equally useful to the English[-speaking] and the Germans...

But so many people to feed, clothe, supply with books, etc.! The gifts from Germany I always use for acquiring new real estate, and the yield from this real estate is to provide for our support, but it is desperately difficult. If we eat a little meat, the flour gives out; if I serve meat more often, the livestock gives out. But, no, it must be sufficient, and really always has been. God's blessing is visibly present; although we have increased by 20 men each year, the cattle and sheep and pigs have also increased, and every year we grow more grain, and the fruit trees we planted are beginning to bear fruit, and the house gets ever larger! Thanks be to God!

CHAPTER FOURTEEN
The Death of Fr. Plazidus Dötl.
Sisters from Eichstätt come to St. Mary's.
The Report on the year 1852.

If we were to assert that Fr. Boniface always achieved the right thing in all his plans, that all his undertakings had a successful outcome, that all his brothers walked on the earth like angels, any reasonable man would doubt the truthfulness of our report.

For at least ten years Fr. Boniface held fast to the hope of being able to establish monasteries and schools also in Carrolltown, St. Marys, and Indiana, with the same success as he had done at St. Vincent, provided that Providence would send him suitable candidates in sufficient numbers, and that his brothers would be able to support these monasteries by means of farming. Based on this thinking, he bought a large house in the little town of Indiana and a farm outside the town. After a few years he erected a chapel on the latter, as well as a solid house and a barn. Eventually, however, he had to admit that at this place his plan could not be realized. In St. Marys, on the other hand, he pursued his work untiringly, in the belief that there he was coming closer to his goal with every year. It is interesting to read his detailed report to the mission society on August 9, 1852, from which we learn the following:

> "Since I have again been supported by the charitable contributions of the Ludwig Mission Society this year, it appears only right that I should give a kind of accounting of the use of the donated alms by way of a short report about the state of my monastery.
>
> I do not have anything great or glorious to report, but perhaps still a few things which might be of interest, especially for all those who share my view that without monasteries and seminaries for the formation of an indigenous clergy nothing lasting can be accomplished for the Catholic Church in this country.

This year again I have with all my might pursued the idea of introducing our Order into the United States, anchoring it firmly, and spreading it abroad, as well as of turning our monasteries into seminaries, partly for young monastic candidates and partly for candidates for the diocesan priesthood, and beyond that of meeting the spiritual needs of our German compatriots and Catholics in general through regular ministry.

I have the consolation of being able to report that three components of beneficial effectiveness have increased significantly during the past year: personnel, material, and the sphere of influence. I may add that the most important ingredient, the spirit of the personnel, does in no way lag behind the other progress. Death tore from us the very reverend Fr. Placidus Dötl, who for two years had filled the position of prior and at the same time was master of novices. Fr. Placidus was a very kind priest, untiring in carrying out his office, a model for all the monks; and to me personally he was as a good son to his father, childlike and loyally devoted. He was sickly for a long time but his poor health did not completely break down until the month of May. He was carried away by his zeal one Sunday when he was feeling a little better and I was away, and he celebrated high mass and preached, although he had already been sitting in the confessional all morning. He experienced a violent hemorrhage, as a result of which he died a few weeks later, much to the deepest sorrow of the whole monastery as well as of the parish. He himself welcomed death, and he was well prepared for it.

Now we are 14 priests and 16 clerics. The number of brothers stands at 77, of whom 20 will receive their habit next week. Out of their midst also death has taken two victims. Among these 77 brothers are 5 blacksmiths, 5 carpenters, 5 woodworkers, 4 masons, 2 tanners, 1 saddle maker, plenty of weavers, 6 shoemakers, only 2 tailors along with a few dabblers, 3 bakers, 1 gardener, dairy men, 1 belt maker, 1 miller, 1 bricklayer, cooks, brewers, and many farmers. Some of them are multiply gifted and can practice two or three trades if need be. Many are also musicians. It is a rule for the brothers that they must allow themselves to be used in any job, and therefore I can actually use them for almost all jobs which do not require a special skill.

Moreover, we are never wanting for work. For one, we have to put up new buildings every year, for which we make the bricks ourselves, break and burn the limestone, cut the boards. Secondly, since we have only poor parishes in the countryside, we must mostly live off our agriculture. One gets fields here only if one first clears the brush and trees that grow on the land; and that takes much labor and effort, as well as time.[1] Thirdly, having so many people living in one place requires a lot of household services, and therefore we need many workers. Another concern is how I can feed so many people, especially so many brothers, particularly when they become elderly. Then, these 77 brothers, 16 clerics, and 14 priests are not all there is to our family. By the close of the past school year, which ends here on July 4th, the anniversary of the Declaration of Independence, we also had 50 students, and I am certain that by the close of the next school year we would have 70 or even more, if I have room for them. Only roughly a quarter of these 50 pay a moderate tuition, not half as much as is being required in all American residential schools. The others are all poor boys and need not only to be fed for free, but often also to be supplied with books and clothing.

These problems have been on my mind often, but for now, that is, as long as there will not be many more of us, they are pretty much solved. I have used the money which I have received from the Mission Society, from his Majesty King Ludwig, and from other benefactors, to buy sufficient land to support a few hundred people, if it be properly cultivated. When we arrived here, the church farm was in such a condition that the people from the area used to pick their supply of black berries on it.[1] Now these two pieces of property supply the monastery with most of its means of subsistence, and I hope to make them yield even far more with our continuing industriousness. They are our main source of support, and as long as the current laws remain in effect, they can never be lost to the monastery.

The construction of the monastery is still far from completed. The main building is now 136 ft. long and 3 stories high, and we make do, accommodating everyone inside. The priests each have their own rooms; students and brothers are together in large study and dormi-

---

[1] In other words, the fields were becoming overgrown.

tory rooms. The library grows a little each year, and the sacristy no longer looks so poor either. Thanks to the many benefactors! However, of books, vestments, chalices, etc. there are never enough, because I always need to give of these things to the newly established priories and country churches. At any place we take over, there never is anything, neither in the house, nor in the stable, nor in the barn, and most often there is actually neither a house nor a barn. The poorest places are always the churches. Thus there is never an end to the need for buying things, and there is never enough of anything, sometimes not even of patience, which I need to give all the time and don't have enough myself.

It is a good testimonial for our young institution that not only poor, but also well-to-do boys, are applying for admission in such large numbers that we cannot accept even half of them. Our daily life is still the same. We do not suffer any want, though we have the barest necessities in every respect of what is needed in food and drink and shelter. There is plenty of work for priests, students, and brothers, but also time enough for spiritual exercises.

The second place we occupy is the little monastery at Carrolltown, which consists of a wooden farm house and a chapel."

The Sunday after the Feast of Corpus Christi in 1849, the corner stone was laid for a beautiful church built of brick, 110 ft. long. The stately building went up quickly, but the blessing of the church took place only at Christmas of 1850. It was performed by Fr. Celestine, who had been authorized to do so by the bishop. Fr. Lemke has also joined the Order now, after he had seen the fulfillment of his wish, that is, the establishment of a monastery in Carrolltown.[2]

The parish is mostly German and has about 200 families, good and honest people who live in an area of approximately 10 miles in diameter that surrounds the church... In addition to Carrolltown, our priests also take care of Glenkonnel, where a church was built under the leadership of Fr. Peter Lechner in 1849, and of the German parish in Loretto, where, by the way, an English speaking priest is in

---

[2][original footnote] Published by him are a) a translation of *Defense of Catholic Principles* by Demetrius A. Gallitzin, Reading, 1850; b) *Life and Work of Prince Demetrius Augustine Gallitzin* by Fr. Heinrich Lemke, Capitular of the Benedictine Abbey at St. Vincent. Münster: Coppenrath, 1861. 120. p.380.

residence for the English parishioners. Furthermore, our priests also minister at the small parishes at Clearfield, Frenchville, Cooper Settlement in the large, rough Clearfield County, which constitutes the eastern border of the Diocese of Pittsburgh. Fr. Celestine Engelbrecht is the prior of the house. Fr. Carl Geyerstanger and Fr. Lemke (the latter invested on February 1st) support him.

Fr. Lemke

To the north of Carrolltown is our third place, at St. Maria, about 80 miles from the former. The parish there has about 400 families, all German and mostly Bavarians. Nine miles to the south of this is another Catholic parish, with 56 Irish and 28 German families. To the east a German settlement of 25 families has been started at Williamsville, all of which are entrusted to our care, along with another few families that live scattered about the area. At the present time I have 2 priests at St. Maria, along with 18 brothers.

Once I was certain that I would settle permanently at St. Maria, I also wanted to bring nuns to the area, and turned to the Prioress of St. Walburga in Eichstätt and to the very reverend bishop there. Recently a prayer society has been established in Germany whose main purpose is to prevent the extinction of the Benedictine Order in Europe by means of their prayer. I, too, along with my people, was invited to join this association and did so most gladly. However, I believe that, "one who will not be counseled, also cannot be helped," and there is reason, too, for the American proverb, "Help thyself." In consideration of this I have always thought, and also said everywhere as often as I could, that the Benedictine Order had to participate in the work of the missions, or it would perish. This I had also said to the dear nuns at St. Walburga during my visit at Eichstätt in the past year, and tried to enthuse them for the missions. The good nuns and sisters were more enthusiastic than I had anticipated; and they readily agreed to help out if they were needed, in order to transplant also the female branch of the Benedictine Order to the New World, and to expand it there. My formal invitation to the work of the missions was therefore most gladly received, and only the permission of the most reverend bishop was needed in order to proceed to the actualization. I am very grateful to the very reverend bishop that he quickly gave his consent and sent two capable nuns along with a lay sister as a first, small start. They just arrived here on July 15...

During my most recent stay at St. Mary's I was almost bitten by a rattle snake; no one had ever seen one there before. I went with Brother Philipp, the carpenter,[3] to inspect the school house near the church that had burned down.[4] When we found the door locked, we walked around the building in order to look in through the side window. While the brother tried to get a look at the inside through the side window, I walked all the way around the house where a pile of rocks made it easier to look in through the rear window. No sooner had I put my arms on the window sill, than I heard a considerable noise to my left, some-thing like that of large grasshoppers, only more shrill. I looked around and saw the nasty animal not two feet from me, curled up and ready to strike. With one jump I was outside of its reach and the Brother came right away. We reached for stones and threw them at the snake, who for its part, tried to hide under the rocks or to crawl under the house. When we saw that we had hit it hard a few times, but not killed it, I reached for a slat from the nearby fence and crushed its head with it.

The parish in Indiana has close to 80 families, but is not one of the best. I have suffered more on account of this place than at any other time in my entire life. The place was relatively my most expensive one, and is yielding the least. The efforts of ministry seemed not to be very fruitful for a long time; but the parish has been growing considerably in recent times... So far, I have not been able to use the small brewery I acquired here, because it is believed that it is not proper for monks to be brewing beer and selling it...

In addition to caring for the little town and its surroundings, the two priests in Indiana care also for a very small, widely scattered group

---

[3]This was Br. Philip Bernhard (1822 – 1907). In 1863 he was stationed at the priory in Carrolltown. He eventually became part of the foundation of Belmont Abbey in North Carolina and is buried there.
[4]The church building burned down in May 1850.

of parishioners along the Mahoning river, 20 miles from the town... In the town itself they conduct a school for the Catholic children, which is very well attended, in the hope of saving the younger generation, because there are few favorable prospects for saving their elders, at least until now, though there are laudable exceptions..."

Boniface Wimmer

CHAPTER FIFTEEN
Fr. Boniface will not relent on manual labor.
A prominent guest. A Letter to the
Rev. Archbishop of Munich. Journey to Rome in 1855.

By laboring, the brothers are to prove that they do not enter the monastery to devote themselves to a life of comfortable leisure, but rather that they are endeavoring to "enter through the narrow gate," that they do not recoil at the word of the Apostle, "He who does not work, also shall not eat," nor at Chapter 48 of the *Rule* of St. Benedict, where he says, "When they live by the labor of their hands, as our fathers and the apostles did, then they are really monks."[1] Though the days are long past when the young prince Columba sat on the same bench in school as the carpenter's son, Kieran, at the Abbey of Clonard, and along with him sifted the grain and, like the other students, when it was his turn, helped to take care of the simple needs and support himself and the community, so Fr. Boniface nevertheless wanted to take him as his model. For this reason, he had his scholastics, novices, and clerics work along with the brothers in the fields at certain times, such as at planting and harvesting time. Every Order has its traditions, and when these are maintained, it is all the more respected. In this regard, Fr. Boniface followed the example of famous Benedictines, saints as well as scholars. "When St. Boniface was studying grammar, poetry, and history at Exeter Abbey, in preparation for the study of the sacred books, he never shirked the manual work prescribed in the *Rule,* when he had a break in his studies," reports his biographer, St. Willibald. This schedule of studying as well as doing manual labor he introduced at Fulda. St. Bernard always counted manual labor among the very important duties of monks. "Work, seclusion, voluntary poverty, these are the characteristics that distinguish monks, these tend to ennoble monastic life," he says (Ep. 24). However, this type of enthusiasm for imitating the monks of the Middle Ages suffered some changes over the years at St. Vincent, *tempora mutantur.*

On December 9, 1853, the Papal Nuncio, Monsignor Cajetan Bedini, visited St. Vincent as he was travelling in the area. A solemn reception was prepared for the prominent guest. The novices, scholastics, and clerics, as well as the secular students greeted him with speeches, each group in a different language. How impressed he was

---

[1]RB 48:8; translation of *RB 1980*, Collegeville, MN, 1981.

with St. Vincent is revealed in the report he made to the Propaganda, in which he mentions that he visited the Benedictine monastery near Latrobe, in the Diocese of Pittsburgh. The superior (Fr. Boniface) was very active and enthusiastic, he reported; he had about a dozen professed monks, and as many novices. They engaged in music, farming, manual labor, art, and theological studies, but everything was still relatively impoverished. The monks were intent upon obtaining an abbot, but that seemed to him to be premature, because the whole thing still appeared to be yet too much in its infancy; though it did appear to deserve encouragement.

In 1854 Fr. Boniface built a grist mill, which became very useful for the monastery. What else that year brought, he reports in his letter to the Reverend Archbishop of Munich in the following manner:[2]

St. Vincent, 7 August 1854

Most Reverend Archbishop! With heartfelt gratitude I received the message that we will be remembered again this year with a generous stipend of 7,000 florins from Your Excellency. Through this help, the holes made last year by various endeavors and mishaps will again be partially patched. Current difficulties, to which I fell heir because of hail, fire, and rising costs, have not caused any lull in our work because here credit is often as good as cash. I simply had to open one hole in order to patch another, and in this way, I got by well enough. The number of students in the lay and clerical seminaries increased each month and will grow even more next year so that I will again have to extend our house by 53 feet...

Like Noah's ark, all sorts of creatures from everywhere gather under our roof. Often, too, useless guests come, who disappear after a while or get sent away. To him who knocks, the door is opened. Some leave soon, others only after months. Some even return and are admitted again. Whoever stays is good.

Things are expensive this year, and the price of food is rising even more after the bad harvest. On poor soil, people did not even get seed for the winter grains, especially wheat. On good soil, they got only a half or a third of the usual crop. We are far behind, and what is worse, after a very cold, dry winter we have had an exceedingly hot summer...

---

[2]The full text of the letter can be found in Boniface Wimmer: Letters, 2008: 143-146. The Archbishop was Karl August von Reisach. He had been bishop of Eichstätt, 1836-1846; became archbishop of Munich-Freising and hence also president of the Ludwig Mission Society, 1846-1855; then became cardinal and official of the Roman curia, 1855-1869. He had celebrated Mass for the band of missionaries on 25 July 1846 when they set out on their journey to America.

If we meet with no great misfortune, we will go far with buildings and agriculture each year, so that we will always be able to take pupils. Without a doubt, St. Mary's, because it is in another diocese, will soon be a rival of St. Vincent, and similar efforts will be made there. I believe I already reported that we would take over [the parish at] Butler and Butler County, where Fr. Utto and Fr. Kilian are stationed with a lay brother...

Otherwise, things are going along in the normal way. Most of us are well, happy, and satisfied. Next to me, Fr. Demetrius (Count Marogna) is most in demand in the house... I have only 5 priests here with me until more are ordained. Everyone is overworked , especially on Sundays, when two, and sometimes three have to go out...

May God reward your goodness to us. We will beg Him to do so daily. With deepest reverence, your most humble,
Fr. Boniface Wimmer, O.S.B., Superior

After serious deliberation, Fr. Boniface made the decision to travel to Rome himself in order to report on his work to the Holy Father. For this purpose he assembled precise statistics about his monks, about the educational establishment, about the activities of his priests in their ministry, as well as about the material possessions of his community. On December 18, 1854 he wrote a letter to his eminence, the Cardinal Prefect of the Propaganda,[3] in which he presented his wish, namely that the St. Vincent Monastery might be elevated to an abbey, so that his foundation might be secured for the future. In this letter he said among other things that the cardinal might perhaps find it surprising that he put so much weight on the title or name of abbot, when his foundation had repeatedly been made secure through the fatherly protection of the highest authority by which his Eminence customarily assists such institutions. "If it is true," he continues, "that where your treasure is, there your heart also is, who can be surprised when that which we have brought about by such great efforts, when we, who are Benedictines, consider our Order, our monastery that treasure that is closest to our hearts, that we wish to see it secured on all sides? Is it any wonder if we burn with the desire to enjoy all the rights and privileges that we are entitled to according to the privileges of the Order, when we see how other religious Orders and associations live under their lawful superiors? Of course, we know that the abbatial office is a grace, which we cannot demand, but which we can only ask for in humility."

---

[3]See Wimmer, *Letters* (2008) 146-147 for the full text of the letter. Giacomo Filippe Cardinal Fransoni (1775-1856) served as Prefect of the Sacred Congregation for the Propagation of the Faith.

Since the Sacred Congregation customarily supports and promotes all good foundations that are useful to religion, then as long as the above-mentioned favor, for which he had humbly petitioned, would be denied, writes Fr. Boniface, he would have to fear that the Sacred Congregation did not deem his monastery to be a good and useful work, or a least not that good and useful that it would be worthy of designation as an abbey and of final confirmations. If that were the case, he would really begin to feel discouraged and to entertain serious doubts about the successful outcome of that which had been started, since he, having done his very best for such a long time, would appear to not have done enough...

In February 1855 Fr. Boniface started on his journey. He wrote to the Central Administration of the Ludwig Mission Society that he hoped that his journey to Rome would succeed in getting the St. Vincent monastery recognized as a permanent foundation, which would be able to meet the double purpose for which he had founded it according to the wishes and the support of the Society, that is, to be a mission institution and a training institution for missionaries.[4]

It is undeniably inherent in the nature of the situation, and supported by the history of all Orders, [Fr. Boniface argued] that his foundation would not be able to exist in isolation. It had life and energy, and these, in turn, would bring about life. Regardless of whether he would remain in charge or if it would be another, "Forward!" would have to be the motto of any superior of St. Vincent! Anyone who would calmly contemplate the situation would eventually also have to come to this exclamation: "The harvest is great and the laborers are few," and these few are not always the best and most skilled. However, even if there were many, duty and the instinct for self-preservation would force them to spread out and to take firm root in a large area, so that the first storm or blast of wind would not knock the tree down and uproot it.

Beyond this, Fr. Boniface expressed the hope that his efforts would not have been fruitless in deeply implanting in all those who had taken the habit of St. Benedict under his leadership, the greatest respect for their Order and the conviction, grounded in history, of its very special vocation of always working for the preservation and propagation of Catholicism. He also hoped that his successors would do whatever was in their power to actualize his leading idea, namely, to make the Order in America that which it was in the Middle Ages of the Church in Europe; and that they would not just act on behalf of self-preservation or to promote religion in general, but would act out of love for their Order and with a certain zeal for its honor.

With this Fr. Boniface wanted to express the hope that the gifts which the Central Administration of the Ludwig Mission Society had given him, and would still graciously consider giving him in the future, would be fruitfully invested for the long term. He furthermore hoped that he would not be far off the mark when he dared to hope that St. Vincent was capable of achieving in the next ten years ten times as much as in the first ten

---

[4]The *Annalen*, Vol. 23 (1855) 428-430 printed an excerpt of this letter of Fr. Boniface to the Society under date of 25 March 1855.

years of its existence during which it had already provided nineteen Benedictine and ten secular priests for America. The Orders have great riches, in spite of their poverty, in these words of our Lord, which he had always firmly believed, "*Centuplum accipietis*—you will receive a hundred-fold," and, "*Ego et pater unum sumus*—I and the Father are one." This was his wisdom which had never caused him to go wrong, and never would, because it was grounded on the words of the Lord.

However, he also had not disregarded human wisdom. As the monastery existed right now, it would stand firm if the Holy Father would lay his hand on it. He had pretty much reconciled himself to not receiving any further help from outside, because he feared the outbreak of a war. Of course, he would be significantly affected by such a loss of funding, and be seriously limited in expanding his sphere of activity. However, his work would not fall apart—provision had been made to prevent that. He was also considering—with trust in God—to take some bold risks in the future, if it were to become necessary and if he would have to work longer. In doing so, he was planning to make such good use of his small capital of experience and knowledge of people and things that the risk, aimed for the greater glory of God, would not be likely to lead to failure. He was firmly convinced that if something good was to be done, it could be done, as history teaches.

Once he arrived in Rome, Fr. Boniface had soon to learn that the reports he had submitted were by no means judged and accepted as favorably as he had expected. What had happened in the small town of Indiana in the preceding three years, the purchase of an inn as well as the establishment of a small brewery in connection with it, weighed in as a heavy reproach against him. All these business transactions in which he had allowed himself to get involved in Indiana were seen as actions that demonstrated a lack of good judgment and discretion on his part. He should have realized that public opinion would go against him, that the honor and good reputation of religion in general, and of his Order in particular, would be damaged in the eyes of the Catholic as well as the Protestant population.

Fr. Boniface, in his defense, cited the long-standing custom of monasteries of various Orders in Germany who also operated breweries. Besides, he had actually abandoned all secular businesses in the little town of Indiana more than a year before. The only thing which he tried to hold onto in these unpleasant negotiations was permission to eventually establish a small brewery at St. Vincent. The remainder of the material he had submitted was then passed on to Abbot Angelo de Pescetelli, the Procurator General of the Cassinese Congregation, with a request for his evaluation. This man, a skillful lawyer, who had been teaching Canon law at the University of Parma for many years, evaluated the material in great detail and in an excellent manner, according to Canon Law. Since these proceedings were pivotal for the whole undertaking of Fr. Boniface, they are of greatest importance for his biography. For this reason, the following chapter is devoted to the highlights of this evaluation.

CHAPTER SIXTEEN
Abbot Pescetelli's Evaluation of
Fr. Boniface Wimmer's Foundation.

Don Angelo Pescetelli, then abbot of St. Paul Fuori Le Mura and Procurator-General of the Cassinese Congregation, presented his evaluation of the foundation of Fr. Boniface Wimmer to his Eminence, Cardinal Fransoni, Prefect of the Congregation for the Propagation of the Faith, on March 12, 1855.[1] In the introduction he said: In order to carry out the prestigious assignment, which the Cardinal had entrusted to him, with all the more diligence, he had repeatedly read the letters and petitions of the Bavarian monks in Pennsylvania, as well as the two reports of the most reverend Michael O'Connor, Bishop of Pittsburgh. In addition he had discussed the case with others in similar positions in his Order and also compared it with the ecclesiastical constitutions, as contained in the *Corpus juris vel extra*.

The monks petitioned:

1) That the monastery of St. Vincent be canonically established as an abbey;

2) That the community be permitted to elect an abbot according to the sacred canons and the special constitutions of the Bavarian Benedictines.

The Bishop of Pittsburgh, he reports, had reservations and favored neither of the petitions. Instead he posed two questions, one of them being a question of principle, the other, a personal one. These questions arose 1) from doubts regarding the Bavarian constitutions of the Benedictines, and b) in reference to the right of the bishop to designate a part of the students to be accepted into the seminary.

In order to reach a conclusion, he asks if His Eminence would permit him to examine the petitions of the monks and the concerns of the bishop in the greatest possible brevity.

I. The Elevation of St. Vincent to an Abbey

In the petition which the monks were humbly submitting to the Holy See, their wish was justified by a number of reasons, which he did not want to repeat here.

See Oetgen, *Mission*, 103-105 concerning Abbot Pescetelli's role in this matter. Pescetelli's report makes up the bulk of this chapter. Fr. Oswald's treatment of the report is extensive but is a paraphrase of the main points rather than a direct translation. It is somewhat tedious to read through, and much of the canonical legislation it references now has long been superseded, but it testifies to Abbot Pescetelli's great efforts which, after all, contributed to a successful result.

However, the main ones were: that the community already had 42 monks and 81 lay brothers; that their property consisted of 3600 acres of land, three mills, and many buildings; that they had already rendered significant services to the Church and the people; that they followed the *Holy Rule* conscientiously—all of which meet the conditions prescribed by the papal and monastic constitutions. It was the wish of all monastics to live always and everywhere by the above rules, with the same practices, and with the same steps of the hierarchical order.

It was a providential law that aimed not only for the preservation of the religious institutions, but that also gave each one of them a certain character and stamped upon it a special face. Furthermore, it seemed that this law evolved as it was influenced by the period of history during which this foundation occurred, both by its reputation as well as by its importance. Thus it was natural for a Benedictine, so to speak, that he live in an abbey which he loved as his country and his home. In any other house, be it ever so large or luxurious, he would always be discontent. He would always imagine that he was inferior to his confreres and did not belong to the large family of the patriarchs of the West. This could be considered so true that, if any further proof were needed, the repeated petitions from the monks of Pennsylvania should convince anyone. The Holy See which approved the establishment of 52,000 Benedictine Abbeys (see *Histoire literaire de la Congr.*, d.s. Maur, p. 10) had often been indulgent in all canonical requirements. However, it had always been forceful in overcoming any hindrances which got in the way of their uniform and universal application, in order to benefit not only what was good, but also that which gave promise of becoming something good.

A good example of this was the establishment of the Abbey of Solesmes in France, under Gregory XVI in 1837. That monastery was at that time a long ways from having the number of monks and as much property as St. Vincent currently had, and the establishment took place in the face of numerous obstacles that were put in its way, partly by the government, partly by the population, and partly by the episcopate.

Everyone knew of the great benefit that had arisen from this abbey for the Church and what consolation for the Holy Father. He should be able to see what happened in France in 1837 could now happen in America. America was a youthful land which could produce Catholic institutions of all kinds as it expanded. In it the models of the Middle Ages could come to life again, when the abbeys were almost the only institutions that instructed the population in religion, the sciences, the mechanical and the liberal arts, and in agriculture. Actually, that was exactly what the monks in Pennsylvania had already brought about. When we read their reports about their monastic practices, their scientific endeavors, their activities in the arts and in agriculture, they brought to mind those long ago days, which were so glorious for the Church. Might, therefore, these very deserving monks have their petition granted, so that they would thereby be newly inspired in their zeal for the honor of the Order and for the propagation of Christianity and true learning in America.

II. Authority to Elect an Abbot

The name "Abbot" is so ancient, so venerable, and so inseparable from the history of the Benedictines and their establishments, that they could neither imagine a superior, nor respect one, who is not honored with this title. That the community was entitled to the election of an abbot was clearly found in the words of the *Holy Rule:* "In choosing an abbot, the guiding principle should always be that the man placed in office be the one selected either by the whole community acting unanimously in the fear of God, or by some part of the community, no matter how small, which possesses sounder judgment" (RB 64: 1-2). St Gregory, in chapt. 5, caus. 18.9.2 *de libertate Monachorum* (which is recognized as genuine in the Maurist edition, near the end of the letters of the Pope) prescribed that "following the death of the Abbot of a monastic community, no outsider shall be elected, but rather the one from the same community whom the community of brothers has elected for themselves by their own will." The above principle was supported by a number of [papal] bulls and by all the monastic constitutions of the various Congregations, to the effect that confirmation by the Pope, or the general chapter, or sometimes by the bishop, acting in the capacity of Apostolic Delegate, was required when the monasteries stood in isolation or did not belong to any Congregation, of which there were some in Germany (or Austria).

The application of this law had been quite opportune in many complicated cases. To mention a more recent example, he [Abbot Pescetelli] reported that in the past year a question was settled in this manner, which had gotten the Benedictine Congregation in Brazil into difficulties. Indeed, it really could not be any different; since the monastics knew each other, it would be expected that they would always elect the most worthy monk and the one most suited for the governance. If, on the other hand, an outsider were to be elected who was not acquainted with the interior structure of the monastic association, who would weigh and judge everything in light of his own interests and often also his prejudices, one would have to be very fearful that even with the best intentions much would be destroyed that had been built up with much toil and effort. For this reason the wisdom of the popes in Rome is deserving of our greatest admiration, because they had always adhered to this rule and protected it, except in a few extraordinary cases, as was clearly evident from the history of monasticism.

May the group at St. Vincent, accordingly, be granted the authority to elect an abbot for themselves, provided [their choice] meet with the approval of the Holy See and [be in line with] any other restrictions which the wisdom of the Holy Father might wish to impose.

III. Two reports of Monsignore Bishop O'Connor

are presented, the first one dated April 12, 1854 and the second one without a date, but presumably written this past December [1854]. First and foremost he [Abbot Pescetelli] agreed with the feeling of esteem and respect which the monks of St. Vincent paid his hallowed person in all their reports. He [Abbot Pescetelli] was also very grateful for all the good things which the Bishop had to say about the institution of the Benedictines, when he commented that it would become one of the most important institutions in the country, provided it would have good leadership. He added, "I can say that it seems to me that there is no institution in the country which promises to be so successful in the formation of a young clergy, as the institution of the Benedictines at St. Vincent." However, he [Abbot Pescetelli] could not agree with him [Bishop O'Connor] on the proposition to set up an abbot with sufficient power and also the title of abbot, who, however, was not elected for life and was not exempt. It seemed to him [Abbot Pescetelli] that this type of abbot would be an illusion, which one could find neither in the *Holy Rule*, nor in the history of the Benedictines. Furthermore, if the wisdom which guided the Holy See in all its undertakings would delay the favor which the monks were requesting with such longing, it seemed certain to him [Abbot Pescetelli] that it [the Holy See] would create something that at the same time was and was not. It should not be said that the novelty of an exempt Abbot in America would cause more harm than good.

It was to be expected that America would observe the customs of Rome in such matters, and not Rome those of America. Thus it would also happen that all the different levels of the ecclesiastical hierarchy would exist there with all their privileges of honor and jurisdiction. They would get accustomed to the observance of the canons and bulls which lend some importance to the office of an abbot, which prescribe the celebration of an abbot's blessing in the Roman Pontifical to be carried out with great solemnity and splendor, and many ceremonies, which set aside a part of the breviary and the Roman Missal for the *Commune Abbatum,* and which always accorded the title of abbot such respect as was often associated with persons of higher and more noble rank, such as bishops and cardinals and, at times, even the Pope.

All the Benedictines knew and understood this and would not consider any other title (such as provost, rector, guardian, or whatever) as proper for their superior. For this reason it seemed to him that in regard to this point also the old canons should be observed, among others the third canon, *Abbatis de privilegiis* in 6, cited by Giraldo *sectio* 888, with the addition of the decree of Alexander VII (September 27, 1659) in regard to the use of the pontificals for prelates of lower rank than bishops. If the strict and exact observance of these decrees were prescribed for the new abbot of St. Vincent, no one devoted to the Holy See would find any reason for complaint. And should someone here or there not consider this timely, let him remember all the good that religion and the people of the country would gain from it, and the greater good which the monks would be able to bring about, if they could organize themselves under their own rules and thus establish a well-governed institution. Such results had actually been observed in France, after the Holy See found it appropriate to name Dom Guéranger abbot of Solesmes in 1837. The former French episcopate did not consider it opportune that an exempt abbot make a new appearance in France... However, Abbot Guéranger, a wise and learned man, defended his cause with modesty and with strength. He choose as his motto the saying (which can be found in the title of each of his works), "*Sanas Pontificii juris et sacrae Liturgiae tradiciones labescentes confovere.*" By doing this, he proclaimed from his seclusion at Solesmes, which is directly subject to the Holy See, the principle of unity and submission to the Supreme Shepherd with such power and erudition, that one could say without fear of contradiction, that the great movement for unity in liturgy and doctrine which took place in France was to a large extent the result of his zeal and his devotion to the chair of St. Peter.

Now he [Abbot Pescetelli] asks, suppose the Holy See had, contrary to its custom and its well-known wisdom, listened to the narrow-minded and timorous advice of some, would it have harvested such bountiful fruits in a church which, often under the cloak of supposed freedom, would have deeply grieved the heart of the Pope?

One must not imagine that the abbot of Solesmes was completely exempt from the jurisdiction of the bishop. Rather, the latter could, in the role of an apostolic delegate, visit the monastery, keep watch over its discipline, eliminate abuses, and finally bring his complaints before the Holy See and call on the fullness of his power. It would seem to him [Abbot Pescetelli] that the aversion toward a new abbot was directed less against the latter than against the Holy See, for history teaches that in bad times and severe trials of the Church, the Orders always unite themselves all the more to the Holy See and join themselves to it more closely. This was a result of their life, their influence and their importance. The wisdom of the great Pope Gregory VII had established and organized monastic institutions all over Europe, and it was from this very fact that he received devoted support and loyal assistance in the time of tribulation.

It was to be feared that if the nomination of a new abbot were delayed any longer, the important Benedictine colony in Pennsylvania might dissolve itself or become subject to some of those irregularities which easily creep into religious communities where no one was clearly in charge and given the authority which made him respected by those subject to him.

It was to be feared that the community at St. Vincent, which, according to the testimony of Bishop O'Connor was so devout, so edifying an inspiration, and so useful to the Church, might perceive this postponement not as a disapproval of their conduct, but as censure of Fr. Wimmer, the founder and superior of the foundation. Should these doubts, which, judging from the latest letters, were already surfacing, take root in the minds of many, should passions and vain ambition awake in this community which was not yet securely organized, then the good which had already been accomplished, might suddenly be lost, along with the greater good which one could expect in the future from these such active and intelligent workers.

May, then, the authority be granted to elect an abbot, who, to the extent that this would appear desirable, would be dependent on the diocesan bishop; may the repeatedly expressed wishes of such zealous monks be fulfilled; may their apostolic and civilizing labors in the New World be rewarded, as even the legislature of the State of Pennsylvania has done, in that it assured them of their civil rights as a corporation by giving them a charter; through this favor may there be an increase of courage and zeal for another division of Benedictines who only recently came from Maria Einsiedeln in Switzerland and moved to a state west of Pennsylvania (St. Meinrad in Indiana); may a Pharus [harbor lighthouse] be erected for the monks of the old Europe, to which they might look for security and where they might seek refuge, if the devastating hand of the Revolution would drive them out of the old abbeys, as is currently happening in one of the most important provinces of Italy.

IV. Who is to be abbot?

Fr. Wimmer delayed his petition until he had formed monks who would be suitable for this honor, so as not to create the appearance that he was inordinately ambitious by demanding this rank for himself.

There were three members who in all probability might win the election. One of them was described by Bishop O'Connor as a man who distinguishes himself in piety, knowledge, and intelligence. He was between 35 and 40 years of age, and currently prior of a house which, after St. Vincent, is the most important one. The second one was suggested by Fr. Wimmer. His name is Demetrius. He is of Italian descent, born in Bavaria, a member of the family of the counts of Marogna. He is of advanced age, very learned, pious, humble, and well versed in business management. He is presently Prior at St. Vincent. The third one is Fr. Wimmer, the founder of the colony and approved as its superior by a decree of May 21, 1852.

May he [Abbot Pescetelli] be permitted to express some justified praise for the last and to offer this worthy confrere his due admiration for being able to accomplish such great things for the glory of God and the Order of St. Benedict in such a short time. Fr. Boniface Wimmer, following the inspiration of the zeal of his soul and encouragement of the Ludwig Mission Society in Munich, left Metten, an exemplary abbey in Bavaria, with four clerics and sixteen lay brothers, with the intention of bringing spiritual aid to the German immigrants which were settling in large number in uninhabited stretches of land in the United States, and to form a monastery and found a seminary. After arriving in New York on September 16, 1846, they were cordially welcomed by Bishop O'Connor. Already on October 24, the bishop named Fr. Wimmer pastor of St. Vincent and gave him two estates, from which, however, the man who was the priest until that time, and who had now ceded his place [to Fr. Wimmer], had been able to support himself only with great effort. The priest's living quarters consisted of only two rooms, and Fr. Wimmer and his companions needed to set up their sleeping area in the attic during six months of a very cold winter. In spite of the bitter weather and a distance of 300 steps, he never failed to go to the church six times a day in order to recite the Divine Office with his monastic companions, starting at 4 o'clock in the morning. The first eleven months he spent in such poverty that 100 Gulden, which he received from Bavaria, seemed like a great treasure to him.

In October 1847 Fr. Peter Lechner, a Benedictine from Scheyern, arrived with twenty candidates and a sum of money. Thereupon he began to think seriously of building a monastery. A difference of opinion arose between him and Peter Lechner, who wanted to abandon the educational aspect and the missionary activity, and to establish a monastery in the mode of the Trappists. Wimmer opposed this and called the dissatisfied ones to order, who then repented and apologized. With the means provided by the Ludwig Mission Society, he bought land, built a monastery, established three priories, built mills and several houses, which he staffed with monks and lay brothers. He subjected all of them to strict monastic discipline, imparted to them the spirit of his own active vision, and assigned a task to each one of them, either preaching, or teaching, or manual labor. He had opened a college and a seminary, which were to be especially accessible to the poor. He also had undertaken a journey to Bavaria and received 10,000 Gulden from King Ludwig for St. Vincent and 8,000 Gulden for a monastery for Benedictine nuns, whom he brought from Germany to teach poor children. He had established a school that offered a classical education, where the old and modern languages were taught, along with grammar, rhetoric, philosophy, medicine, dogmatics, moral theology, canon law, and church history, using textbooks by the most proven authors. To many a monk or lay brother who had acquired skills and knowledge in music, painting, sculpting, and gold smithing in Germany he gave opportunity to develop these and make them useful.

He leads a community of 81 lay brothers in manual labor and farming with great order and discipline, without sacrificing any of the monastic exercises, which is deserving of the greatest admiration. When he wrote his most recent letter, dated December 10, 1854, he had 42 monks, 18 novices, 81 lay brothers, and 100 students and seminarians. In addition to the main monastery, three priories are subject to him, located 28, 55, and 115 miles from St. Vincent, respectively. His monastery owns

3600 acres of land, an art gallery, a library, all kinds of musical instruments, and all kinds of trade tools and farming machinery. All sums [of money] which he had received from the Ludwig Mission Society or from the king himself, and for which he gave an exact accounting, he had used for the purchase of land. The support for the monks, the lay brothers, the seminarians (which he maintains almost for free), for the priests in the monastery who teach, for the poor and for the transients, he obtains solely from the farming operation, harvested by the sweat of the lay brothers, and often by the monks themselves.

He has spread the blessings of the Gospel and the consolation of religion over a territory as large as the Grand Duchy of Toskana, and with much benefit, as the bishop himself attests. He is very experienced in the management of the business aspects and wise in the governance of his large monastic family, as the bishop himself (in a letter of April 12, 1854) asserts, "the society would not be able to make such progress under the leadership of another [person]..." Would a man, who in the brief space of eight years, brought about such miracles, not possess the good sense which an abbot is supposed to have? Would not a man who has guided so many to a monastic vocation, who formed them and accustomed them to such a strictly disciplined life, which is wholly devoted to the glory of God and the love of neighbor, be well able to manage not only the temporal but also the spiritual affairs.

It was true that there was a report in existence which bore testimony to some imprudence on the part of Wimmer. This was a situation that was well known to the Sacred Congregation, regarding some business activities in the small town of Indiana. However, this incident was in part the result of disloyalty on the part of a third person, and occurred against his [Wimmer's] will. He [Wimmer] also had straightened the matter out partially before the decision from Rome had reached him. However, even if it were acknowledged that this incident did not bring much honor to Wimmer's wisdom—if one examined the thousands of actions of a man who undertook so much and accomplished so much, a single mistake would present weak evidence against him. This incident should therefore not be a reason to exclude Fr. Wimmer from a position which he had filled so honorably thus far. It should provide even less reason for him not to be elected, for otherwise it would be impossible to fill any ecclesiastical position. He [Abbot Pescetelli] was inclined to assert that there was no man in all the world, no matter how wise he might be, who had not committed some unwise action, because he did not take into consideration the judgment of individuals which seemed to him to be less favorable.

V. As regards the objection and concern

in reference to the Bavarian Benedictine Congregation, one may look for counsel to the *Bullarium* of the revered Pope Innocent XI, where the relevant constitutions can be found on p. 340 and p. 366, *Const. Cirumspecta, et Const. Militantis Ecclesiae.* Serious opposition might be raised against the Benedictines in America if they were to be dependent upon a stranger for a superior. However, he [Abbot Pescetelli] did not know what reply could be made to this [opposition], since he [Abbot P.] did not grasp its significance. He did hope, though, that this opposition would not extend to the dependence of all monastics on their superior-general, who resided in Rome.

VI. In regard to the tuition-free acceptance

of a certain number of English-speaking seminarians, one needs to remember that the Mission Society had sent Fr. Wimmer primarily for the Germans, which were very numerous in Pennsylvania: *missus eram, ut Germanis providerem* (Letter to his Eminence Cardinal Morichini). The question regarding this point was already raised at the start of the mission, in June 1847, when Fr. Wimmer and his companions came close to leaving St. Vincent. They stayed only as a result of a contract which they entered at the time, and which, it appears, was to be honored. Regardless of this, the monastery had always accepted such students into the seminary, however, without obligation...

As regards the estate belonging to the parish of St. Vincent, it may be pointed out that in December 1854 it was worth no less than 20,000 scudi... While in the year 1846 (at the time of the take over), it barely supported the priest of St. Vincent. Indeed, during their first year there, it did not supply the necessary bread for Wimmer and his companions, either.

Since state and county taxes were always assessed and imposed according to the yield of the estate, they offered the best proof of the worth of a land-holding at a given time. In the year 1846 Fr. Wimmer had to pay only 16 dollars in taxes for the property, by the year 1855, already 200 dollars. Everyone knows that the value of virgin soil or uncultivated land can increase ten fold, as soon as it is subjected to diligent and competent cultivation. Thus it was possible that this property attained the above mentioned value after it had been diligently cultivated by the Benedictine lay brothers over the course of eight years.

VII Conclusion.

After weighing the matter to this point, it was his [Abbot Pescetelli] humble opinion that the St. Vincent monastery should be elevated to an abbey; that the community be authorized to elect an abbot, who would be confirmed by the Holy See; that the election should take place three times, i.e., at the end of every three years; and that, if the same person was elected, with two thirds of the vote, the thus chosen person should govern the abbey for life; that the abbot should adhere strictly to the decree of Alexander VII of September 27, 1659 in regard to the issue of *pontificalia;* that he should not wear the pectoral cross outside the monastery, as is customary in Germany; that the monastery be exempt from the jurisdiction of the bishop in both its spiritual and temporal governance, though the bishop should have the right of visitation, during which he was to act as an Apostolic Delegate, according to the mind of the Council of Trent. Finally, may it be proposed that in order that this small, budding community does not remain isolated from the rest of the Benedictine Order, it be affiliated with the Cassinese Congregation, as was also done for the French Benedictine Congregation, with these words, "In order to honor the head of the sacred mountain from which the Benedictine Order originated, and in order to give the progress of this restoration some dignity and protection, the French Congregation has been declared to be affiliated with the Cassinese Congregation.[2] (Chap. 22, #90 of the Constitution of the French Benedictines, confirmed on a brief of 1 Sept. 1837).

Being that these and the previous regulations, as noted in pages 90-100 in the above mentioned brief, have brought about such auspicious success in France, and were able to lay to rest any of the concerns that existed in that country, how much more should they satisfy those who are so well known for being sincerely devoted to the Holy See.

The decree of September 27, 1659, to which Abbot Pescetelli was referring, determined the exact limits regarding the use of the *pontificalia* on the part of abbots, in order to distinguish them from bishops. There were 21 points listed, the most important of which may be given space here:

• Abbots should not place a seventh candle stick on an altar, at which they are celebrating [mass].

• They should not have any permanent thrones in their churches, or any immovable abbatial chairs. Instead, on the three days a year on which they are permitted to officiate they should use a portable chair, which they may cover with a plain cloth, made of silk, in the color which corresponds to the feast, but never with material containing gold threads or splendid embroidery.

• They may erect a canopy above their seat, but not a precious or golden one, but a plain one which is inferior to the one above the altar, both in regard to material as well as workmanship. No more than two steps should lead from the floor of the sanctuary to the seat.

---

[2][original footnote] The meaning and significance of this affiliation is explained in the so-called Aggregation–Bulls given to such abbeys at different times, at their request, by whoever were the president and definators of the general chapter of the Cassinese Congregation at that time. In these documents it is stated that the affiliated monasteries shared in all good works and spiritual merits of the [entire] Cassinese Congregation, for the present, as well as for all eternity. In this manner the monastery of Mondsee, for example, was affiliated with the Cassinese Congregation by a decree issued by the general chapter of Perugia on April 23, 1690. The text of this aggregation-bull is recorded in the *Chronicon Lunaclacense* of 1748, p. 425. This was additionally reinforced by a papal decree of Benedict XIV, on April 11, 1741, in which it is declared repeatedly that the affiliation offers a participation in the privileges only in regard to spiritual graces. l.c. p. 454.

• They should have only a small credence table set up for themselves on the epistle side, on which are to be placed two candle sticks with candles, along with the mitre, the chalice, the missal, the censer, the incense boat, and other necessary items. The crozier is to be placed near this table also.

• The days on which they are permitted to officiate with *pontificalia* are to be obligatory feast days or else the patronal day of the church, the feast day of the founder of the Order, or the anniversary of the dedication of the church. At the Divine Office for the dead or a requiem they should not officiate, no matter what the day, even if it is an obligatory feast day.

• When they are going into the church, in order to officiate, or when they return after the worship service they should not permit their canons or monks to walk with them, as is the custom with bishops.

• They are not allowed to use a precious mitre unless they have special permission from the Holy See. Their crozier should be covered with a white veil. In addition, they many not use *pontificalia* in churches that are not under their jurisdiction, even with permission of the bishops.

• The Order prelates are not to wear a rochet unless it is part of the habit of their Order (as it is for the lateran or regulated canons).

• In the presence of a bishop, abbots do not give the blessing, even if they are the ones who are officiating.

• Except on the three feast days mentioned above, the abbots should never use the *pontificalia* either when they administer minor orders or in the investiture professions of the monks, unless they have special permission from the Holy See.

• They may bless sacred vessels only for their own churches.

• Abbots may bless neither bells nor chalices which are not designated for their own churches or their own subjects, even with permission of a bishop. The same applies to minor orders.

• In regard to private masses, abbots are no different from any other priest.

However, when the Procurator General of the Cassinese Congregation presented a petition requesting that the Abbey (Nullius) of Cava be given the special privilege of using *pontificalia* for the burial of certain noblemen, this monastery was granted an exception in regard to the fifth directive. Also, monasteries of the Cassinese Congregation were granted exceptions in regard to directives six and seven, so that those abbeys were permitted to use the mitre during consecrations for minor orders and during the benediction, when anointing with the holy oil was involved. However, it was stated that the remainder of the above decree be strictly observed. Given July 20, 1660. Furthermore, Popes Clement IV and Benedict XIV directed that abbots were to wear a plain mitre during provincial council meetings and synods.

CHAPTER SEVENTEEN
A Letter from King Ludwig.
St. Vincent becomes an Abbey and Fr. Boniface abbot
for three years. The Apostolic Brief.

Though the evaluation by Pescetelli could hardly be expected to fail in bringing about a favorable disposition in regard to the concerns of Fr. Boniface, he received further support from the circumstance that his influential benefactor, King Ludwig of Bavaria, was present in Rome at the same time. He, who, in keeping with his generous disposition was always willing to promote a good cause, now also took a keen interest in the difficulties facing his protégé, and therefore made every effort to recommend that the cause of St. Vincent, as whose principal benefactor he was known, be brought to the longed-for conclusion. However, before a result could be achieved, he had to leave Rome, in order to attend a meeting with his son-in-law, the Count of Modena, in Reggio. Nevertheless, he had the great satisfaction of receiving a favorable reply from Monsignore Barnabo regarding the above matters shortly before his departure. In order to offer his protégé at least some consolation, he sent him the good news as soon as possible by way of the following letter:

Ascagnano, May 26, 1855

Most reverend Sir!

His majesty, King Ludwig, would like to inform you that His Highness immensely regrets that he has not been able to see you one more time before his departure in order to tell you in person that His Majesty had spoken to Monsignore Barnabo and strongly recommended your affairs to him. In response, Monsignore Barnabo had given him his promise to do everything he could in keeping with your wishes. This reassuring message His Majesty wanted to bring you in person on the last day, as noted, but so much was happening that His Majesty found it impossible to get to it, and it is for this reason that he has given the pleasant task to me, with the addition of giving you his kindest good wishes. May you fare well and continue in your good regard towards your most devoted servant, who waits on you with most excellent respect,

Jon Gmainer
Serving Aide-de-Camp

Near the end of the month of July the consultations were finally brought to their conclusion, and Cardinal Fransoni submitted the result to the Holy Father Pius IX for confirmation during an audience on July 29 [1855]. Accordingly, the monastery of St. Vincent was elevated to an abbey and Fr. Boniface was named its abbot for three years. Though he received this gratifying news the following month only orally for the time being, but from a reliable source, he did not want to wait until the relevant documents were issued, but hurried to convey the fortunate outcome of this matter immediately to King Ludwig, whereupon he received the following autograph:

Leopoldskron by Salzburg, August 22, 1855

Rev. Abbot,

It is very gratifying news that you convey to me regarding St. Vincent Abbey in North America and that Wimmer is its first abbot. Indeed, a more suitable one than you could not have been named for this honor. The most recent mail brought me your letter of the 19th of this month, the content of which would not have been expected on the basis of your letter of June 4. From that one, it seems that the opinion had been disseminated in Rome that I had decided on my departure quite suddenly, though I had informed the Cardinal Secretary of State of this ten days earlier, and I never had the intention of staying longer, which I actually could not, if I still wanted to meet my daughter, the Countess of Modena, in Reggio. That I have had a special love for the Benedictines, that excellent Order that has distinguished itself in both religion and science, is well known. You, however, may not know that when I was the Crown Prince, at the time that Salzburg and Bavaria were joined, I assured the continuation of the two abbeys in the region, St. Peter in Salzburg and Michelbeuren, by decreeing that they were permitted to take in novices. May God's blessing rest on the Benedictines of North America.

With this wish,
[I remain] Your well disposed
Ludwig

Steep banks make the area around a river romantic; and sudden, unexpected bends make it lively and interesting; while a river whose course flows towards its estuary through a uniform, unbroken plain in straight line, is more like a monotonous, boring canal. It is similar with the course of a prominent man, whose undertakings are often limited and hindered by unexpected difficulties, and whose plans at times are suddenly frustrated by seemingly insurmountable obstacles. A riverbed may at times be so completely enclosed by mountains, as for example the Hudson at West Point, and look so deceptively like a lake, that a traveler unfamiliar with the area may look in every direction in order to detect an opening between the mountains for the continuing flow of the river. The traveler may then be all the more pleasantly surprised when he is suddenly able to see the opening quite close and at a totally unexpected place. After a long wait, such a welcome opening presented itself to Fr. Boniface and his monastic family on the last day of September 1855, when the following documents were presented to him:

> Apostolic Brief
> In eternal remembrance Pius P.P. IX
>
> Among all of the spiritual obligations which fall to us in carrying out the office of shepherd, the greatest and most important is that of caring for the eternal salvation of Christians, wherever their residence may be on the earth, and that we most zealously promote all that may be useful toward that purpose. Among that which has occurred for the prospering of religion in the United States of America in recent times, with the help of God, we justifiably believe that we may count the monastery of the Order of Saint Benedict, which has been built on the hill of St. Vincent, by the efforts of our beloved son, Boniface Wimmer, with the approval of our reverend brother, Michael O'Connor, Bishop of Pittsburgh, in the Diocese of the same, and been approved by the authority of the Holy See. Being that the way of life of the students living there has been properly established according to the guidelines of monastic profession, and that several lay brothers – also called conversi – have been instructed in the same required, valuable behavior, and have been incorporated into the Order, with consideration for the special conditions of the area, the goal has been achieved that it is not only possible to observe the prescriptions of the *Rule* of St. Benedict there, but that the monastic priests are exerting their influence also in the formation of clergy and in ministry in the parish of the above named monastery on the hill of St. Vincent, as well as in the immediate vicinity.

In the name of the above mentioned Boniface Wimmer and the monks of the monastery, a petition was therefore presented to us that we, as has elsewhere occurred for the prospering of the Order of St. Benedict, ensure the permanence and well-being of the undertaking by proper decrees regarding the monastic governance, by means of our Apostolic Authority.

We, therefore, elevate the above named monastery on the hill of St. Vincent in the Diocese of Pittsburgh to an abbey with exemption in the least rank, after we have given serious consideration to everything, together with the council of our reverend brothers, the Cardinals of the Holy Roman Church, who preside over the affairs of the Congregation for the Propagation of the Faith, by the power of our Apostolic Authority and this document. We also have decided that the monks of that monastery, the current ones and the future ones, are to form a special Congregation of the Order of St. Benedict, which Congregation is to observe, in addition to the general *Rule* of St. Benedict, those special constitutions which our predecessor, Pope Innocent XI of blessed memory, approved for the Bavarian Benedictine Congregation, by the means of the Apostolic Briefs, starting with the words, *Circumspecta* and *Militanti ecclesiae,* and that this Congregation be joined to, or affiliated with, the one that carries the name of Monte Cassino.

We also want, by means of our Apostolic Power, that the election of the abbot be executed by a monastic chapter, and that the documents about which are to be sent to our Holy See in order to receive confirmation by the same. Every abbot is entitled to all the rights and privileges which are granted to exempt abbots in the Order of St. Benedict, and according to the above mentioned constitutions, especially as it concerns the time in office, and in observance of the decree of Pope Alexander VII, our predecessor of blessed memory, in regard to the insignia and honors. Finally, in consideration of the special local conditions and especially the prevailing lack of priests, we declare that in regard to priestly ministry the principles generally applicable in the mission field are to be observed in addition to the general church law. The monastic seminary that exists in the St. Vincent monastery is to continue, and diocesan clerics are to be accepted also, in exchange for tuition to cover the cost. The bishop, in his capacity as papal del-

St. Vincent 1869

egate, has the right to watch over the studies and the morals of the clerics.

(Here follow the usual formulas and wording of confirmation.)

Given in Rome at St. Peter, sealed by the Fisherman's ring.
August 24, 1855, in the 10th year of Our Pontificate.

(L.S.)   V. Card. Macchi

Decision of the Sacred Congregation for the Propagation of the Faith.

Our Holy Father Pope Pius, by the grace of God the ninth by this name, on July 29, 1855, after the vote of the Congregation for the Propagation of the Faith, has approved and supported with the force of law many things regarding spiritual governance of the monastery belonging to the Order of St. Benedict on the hill of St. Vincent, in the Diocese of Pittsburgh, and his Holiness has then deigned to publish a brief regarding this on August 24 of this year.

However, in consideration of all that the most reverend Fr. Boniface Wimmer has wrought praiseworthily for the growth of this monastery, according to a second decision by the Sacred Congregation, His Holiness has deigned to decree that this first time the directives regarding the election of an abbot not be enforced; and he has elevated said Boniface Wimmer to the position of abbot, and designated him as abbot of the aforementioned monastery for the duration of three years, as though he had been elected according to the customary lawful regulations. However, at the end of the three years the election of an abbot shall proceed according to regulation.

His Holiness ordered the preparation of the present decree by the Sacred Congregation.

Granted from the Palace of the Sacred Congregation at Rome on September 17, 1855.

(L.S.)   J. Ph. Card. Fransoni, Prefect
                 Al. Barnabo a Secretis

[Here follows the]Letter of His Eminence Cardinal Fransoni to Abbot Boniface Wimmer.

Most reverend Father!

Your Reverence is receiving with this letter the enclosed Apostolic Brief, by which the monastery on hill of St. Vincent has been graced with the honor of becoming an abbey, and wherein several things regarding its governance are noted; furthermore, enclosed is the decree by which you have been elevated to the honor of abbot, and named abbot of said monastery for three years. From all this your Reverence and your other monastic priests and brothers can see with how much care and apostolic zeal the Holy See makes it their concern to promote and support that which causes religion to thrive and brings salvation to souls. At the same time this is to serve for your encouragement, to inspire you to achieve "even greater gifts," so that that monastery, as it is being elevated for greater esteem and honor, may also become a shining light by setting an example for virtue and praiseworthy deeds. Finally, I pray God for the richest blessings for your Reverence, etc.

Rome, from the Palace of the Sacred Congregation for the Propagation of the Faith, September 27, 1855

J. Ph. Card. Fransoni, Pref.

Al. Barnabo a Secretis

Who could describe the joy and the gratitude with which the new abbot now left the Eternal City! He first went to Munich, to prepare there for the return trip. On November 2 he embarked at Bremen, and on December 6, 1855 he reached St. Vincent, where a festive reception was being prepared for him. Most of the priests from the outlying parishes had hurried over to bring congratulations and good wishes to their spiritual father.

When he notified the bishop of Pittsburgh of his arrival and of the success of his undertaking, he, too, congratulated him on the favorable outcome of his endeavor. The bishop commented that though he himself considered the elevation of the monastery to an abbey premature, he nevertheless gave his sincere approval to the action as soon as the Holy See considered it wise to take this step. He, himself, had always considered it a matter of time when this should occur; and it actually was much more appropriate at the present time than back when it was first proposed. He firmly trusted that the abbot would direct everything in the best order by his discretion and wisdom.

CHAPTER EIGHTEEN
Expansion of the Order in 1856.
The First Abbatial Election in the year 1858.

For ten years Abbot Wimmer had labored with his confreres at St. Vincent; for ten years they had been sowing with tears, so to speak.[1] The joy of the harvest still lay in the distant future, but they did obtain one crown: their foundation was secured; the Holy Father himself had given them his blessing. The monastery was now visibly increasing in both the number and the achievement of its members. When, therefore, several offers were made to the abbot from the Far West to establish missions among the German settlers in Minnesota and in Kansas, he considered it an indication that Providence was at work and wanted to assign a wider sphere of influence to his Order. Besides, he believed he could find a mission field in these newly opened territories that was most compatible with his original plans. The foundation of these two colonies dates to the year 1856.

The abbot communicated this intention to his benefactor in Munich in the following manner:

"The question of whether we should think about founding new monasteries in the West now or only later is a vital concern to us. There are reasons for it and against it. I would not be in America if I had not been firmly convinced that there was a need to expand the Benedictine Order and that it was the right time to do so. I am still of that opinion now, because I believe that it is easier to close the gates of a fortress to an enemy when one beats him to the occupation of the same, than to throw him out of the fortress when he had been able to get there first. Discipline also seems to be observed more strictly on the battlefield than at fixed quarters, if the general is not very careless. Thus, I will not miss any opportunity in order to found a new colony of our Order in the West, where the stream of immigrants is now pushing..."

---

[1] The allusion here is to psalm 126:5 "Those that sow in tears shall reap rejoicing."

The following year (1857) he himself traveled to Doniphan in Kansas and also to Minnesota for a visitation. On this occasion he wrote about what he thought of the West to both the Archbishop of Munich and Court Chaplain Müller, to whom the observed, among other things that, "The new foundation would be necessary in some respects, though inconvenient in regard to the money situation. The West really should become our sphere of influence because that is where the most Germans and the fewest priests are, because conditions there are just beginning to unfold and religion should not be lacking an influence in this. I can at the moment not do much about this, but I am doing what I can. Also, the Bishop of Kansas keeps urging us all the time to send him more help. It is as far to go there as to Minnesota, but Kansas is not as healthy. God will decide and show us the way. I am now well supplied with instructors. Good superiors will be formed by experience..."

From the reply of the Court Chaplain, on January 19, 1858, it is evident that neither the archbishop nor he himself shared the enthusiasm of the abbot about the prospects in the Far West that he describes. He wrote:

Munich 19 January 1858

Reverend, dear friend!

I have received both of your letters on the same day, one from Doniphan and the other from Saint Vincent. His Excellency also received his.[2] He is displeased with you because you begin too much and get mired in an enormous burden of debt. It has always been your mistake to make too many plans.[3] If his Excellency does not know America as I do, still I also have to agree with him and say: strengthen first what has thus far been created. If you would no longer be elected abbot, who would be capable of continuing all of this? Who would listen to you if another was giving the orders?

Do not let yourself be so caught up by your enterprising spirit. You have already done more than others could hardly do in fifty years. Look at the [hermits], how slowly everything goes along. Strengthen that which already exists and look more to your school, from which you repeatedly have to withdraw your best men when you accept new places.

Jos. F. Müller

This letter, the witness of a friend who was as candid as he was loyal, was neither complimentary nor particularly encouraging. However, the abbot did not let himself be deterred by this. In the vast regions of Kansas and Nebraska his priests sought out the scattered settlers, joined them into parishes wherever possible, and built over

---

[2]Fr. Müller is referring to Archbishop Gregory Scherr who, since 1856, was also the President of the Ludwig Mission Society.

[3]This is an allusion to Abbot Boniface as the "Projektenmacher."

twenty churches in suitable places. Within a few years they chose Atchison as a central point and erected a church there in genuine ecclesiastical architectural style, and connected their monastery and an educational institution with it.

The missions which had been started in the territories of Minnesota and Kansas eventually grew to a point where they became independent abbeys. How and when they reached that point of development will shortly be reported at the proper place. In addition to the above, the abbot of St. Vincent at this time also took over German parishes in Newark, Covington, Erie, Chicago, and Richmond. In June 1858 he reported to the Court Chaplain in the following letter that he wanted to send some additional priests to Kansas and to Minnesota:

Dearest Friend!

Here I am sending you a picture of my monastery as seen from the east. On the first floor, in the round tower, and two windows to the right and two to the left of it, I live, and often look at the morning sun, which brings me greetings from my friends in Europe into my room. It still shines on a happy, eager, active little flock of Benedictines at St. Vincent.

Now another school year is over, because the sun is getting too hot. On June 30 is the Exhibition (award assembly) for which a large crowd of people from nearby Pittsburgh is expected. The railroad company offers special half-price tickets for the event. It is to take place on the threshing floor of the barn. Our students have already been working on decorating the area and converting it into a beautiful assembly room. Then it will be converted into a small theater, which will also serve as a concert hall, so that samples of the acquired knowledge and skill [of the students] can be demonstrated there. Such a day is a real holiday for the whole area.

During the recent ember days four priests and one deacon were ordained: Fr. Ignatius Trüg,[4] Fr. Edmund Langenfelder, Fr. Bernard Manser, and Fr. Ansgar Frauenhofer; and deacon Edward Hipelius.[5]

---

[4] [original footnote:] Fr. Ignatius Trüg is quite well-known. He rendered great service through his musical work, of which six appeared in print. The Ordinary of the Mass, approved by Pope Pius IX and published in repeated editions by Pustet, he arranged for four voices and organ accompaniment in such wise that he demonstrated his thorough knowledge of ecclesiastical chorale. He is also the inventor of an instrument that he names the Heliorama and for which he received a patent from the United States Patent Office in 1870. This instrument belongs to a class of better sundials and reminds one of the astrolabes which Martin Behaim of Nürnberg made at Lisbon in 1484. It determines the geographical latitude through the meridian altitude.

[5] [original footnote:] The contributions of Fr. Edward Hipelius to this book follow below in the twentieth chapter.

An Irishman, Francis Cannon, became a subdeacon. He and Fr. Edmund are going to Kansas next week to help Casimir. One of them will then probably remain in Kansas. The other one will go to Nebraska with Fr. Casimir, that vast territory which stretches from the Missouri River to the Rocky Mountains and from Kansas to Canada, and which is still largely inhabited by native Indians. There they will settle in Omaha, the capital, and from there take care of the Catholics who are scattered far and wide. They are the only priests in the region.

In September there will be an abbatial election since the Holy Father had appointed me for only three years. If I am not re-elected, I will also go out West. There is a true Benedictine homeland.

On July 11 several novices will make profession, several scholastics will become novices, and several students, scholastics. Several brothers will also be getting the habit, among them two from Scheyern. We now have educated twenty seven diocesan priests and forty-four Benedictines. Is that not a lot for such a small monastery?

Our priests are the outposts of the Catholic Church beyond the Missouri river. Our seminary will again be enlarged this year. Our debts have not become smaller, but also not greater, in spite of these hard times. Our crops are doing wonderfully, but from Easter to the middle of June we had steady rain and flooding, which caused much damage. Now it is very hot, with severe thunderstorms. I have almost never been in so much trouble as this year. There is almost no money and I don't know anyone from whom we might get any; yet everyone wants to be paid.

Otherwise, I don't know anything new [to report]. I believe we are making progress everywhere and work to the best of our abilities. We are also building extensively again this year. Our institution continues to gain ever more prestige, good reputation, and significance. Four bishops have students with us. So we continue with our quickly changing ups and downs. Who on the outside can possibly know the cares of an abbot of St. Vincent with its far flung missions?

However, in all the difficulties and struggles of so many different kinds I have the comforting conviction in my heart that I keep my eyes only on the honor of God and of my Order, and not on me. That is a strong support in all tribulations.

I hope you are in good health and also remember me at the altar, as I always remain with love and esteem,

Your most grateful,
Boniface, Abbot

After the monastery of St. Vincent was elevated to an abbey, all capitulars had to renew their vows according to the statutes of the former Bavarian Benedictine Congregation. In general this did not change anything in the usual daily routine of the house; to the contrary, it actually strengthened it. The regular routine which had already been established previously remained the same, as it is still being maintained currently. The most important activity is worship, the prayers in the choir. Vespers and Compline are chanted daily. Weekly the monks and the brothers, divided into four groups, humble themselves before the Superior in order to do penance by means of confessing external faults.

Conferences on philosophical and theological topics are held weekly, by the prior for the clerics, and by the abbot or the rector for the priests. While the priests lecture, and the clerics and scholastics study, the lay brothers are busy with housework, trades, farming, and preparation of building materials for the expansion of the monastery.

The three years for which Fr. Boniface Wimmer had been named abbot of St. Vincent by the Holy Father were coming to a close. The first abbatial election was to be held by the capitulars of the monastery. Even though the election was again to be for only three years, it nevertheless was an important event. The abbot himself describes the course of the election in a letter of September 19, 1858, addressed to his loyal friend in Munich:

Dearest fatherly Friend!

Since I can imagine that you are somewhat in suspense regarding the abbatial election, I am hurrying to report the result to you speedily. It took place yesterday, September 18. There were 48 Capitulars who were eligible to vote, though only 34 were present in person; 8 were represented by a procurator, while from 5 no letters had been received, even though they had been invited in plenty of time, and one had sent his vote in openly, which could not be counted since the election was to be done by secret ballot.

Since the meeting of the General Chapter was to follow immediately after the abbatial election, and both were of great importance for the well-being and thriving of the Benedictine Order in America, I called on the renowned Jesuit, Fr. F. Xav. Weninger to give a retreat for us. The zealous missionary agreed gladly and hurried here from the distant state of Michigan, where he had conducted missions for several German parishes. He arrived on September 10 and conducted the holy spiritual exercises, with the anointing special to him, which were a great inspiration to us. Everyone took part, the priests, the younger clerics, the novices and scholastics or postulants, and even the lay brothers. It was just at the time when the work in the fields was most urgent, but I did not want to rob them of the joy and the consolation of hearing the deeply moving presentations of this missionary who is so passionate about God. So there were 150 Benedictines living in strictest silence for a whole week, seriously pondering the most important religious truths and engaging in fervent prayer to God, in order to renew their spirits, and, for those who were to take part in the election and the General Chapter, to prepare themselves, so they would engage in these two most important activities for the glory of God and his holy Church, and for the good of the monastery and the Order.

At noon Friday, September 17, the retreat ended. On the same day, the triennium, for which I had been appointed by the Holy Father to be abbot of St. Vincent, also expired. When I was in Rome three years ago, I asked the Holy Father, in the name of our whole monastery, only for the elevation of the monastery to an abbey and for the right to elect our own abbot. The Holy Father granted this petition gladly and signed the decree referring to this. When our concerns were presented to the cardinals for their review a few days later, however, they petitioned that I should be installed as the first abbot of the new monastery at the same time as its elevation to an abbey. His Holiness responded to this recommendation by deigning to name me the abbot, but only for three years, so as not to completely contradict the earlier decree. After that, the capitulars were to be permitted to freely elect the abbot themselves. The only problem this time was to decide who would preside at the election.

I had turned to Rome already in April in order to receive some guidance regarding the proper procedures and waited every day for a response. However, none came by the time of the election. Since I myself had the right for an active as well as a passive vote, I could not, and did not want to, be the one to preside. Therefore, I requested that the very reverend bishop of Pittsburgh do this. He did come to the abbey the evening before the day of election, but refused to participate in our electoral activities without a formal assignment from the pope, because we are exempt and, according to ecclesiastical law, he was not entitled to be the presider. He encouraged me to preside myself and to let the scrutatores vote. Since all capitulars agreed to this, they all assembled in the chapter hall on September 18, following a solemn high mass. Three tellers were elected by majority vote; they were Fr. Benedict Haindl, Fr. Augustine Wirth from Kansas, and Fr. Henry Lemke. After this, a crucifix was placed on a table between two burning candles, and everyone swore to give their vote to him whom they thought, to the best of their knowledge and judgment, to be the most worthy one. Likewise the tellers swore to collect, open, and read the ballots without deceit or guile.

In a brief speech I admonished the assembled monks to vote according to their oath and not to pay any regard to personal affection or loyalties, because the future of the monastery and the congregation depended to a large extent on the outcome of the election. The discussion about the merits of the various candidates, required by law, had already taken place the day before; (there were 20 of us over the age of 30 years). Each voter was given three ballots, on which the names of the 20 qualified candidates had been written by the novices, in case three scrutinies might be needed. The ballots were all of the same paper, of the same size, and folded in the same way, and since no one had written the names on the ballots himself, confidentiality was completely assured. In front of the whole assembly each person walked to the urn by himself and dropped in his ballot. Thereafter they were opened and read aloud in front of everyone, and the votes were counted. Already in the first scrutinium, thirty-eight of the votes were for me; three, among them mine, went to two other capitulars; one was discounted because no name was marked on it. If the two votes from Kansas and the three from Minnesota (which did not arrive, because the letters apparently are late or were lost) were to be added to these forty-two, as well as the one that was sent open and therefore was invalid, there was a total of 48 votes. Since a majority required only 25, and of the missing 5 votes hardly any would have been lost to me, the vote was nearly unanimous; and so I accepted the election, which now binds me to St. Vincent for life. I do not want to deny that this result has made me happy, and that I would much rather be the abbot of St. Vincent due to the vote of my confreres than by appointment of someone outside. When everything was over I dictated the minutes of these proceedings, had them signed by everyone, and sent them to Rome for confirmation by the Holy Father, only after which everything will be valid. A joyous *Te Deum* and a festive meal afterwards ended the day.

It was exactly twelve years since I, with four students and fifteen farmers and tradesmen, destined to become lay brothers, left New York (having arrived there on September 16, 1846), and set out for the interior of Pennsylvania in order to look for a suitable site for a monastery. Divine Providence led me here, and now I am the head of an abbey which has 43 priests, 12 clerics, 15 novices, and as many scholastics, in addition to over 100 lay brothers. We have a complete gymnasium [classical high school], and lyceum [philosophical – theological college], a seminarium puerorum, and a secular boys' seminary. Our priests minister at many and varied places, from the shores of the Atlantic Ocean to the outer borders of civilization in the West along the great Mississippi and Missouri rivers. There are presently 3 priests of our Order in Newark at a bay of the Atlantic Ocean, in the state of New Jersey; at Bellefonte in the State of Pennsylvania in the Diocese of Philadelphia are 2; at St. Marys-Town are 3 and 1 at Cooper Settlement in the Diocese of Erie; two are staying at Carrolltown, 1 in Indiana, 1 in Greensburg and 2 in Butler in the Diocese of Pittsburgh; 3 are in Covington, Diocese of Covington, in the state of Kentucky; 1 in Leavenworth and 2 in Doniphan, in Kansas; and 1 in Omaha City, capital of the immense territory of Nebraska. The very reverend bishop of Kansas resides in Leavenworth and has Nebraska under his jurisdiction also.

The latter, however, will become a diocese in its own right in the near future, although presently only one priest of our Order is there. It is largely still inhabited by native Indian tribes. Finally, there are 6 priests in the State of Minnesota, (2,000 English miles from St. Vincent) in the Diocese of St. Paul; 1 in St. Paul itself, 1 in Shakopen, and 4 in St. Cloud; they will be getting two confreres this year to support them in their ministry. The rallying point for all these mission stations, more than 2,000 miles from each other, is the mother monastery St. Vincent, where also the heart of our Order in this country is. Everyone here can easily imagine that being abbot of St. Vincent is no sinecure. Indeed, every one of us has work enough, but the heaviest burden does rest on the abbot, especially since I have been sending any priest that I can possibly spare to other places, due to the requests for priests being so numerous. That leaves the care for the governance and the management here mostly to me. Then there is the immense responsibility! Truly, I am a poor, burdened man. I hope you, and all my other good friends, patrons, and benefactors will continue to support me now more than ever, not only with your material, but also with your spiritual charity – your fervent prayers. If I could not have come so far in such a short period of time without their support with money and other needed things, I could do it even less now without the grace of God which I trustingly expect to receive through their intercession. Give my obedient regards to his Excellency, the archbishop, and remain a loyal friend also in the future, to your

Boniface, Abbot

The first abbatial election had thus taken place at St. Vincent on September 18, 1858, and the result was, as could be predicted, that the founder of the monastery, or rather his name, arose unanimously out of the voting urn. The records were sent to Rome, where confirmation of the abbot's election for the following three years was granted.

The activities which the abbot initiated during these years have already been hinted at, but they will be described in greater detail in the chapters that report on the foundation of St. John's Abbey in Minnesota, St. Benedict's Abbey in Atchison in Kansas, and St. Mary's Abbey in Newark in New Jersey.

CHAPTER NINETEEN

San José in Bexar County, Texas. A Ghost Story.
Spiritual exercises. The second abbatial election.
The time of war. The tramps.

San José Mission

In June 1858 the Most Reverend J.M. Odin, bishop of Galveston, came to St. Vincent. The purpose of his visit was to propose a promising plan for the establishment of a monastery in Texas to Abbot Wimmer. His proposal suggested that a monastery, and in time an educational institution, be established in San José as the hub from which the priests could then care for the surrounding German parishes in San Antonio, in Castroville, in Fredericksburg, in New Braunfels, etc.

San José, situated three miles from San Antonio, along the river of the same name, is one of the grand monuments that witness to the living faith of the Spaniards of yesteryear and their willingness to make sacrifices. The Spanish government had established eight missions in Texas at great expense, and that not for the establishment of settlements for white immigrants, but solely for teaching and converting the Indians. The beginning of San José dates back to the year 1721; the baptismal records date back to the year 1730. The buildings, church, monastery storehouses, etc. form a quadrangle with the high surrounding walls that measures 600' in length and 400' in breadth. Not only the upright walls, but even the arches of the church and the flat roofs were made of large quarried stones. The mission was run by Franciscans from Mexico and was exceptionally beneficial for the Indians.

> "To the place where the blue waters of the Antonio rush,
> There, to San José, the Lipan moved,
> To the good white man, to listen to his words,
> To exchange the arrow for the plough."
>
> Fr. Alto Hörmann[1]

---

[1] Fr. Alto Hörmann (1829-1867) had been a student at Metten who came to Saint Vincent in 1852, made monastic profession in 1854, and was ordained in 1855. After ordination he volunteered for the mission in Texas. He served as its superior for most of the length of its existence, 1859-1867. The mission suffered due to the disruptions of the Civil War and because many of its members contracted tuberculosis there, Fr. Alto himself succumbing to the disease in 1867 after returning to Saint Vincent. See Oetgen, *Mission to America*, 95, 115-116.

However, in time another spirit pervaded the Spanish rulers, which did not rest until all the houses of the Franciscans were suppressed. This occurred in the year 1812. The result was that the Indians scattered and the buildings fell to ruins.

The abbot of St. Vincent accepted the offer of the most reverend bishop and sent several priests and brothers to Texas the following year. The reports which these missionaries wrote to the abbot already in the first few years were so gratifying that, together with the chapter that was assembled at the abbey in September 1862, the abbot decided to present a petition to the Holy See to have the mission at San José elevated to a priory.

For ten years 6 priests and a number of brothers from St. Vincent worked steadily at the above named missions in Texas. The first superior, Fr. Alto Hormann, immortalized San José in his historical novel, *The Daughters of Tehuan*,[2] or *Texas in the Past Century* as well as in his allegorical tale, "Aner's Return."[3]

The Benedictines already had spent fifteen thousand dollars on the restoration of the large church and the monastery at San José, and still the hope of reaching the desired goal lay in the distant future. That explains why Abbot Wimmer eventually arrived at the decision to give up the whole undertaking in Texas.

A Ghost Story

They would be much mistaken who imagine that Abbot Wimmer had had only warm days of sunshine and blooming and thriving fruits from his labor since he had received the mitre. To the contrary, he was to experience now that a portion of those difficulties and worries which come along with honors and office had also been reserved for him.

When it happened at times, as was to be expected, that unworthy persons misused the well known magnanimity and generosity of the abbot, he did not let himself be deterred from continuing his customary way of behaving but consoled himself with the thought that it really was better to suffer hurt than to inflict hurt on others.

Once, though, he came across a situation where he was so badly deceived that he still felt the disappointment years afterwards. In his innate kindness he granted a young man, who came unannounced, acceptance as a candidate for the novitiate on August 10, 1859. The man was 24 years old, had devoted himself to classical studies for a time, and had a confident manner about him. When it was learned later that he had already worked professionally on the stage, it was no longer counted against him, because he had managed to obtain the abbot's favor by his engaging manner.

After some time he became sickly and was therefore placed in the sick room, where several of his confreres compassionately cared for him. He also received dispensation from participating in choir and from other physical activities. While he could now enjoy some leisure in this manner he hatched his devious plans. Gradually

---

[2] *Die Tochter Tehuans oder Texas im vorigen Jahrhundert.* Benzinger Brothers, Cincinnati, 1866.

[3] *Anêrs Rückkehr. Landshut, 1864.* English translation: *Anêr's Return: or the Migrations of a Soul, an allegorical tale.* Trans. Innocent A. Bergrath. New York: P. O'Shea, 1869.

he spun some mysterious tales for his trusting caregivers, similar to the usual ghost stories. He claimed that a ghost who was a monk had appeared to him and begged him to free him. In gratitude for the student's willingness to do so, the spirit would provide certain revelations from time to time about the destiny of the monastery and its inhabitants. These mysterious communications continued quietly for some time, until the ghost-seer met with his deserved fate, being found out as a charlatan and dismissed on November 15, 1862.

Spiritual Retreats and The Second Abbatial Election

So that each division of the large monastic family could enjoy the benefit of a retreat at least once a year, the abbot had initiated a standing arrangement by which the lay brothers would have their retreat between Christmas and New Year's Day, the novices, at the beginning of [summer] vacation, the clerics around the middle, and the priests near the end. The scholastics and the students made only three-day retreats at the start of the school year.

Now, that the term for which the abbot had been approved by the Holy Father was ending, he scheduled the second abbatial election to follow upon the retreat that was held at St. Vincent in September 1862. The result was the same as that of the first election, as no name other than that of the incumbent emerged from the voting urn. The records were sent to Rome, but his Eminence, the Cardinal Prefect of the Propaganda, gave his reply only on April 13, 1863. It stated that Boniface Wimmer was confirmed as abbot of St. Vincent *ad beneplacitum Apostolicae Sedis*,[4] that is, for an undetermined period of time, while it had been expected here that the confirmation, if not for life would at least be for three years.

The Civil War

Though the abbot of St. Vincent had adopted the Cassinese motto, "Pax," he and his monastic family were nevertheless drawn into involvement with the War of Secession, for, when the number of volunteers proved insufficient for an effective war effort, universal conscription was begun. Some of the Benedictines on whom the lot fell could be redeemed by substitutes, such as Fr. Valentin Lobmayer of Johnstown, for example, or Fr. Meinrad Jeggle from Erie, while Fr. Benno Hegele, also chosen by lot, was not drafted into the service due to weak eyes. The lay brothers Leo Christ, Bonaventure Gaul, Ildephonse Hoffmann, George Held, and Ulrich Barth did have to join the army, but were soon assigned to the care of the wounded, due to a special intervention by President Lincoln. Brother Martin Beck, sacristan at Carrolltown, was bought off by the parish. The Reverend Emmeram Bliemel was caring for the German parish at Nashville in Tennessee when the war started. Since the 10th Tennessee Regiment (Confederate Army) had a significant number of Catholic soldiers,

---

[4] Latin: at the pleasure of the Apostolic See.

Irishmen as well as Germans, he felt obligated to join them as chaplain. According to all reports by eye witnesses, he devoted himself to his dangerous service with complete dedication and fearlessness, until he eventually lost his life in the battle of Jonesborough, near Atlanta in Georgia, on August 31, 1864, due to an exploding bomb.

The Tramps

Abbot Wimmer introduced hospitality in his monastery, according to the *Rule* of St. Benedict, and he took care of even the poorest travelers, the so-called tramps. The abbot of St. Vincent had made it his mission to establish a Benedictine monastery modeled on the monasteries of the Middle Ages. All his other plans, such as the establishment of a seminary for the formation of priests who would take care of German immigrants, etc., were considered to be only incidental to his foundation. It was his ideal to establish a house whose members observed the evangelical counsels of obedience, chastity, and poverty, and did not live from alms, but rather, in keeping with the *Rule* of St. Benedict (RB 48:8), "When they live by the labor of their hands, as our fathers and the apostles did, then they are really monks." Moreover, they were to take care not only of their own needs, but also kindly receive and serve as a guest each poor person who comes knocking at the gate of the monastery without regard to his religion or nationality, welcoming him (RB 53:1:) "as Christ, for he himself will say: 'I was a stranger and you welcomed me' (Matt 25:35)." True to this principle he ordered that at St. Vincent abbey hospitality be extended even to the lowest class of unemployed wanderers, the so-called tramps. Such guests, then, turned up at the monastery daily, and often as many as fifty in number.

This his treatment of the tramps Abbot Wimmer considered of utmost importance, because he recognized that it was one of the weaknesses or vulnerable aspects of modern times that poverty was seen as the greatest evil and as such was subject to being generally looked down upon. True to the tradition of his Order he took care of the poor, without seeking to determine if their poverty was their own fault or not, if they were worthy of alms or not.

Right from the start of his foundation he therefore endeavored to inculcate in his disciples, by word and example, the teaching of St. Paul, "I have never wanted anyone's silver or gold or clothes. You know well that these very hands have served my needs and those of my companions. In every way I have shown you that by hard work of that sort we must help the weak, and keep in mind the words of the Lord Jesus who himself said, 'It is more blessed to give than to receive'" (Acts, 20: 33-35).

"Gentlemen," he used to say to his priests at times when a large number of these poor travelers would come to the monastery, "this brings blessings to our house." And "This will be our consolation on the Day of Judgment when the Lord will say, 'whatever you did for one of these least brothers of mine, you did for me' (Matt. 25: 40)."

The cultivation of hospitality, especially toward the poor, was always considered not merely a sacred duty, but also a rich source of spiritual as well as material blessings in Benedictine monasteries. Often one could find series of inscriptions like these on the walls of the hall ways, near the entrances, or in the refectories of the old monasteries like these: "whoever cares for the poor lends to the Lord, who will pay back the sum in full," (Proverbs 19: 17). "To the poor also extend your hand, that your blessing may be complete. Give your gift to all the living…" (Sirach 7: 32-33a). "Human goodness is like a signet ring with God, and virtue he keeps like the apple of his eye." (Eccl. 17: 22).

Even the grace at table in the refectory is to remind the Benedictine daily to remember the poor, "*Edent pauperes*…the poor will eat and will be satisfied and will praise the Lord."

The Protestant neighbors, however, had a different view of the magnanimity of Abbot Wimmer toward the poor unemployed travelers. They also did not fail to inform him from time to time that they could not appreciate his actions of neighborly love toward this "feared" class of people.

As often as a theft occurred, something that had been unheard of in this area earlier, but now was not uncommon, they suspected the tramps. That the tramps came to this area in such large numbers, moreover, they blamed on Abbot Wimmer, whose monastery was known far and wide as the main point of attraction for these feared guests, and still is. Forty years ago, they claimed there had been no tramps in this area, and in the following decades only a few were seen here and there, while now their number had increased to such an extent that it made the area unsafe. The abbot of St. Vincent however, explained to his neighbors on such occasions with great friendliness, how one could actually only wish that many such monasteries would exist everywhere in the land which could alleviate at least the immediate neediness of these poor ones, as is done daily at St. Vincent. In this way not only their number would be diminished, but their moral character could be improved as well, as their three-day stay at the monastery was a good way to influence their religious life in a beneficial way. Some of them also found work and pay in the fields and gave up their wandering about.

Actually, the objections of these neighbors to the actions of the abbot regarding the tramps can be examined a little more closely, without any fear that he might have deserved them. We do have to admit that the monastery is indeed a special point of attraction for these poor men, because they know that they will be served a substantial meal at any time. Furthermore, we must agree with the neighbors that in former times, for example forty years ago, this area was indeed free of such hungry travelers.

However, who would seriously draw a conclusion such as this: The abbot or his monastery feed the hungry; therefore there are so many tramps? That would actually be the, *"post hoc, ergo propter hoc"* in its purest form! To blame the monastery for the fact that the area is overrun by tramps would be extremely inaccurate, or a barely unconscious twisting of the truth. The source of this bad situation is not the monastery, but something entirely different, and thinking people have realized it for a long time.

The reasons why this area was completely free of these poor travelers forty years ago is very simply this: in those days the inhabitants of this area were exclusively farmers, with the exception of a few shopkeepers. The large guild of tramps, on the other hand, came into existence mainly thanks to the mines and the factories, where often a large number of workers is laid off suddenly and thus robbed of an income. If, as we know from history, the active love of neighbor of the Christians in apostolic times made such a deep impression on the minds of unbelievers, one might be justified to conclude from that that the magnanimity and practical generosity of the abbot of St. Vincent might have the same effect on at least the immediate neighborhood of his monastery. One should be able to expect that those who have been eye witnesses for more than forty years of such willingness to make sacrifices and of such devoted Christian love-of-neighbor might be compelled to feel that, "By its fruits one will know the tree." Such works only grow from true faith.

Alas, who can measure the power of prejudice! In the present case it truly seems impossible to overcome it. Apart from his charity toward the tramps, the magnanimous and kind hearted spirit of the abbot was expressed in a hundred different circumstances, such as helping needy students, as well as afflicted people in various other situations, nearby as well as far away. Unfortunately we cannot conceal, either, that his generosity did not always receive the deserved appreciation. The reason for this was known to him also, but he did not want to pay it any heed. He knew that "public opinion," the ruling fashion, judged everything by "looks," by appearance, that many believe only what they can see and expect, and that everyone puts his best foot forward right at the start. However, the abbot's whole nature bristled against such superficialities. Such exhibition of outer glitter he considered to be incompatible with the spirit of his Order, as well as with the vow of poverty. Therefore he did not want to accommodate himself to this prevailing fashion in either the buildings he erected or in the way he furnished them, nor in any other aspect of the management of his monastery. According to a proverb, words stimulate, but example attracts and often thrills. Well-chosen words can be acceptable, even when they demand a difficult thing; however, it is the magnanimous, heroic example of the leader, the self sacrifice of the general that calls forth an enthusiasm in the ranks of the soldiers that makes them ready for any sacrifice. For this reason the abbot of St. Vincent lived for the consoling hope that the holy enthusiasm for active love of neighbor, which he had instilled in his disciples by word and deed, would be an ongoing inheritance in all his monastic foundations far into the future.

Wherever we linger, wherever we wander,
May our concern always be for others.
Let us help everyone,
Open our hearts to the sorrows of strangers,
Still all cruel pains,
For to Christ himself we do this.

CHAPTER TWENTY
The Second Journey to Rome. The Beard.
A House of Studies in Rome for American Benedictines.
Cause of an Extended Stay.

Toward the end of 1865 the Abbot of Saint Vincent undertook his second trip to Rome. In order to render an account of his almost 20 years of work in America, he had worked out a comprehensive report that he presented to his Eminence Cardinal Barnabo. His stay in Rome, however, stretched out deep into the following year and there exists the following interesting information about this time, for which we have to thank Fr. Edward Hipelius[1] who was dedicating himself to the study of Arabic under Fr. Pius Zingerle.[2] Fr. E. Hipelius[3] writes:

> On a beautiful March morning in 1865 I sat in my room in the Abbey of Saint Paul Outside the Walls; the little window was open and the friendly spring sun supplied *gratis* heating service for my cell, while fragrant aromas *sans façon*[4] made their way in to me from the monastery garden. There was a modest knocking at the cell door. *"Entrate."* *"Buon giorno." "Il Padre Abate vorrebbe vederla."* [5] I went immediately

---

[1][original footnote:] He is known as the author of the following works in Latin: 1) *Album Benedictinum* etc. etc.*Adjecto indice Scriptorum ejusdem Ordinis hac aetate florentium. St. Vincent in Pennsylvania*, 1869; in octavo. 2) *Caeremoniale Monasticum. Saint Vincent in Pennsylvania*, 1875, in octavo.

[2][original footnote:] Fr. Pius Zingerle, from the Abbey of Marienberg in Tyrol, published valuable translations from the Syriac and scholarly commentaries of various works of the holy Fathers Ephrem, Clement, and others. Pope Pius X called him to Rome in order to entrust him with a chair for oriental languages at the Sapienza University.

[3]Charles (Karl) Hipelius was born on 7 February 1836 in Stadtlauringen, Unterfranken. He came to Saint Vincent at age 15 in 1851, eventually entered the monastery and made profession in 1855 with the name Edward. He was ordained to the priesthood in 1858. He studied in England in 1861 and then in Rome from 1862, leading to a doctorate in canon law. Oetgen, *Mission*, 90-91, records that he taught scripture and canon law in the seminary, served as secretary to the monastic chapter, and became a key advisor to Abbot Boniface. He received a dispensation to leave the Benedictine Order in 1878 to support his younger brothers and sisters. He served as pastor in the Albany Diocese, retiring to Port Ewen, New York where he died in 1900.

[4]French: unpretentiously, without ceremony.

[5]Fr. Edward gives the brief exchange in Italian: Come in. Good Day. Father Abbot would like to see you.

to the abbot's quarters and saw, upon my entrance, my own abbot. I remained on the threshold in a state of surprise. Seeing him again was not unexpected, but the expression of embarrassment and anxiety that I saw on him, and that I not was accustomed to see on him, touched me in a painful way.[6]

After greeting each other we went into the city. The impression I had gotten at first glance in meeting him was given a woeful confirmation in our conversation during the ride. I saw only too clearly that the good man had come to Rome with a heavy heart. I sought to cheer him up, but with little success. I do not know how it came about that we did not take the usual way; we turned to the right at Santa Maria in Cosmedin and we passed right over the Place of Execution, precisely where the guillotine normally stood, as he asked me whether I thought he should cut away his beard. Now, I was never really kindly disposed towards beards, and had the abbot asked me elsewhere, I may have been inclined to pronounce the death sentence. But the place itself was too ominous for me to utter such a far-reaching and heavy verdict. There, where the head of the poor sinner fell into the sack, I did not want to ban the existence of venerable beards. I felt a little awkward in the presence of the colleagues of Maestro Stefano, the chief executioner of Rome at that time. And so I expressed myself in the negative; and the beards remained, blossomed and thrived, and the flowing beard of the abbot especially aroused the admiration of Pius IX, and in the end I am happy that my fear of being compared with the otherwise very honorable Maestro Stefano saved the glorious existence of the beards.

Partly because of his external appearance and partly because of his pronounced predilection for farming, an American prelate called Abbot Wimmer an *agricola*,[7] a name that others were inclined to recognize as well-founded, at least until they had the opportunity to convince themselves that this "farmer" was well-versed in higher studies. The cause for his predilection for farming was sufficiently demonstrated because he saw in it the basic condition of his creation,[8] in that farming formed for him the pivot of the large question of to be or not to be.

---

[6]The style, careful wording, and some elaborate phrasing indicate that this was an essay, composed with deliberation, rather than a letter. Several ellipses, shown by a string of periods, suggest that Fr. Oswald chose to omit parts of an obviously longer text. He does not give any exact citation for the essay, so it seems to have been an unpublished study provided by Fr. Edward, likely requested by Fr. Oswald as he prepared this biography of the Archabbot.

[7]Latin: farmer. The American prelate is not identified.

[8]Fr. Edward uses this word to designate Saint Vincent and indeed the whole Benedictine enterprise in America.

During his 16-month stay in Rome in the years 1865 and 1866, the abbot often attended public disputations in philosophy and theology as well as doctoral exams with the intense interest of a professor. After he had endured for four or five hours at such occasions, he gave evidence of the alert attention with which he had heard and grasped the academic lectures, during conversations with his confreres during the evening. When one evening one of these confreres could not completely hide his surprise over the discovery that the "farmer" could interest himself so earnestly for scholarship, the abbot looked at him with an expression of good-hearted mockery and said: "In philosophy it is said: *prius est esse, quam talem esse*," that is, first one has to eat, otherwise everything ceases.[9] "The saying shone like an electric beam through my philosophy of the unconscious," wrote Hipelius, "and kindled in me suddenly the consciousness of a long slumbering conviction. Certainly, *prius est esse,* first one has to eat! But where the food comes from, that was a question that in my Arcadian naiveté I had considered as rather superfluous...."

The abbot was especially amused one time, when a soldier of the papal Swiss Guard at a public disputation on the thesis *de incarnatione*[10] engaged the doctoral student with an incisive objection. From time to time Abbot Wimmer felt himself tempted to imitate the example of the learned Swiss Guard but he always had too much pity for the poor tortured examinees and so he left them in peace. "It was good that way for their sake," he said in his good-natured humor.

The events of those times offered the abbot so many serious and also bitter things, that spirit-raising intermezzos were only too welcome. I permit myself to immortalize a few of them.

The abbot was a mortal enemy of that nimble but annoying member of the noble guild of blood-letters and cuppers, so common in Rome. It was unfortunately impossible for him to enjoy a beneficial sleep, as long as one of these sharp-nosed creatures found itself in his vicinity. In order to keep himself as far as possible from these little Manicheans, in the early morning he regularly would shake out his bedclothes from the window – we were living in southern lands after all; the win-

---

[9]The saying plays on the proximity of the German word *essen* (to eat) to the Latin word *esse* (to be) to good effect.

[10]This was a disputation concerning the topic of Christ's taking flesh or becoming human.

dow was on the side of the large garden that served as a military exercise area. French military were billeted on the lower floors. One fragrant morning as he attended to this activity of exiling [the insects], a French warrior shouted up to him, "Hey, dear Father, keep those little critters[11] up there, we have enough down here ourselves." The abbot laughed heartily and from then he shook out his bed covers somewhat earlier so that he would not be caught [doing it] again.

One day when he returned from St. Peter's to his quarters in St. Calisto, he was met in a very narrow alley near St. Maria Trastevere by a little donkey with a huge load of grass. There was just enough room for the abbot to get by, but the drover, probably a young man, drove the donkey straight into the abbot. He grasped the situation immediately, and in authentic Bavarian matter-of-factness he unceremoniously grabbed the donkey with its load and shoved it to the other side of the alley. Not even the clerical fog-splitter[12] on the abbatial head was budged from its place. Now there was enough space for him to pass by. Without so much as granting the drover a further glance, the abbot continued peacefully on. But the drover remained standing wide-eyed and may well have wondered, where in the world do they grow this kind of little giant.

Many an evening he came home in such a sad and discouraged mood, that I had heartfelt pity for him. I sought to make the long summer evenings more bearable for him. Each evening we exchanged the experiences we had had during the day. Once I had brought him into a stream of conversation, his Bavarian *Gemütlichkeit* and resilience of spirit returned. Our evening conversations in St. Calisto were often quite amusing. When letters arrived from America, their contents were shared, as far as that was permissible, or fresh American newspapers with news that was three weeks old. Those were for us obviously the most interesting themes, except for our discourses over farming, about which I more often than not launched forth into very ingenious theories. At any rate my theories in this area were often the source of sheer joviality for the abbot, who did not fail in a basically cheerful way to appropriately recognize my famously known giftedness and at the same time great practical experience in this field.[13] My touching innocence on the topic of farming delighted him.

---

[11]Fr. Edward uses the German word Vögelchen, which literally means little birds.

[12]The German Nebelspalter, literally rendered. It was a humorous nickname for a three-cornered hat, a kind of biretta.

[13]This of course is said in mock seriousness and self-deprecating humor.

If we were about to lose the thread, the "Ridge" was the saving angel; and in fact it showed itself to be a real gold mine of material for our evening conversations. As soon as I touched on this subject new life and higher verve and healthy animation came into the conversation. Then he was in the right navigable channel. A more generous use of the snuff box and a livelier pace announced even externally his happier mood. The abbot never grew tired to make ever new plans and designs for the future of the Ridge. It did not escape him for long, that and why I deliberately brought the topic of the Ridge back to the table and indulged in oracles about farming. He also would have forgiven my rascality; he knew my motivation and indeed the tried man needed to be cheered up. I told myself that it would be a bad thing if this item of our exchange of ideas would lose its magnetic effect on the abbot. At times it seemed it would. Many times when he had worked out the future plans in the smallest detail, he would suddenly close with a sigh: "Ach, what is the purpose of this plan-making; it is good for nothing." One evening he came back completely despondent and broken and said to me: "Tomorrow I am sending in my resignation; I am very tired of it all now." "Ho ho, Fr. Abbot," I replied, "resignations don't take place so quickly." And I added to this theme a very emphatic warning about over-hasty steps and attributed the thought of resignation as the precipitous result of an improper and unjustified discouragement. Such a lecture was improper for me to give; but I said it and indeed "with seriousness and zeal," and with the constant respect that I owed him. And my attempt in this area was to my great joy decidedly more successful than my attempts in the area of farming.

Our colloquia were often very learned and many times even crossed over into the quite scholarly; and I often was silently amazed that the abbot had retained his store of knowledge from Munich so well, despite the burdens of farm management and governing [the monastery].[14] Our topics of conversation did not confine themselves to vague theories, but ordinarily also had a practical bent, especially in historical matters in which the abbot developed his own forte. So it happened that we came to speak of the great monastic schools of the Middle Ages [and followed] in natural course down to our schools in the present, and finally we arrived without noticing it to the project of a philo-

---

[14] It will be recalled that before becoming a Benedictine at Saint Michael's monastery in Metten, he had decided to study law at the University of Munich. But after the first year he enrolled at the Georgianum, the theological seminary attached to the university. In 1831 he was ordained for the Diocese of Regensburg, but after a year attending to the pastoral needs of pilgrims at the Marian shrine at Altötting, he entered the monastery at Metten.

sophical and theological educational institute in Rome. These were the first seeds of the future Saint Elisabeth House of Studies.[15] For a long time the discussions in this regard had a more or less speculative character, gradually, however, the issue took on a more concrete and practical form and at that point the question arose: should we or should we not?

It was on a winter afternoon in the year 1866 when we, caught up in a serious discussion of this question, strolled slowly from St. Paul to Rome. The abbot was seized by a more than usual enthusiasm for the undertaking, without, however, being able to come to a decision. We came to the small chapel on the via *Ostiensis*,[16] that was erected on the site where according to an old tradition the two princes of the apostles took leave of one another, when St. Paul was led out to *Aquae Salviae*[17] for martyrdom. There we stood quietly and I listened to the abbot for a while, but then I gathered myself for a *coup diplomatique*, and with the exertion of all my "freshness" and impudence, I said with apparent indifference, "Fr. Abbot, this plan is too good for me to think that you could bring it about." He looked at me with a peculiar gaze and gave what was a perfectly characteristic response for him, "And now it will happen for that very reason."[18] Now the die was cast and I rejoiced inwardly. I could not help making the abbot aware of the venerable classic Christian site on which he made the far-reaching decision, and I pointed out that this site seemed to me to be an omen that prophesied success. The abbot was so kind as to concede that I was correct and agreed with my prediction.

We separated there, where the Apostles parted, and Fr. Abbot went straight to the Vatican where he communicated his decision to Archbishop (now Cardinal) Prince von Hohenlohe and the learned Dominican Fr. Salua, later Archbishop and General Commissioner of the Holy Office, who was at that moment visiting the prince. Both heartily congratulated the abbot on this, and as I had perceived an omen in the [above-mentioned geographical] site, so Fr. Salua saw one in the temporal circumstances, namely that the birthday of the decision was 10 February, the feast of Saint Scholastica. The joy of the abbot was

---

[15]Abbot Boniface established this house of studies in Rome in 1866, sending the first students almost immediately after returning home from Rome.

[16]Fr. Oswald clarifies: on the road to Ostia.

[17]Fr. Oswald notes: about one mile from the patriarchal basilica of St. Paul Outside of the Walls there is the abbey ad *Aquas Salvias* or at the three fountains. Here on the site of the martyrdom of St. Paul the early Christians already in the earliest times erected an oratory.

[18]Fr. Edward quotes him as saying: "Und jetzt g'schieht's grad."

now complete. His confidence in the success of the undertaking was made firm to such a degree that he would let himself be diverted from its execution by nothing more. With his own energy and tough persistence he undertook the necessary steps; the joyful blessing of the great Pius IX rested on the enterprise that already in the fall 1866 came to full realization and without doubt fulfilled a providential task, namely it gave the first impulse to the reestablishment of the famous Benedictine College of San Anselmo.[19] While its prospects are not the most promising for the immediate future, due to the unpropitiousness of the times, he, whom storm and sea obey, has set the time according to his own judgment, when he will let thunder into the roaring storm a sovereign halt, and what is now dark will be light, and the children of the Church who are now oppressed will enjoy holy rest and bliss in the newly arisen light of gracious peace. Facit Deus![20]

The abbot considered his 16 month stay in Rome more or less as banishment, though he willingly admitted that it turned out to be for him a source of many graces and of very valuable spiritual advantage. Being far from the creation in which he had invested heart and soul, the pain of separation grew in that measure that he, an active man used to restless work who had been taken away from it, felt with increasing torment the lack of a suitable object to work on.

Among the graces that he received during this time the abbot named, not in last place, familiarity with the holy life of the blessed Anna Maria Taigi, which soon drew him to a great and confident devotion that resulted in the bestowing of many rich graces and the granting of petitions. His devotion and gratitude eventually led to his writing a book about her life that appeared in 1867 in Regensburg.[21]

The long duration of his Roman sojourn gave occasion at the time to many false presumptions and baseless speculations in many American circles. As often happens in both high and low politics, very simple

---

[19]This allusion helps to indicate the date of Fr. Edward's essay at 1888—1890. The papal brief "Quae diligenter" (4 Jan. 1887) was the founding document; but the "birthday" of the International College of San Anselmo is 4 January 1888. On this date the school opened and classes began on the following day. (See Pius Engelbert, *Geschichte Des Benediktinerkollegs St. Anselm in Rom: von den Anfängen (1888) bis zur Gegenwart* (Roma: Pontificio Ateneo S. Anselmo, 1988) 15-20. Of the first 14 students, three were from Saint Vincent; of the seven faculty members, two were from Saint Vincent (Engelbert, Geschichte, 17). For several years the school was housed in temporary quarters; only in fall 1896 could they move into the current site (Engelbert, Geschichte, 41).

[20]Latin: may God accomplish it.

[21]Bonifaz Wimmer, *Lebensgeschichte der ehewürdigen Dienerin Gottes Anna Maria Taigi* (1769-1837). Regensburg: Friedrich Pustet, 1867.

(not to say simplistic) causes lie at the base of complicated proceedings. So too, what was responsible for the long stay in Rome and
his failure to work out a favorable resolution of the pending matters
was a very insignificant circumstance, even if it was also a detail with
serious consequences. It was namely that simply and solely the abbot had a predilection for a certain comprehensiveness in his reports
and applications. It seemed that he, who was otherwise so short and
compact in speech as well as in his whole being, was simply unable to
maintain this characteristic in his official correspondence with the Holy
See and the Roman offices. Each subsequent application exceeded
its predecessors in scope and formality. This drawback appeared to
rest on him like an ill fortune. The simple result was that the already
over-stressed clerks (*Minutanti*), at the sight of such masses of reading material, were seized by alarm and shoved the stack of paper to
the side until they might have sufficient time to manage it. But before
it got to that point, yet another load appeared; and so one application
piled on top of another, and none of them reached [the stage of] pe-
rusal and proposal.

Cardinal Reisach,[22] who was always well intentioned toward the abbot,
once addressed him sharply on account of the above-mentioned fail-
ing, and said to him in good Munich dialect: "Quit writing so much! No
one reads it and no one can read it all; it would be necessary to assign
a couple of clerks just for you. You are so overwhelmingly fond of
writing. You say so many things that we don't want to know and don't
need to know. Make it short and clear and leave all the superfluous
stuff out; then it will go better." But it took a long time before the abbot
conceded that the cardinal was right. One day as he complained to
me, as he often did, about the eternal and fruitless waiting, I asked him
if he had forgotten what Cardinal Reisach told him. In order to transfer
the thing from theory to useful practice, I suggested to him to make the
superhuman effort to prepare a document for once that was as short
as possible, and commission me to undertake the task of editing and
total completion. He agreed. I must confess that I had not yet taken on
many tasks in the serious but also enthused frame of mind as I took
on this one. I did not have to play the executioner to the extent that I
had expected; the abbot had applied himself to achieve golden brevity.

---

[22]Early on 25 July 1846 it was Karl von Reisach, then Archbishop of Munich and president of the
Ludwig Missionsverein, who celebrated Mass for the little group of missionaries and sent them on
their way that day to America. Called to Rome as a cardinal in 1856, he continued to be a supporter
of Saint Vincent.

Nevertheless I found it advisable to condemn about a third to the scissors.... in short, I exercised my editorial office with happy conscientiousness. I also was mindful of an appropriate outward appearance. I completed the copy with my best calligraphy skills.

The abbot was well satisfied with it and even bestowed mild praise. The document was sent in and behold, already in the following week the ardently awaited decision arrived. The abbot was blissful and I not much less. But I could not refrain from extoling myself a little with the words: "Isn't it true, Lord Abbot, that I'm also good for something?" To this he said, in good spirits, "yes, it could be."

From then on, the settlement of all the matters followed in surprisingly rapid order and the demonstration of apostolic benevolence compensated the abbot more than sufficiently for the long and dreary hours that he spent during 16 months in the city of seven hills.

[Fr. Oswald concluded the chapter:] In the end he obtained his definitive appointment by the Holy Father not only as abbot of Saint Vincent but also as President of his Congregation for life. When after this he also brought about the elevation of the Priory of St. Louis on the Lake in Minnesota to the status of an abbey, he left the eternal city satisfied in order to return to his beloved monastery.

At the farewell audience his flowing beard itself aroused the admiration of Pius X who said smilingly: *"Evviva l'Abate Wimmer colla barba magnifica."*[23]

---

[23]Italian: Long live Abbot Wimmer with his magnificent beard. This final story apparently also comes from Fr. Edward's essay.

CHAPTER TWENTY ONE
Foundation of Three New Abbeys:
Saint John's, in Minnesota, Saint Benedict's in Kansas, and Saint Mary's at Newark, New Jersey.[1]

Saint John's Abbey.

In response to the urgent invitation by the most reverend Joseph Cretin, D.D., bishop of St. Paul, the abbot and the chapter of St. Vincent made the decision to establish a foundation of their Order in faraway Minnesota, where the great rivers, Mississippi and St. Lawrence, have their headwaters, a decision that would have far reaching consequences. To carry out this important undertaking, Prior Demetrius Marogna and two newly ordained priests, Fr. Cornelius Wittman[2] and Fr. Bruno Ries,[3] were chosen, along with several lay brothers. Minnesota was considered a "new land" in those days; it was a territory only recently opened up for immigration. For this reason Abbot Wimmer considered it only right that his western pioneers would be supplied with everything they would need, as far as possible. A significant cargo of boxes was given to them from the abbey which contained a complete set of all that was needed for the altar, sacred vessels and church vestments, a nucleus of books for a library, and many other useful objects. Beyond this they received a substantial sum of money in cash, as well as several land warrants, that is, government issued vouchers for the acquisition of land, each worth 160 acres, which had first been issued in 1846 to soldiers returning from the war with Mexico.

On April 5, 1856, they started on their long journey. In Pittsburgh they boarded a steam boat and went down the Ohio to the place where it meets the Mississippi, from where they continued their journey up stream to St. Paul. From there they continued another 80 miles north, following along the river, and settled down near St. Cloud, which counted barely one hundred inhabitants at that time. From the barren little wooden cabin which initially served as their residence the priests travelled every

---

[1] In the German original, only two new abbeys are given in this title: Saint John's and Saint Benedict. But all three are subject of the chapter.

[2] Fr. Cornelius Wittman was born in Oberengbach, Bavaria on 11 October 1828. He made profession at Saint Vincent on 21 August 1853 and was ordained a priest on 17 May 1856. He died on 22 September 1921 and is buried at Saint John's.

[3] Fr. Bruno Riess was born in Augsburg, Bavaria on 17 October 1829. He made profession at Saint Vincent on 21 March 1853 and was ordained on 17 May 1856. He eventually became part of the group that established St. Peter's, Saskatchewan, Canada. He died on 2 February 1900 and was buried at Saint Bede's Abbey, Peru, Illinois.

week in different directions through the dense woods and over open prairies in order to visit the new settlers scattered widely over the large territory. Their arduous efforts, however, were crowned with such success that in the short span of three years they were able to organize the faithful into small parishes at thirty locations, and to build as many churches and chapels for the service of the Almighty. Of course, only two of these "churches" were frame buildings, the one at St. Cloud and the one at Shakopee. One was of brick, at Chaska. All the rest were only so-called log cabins.

One can imagine that Abbot Wimmer was extremely pleased about the quick success of his zealous missionaries in the Northwest. He had such a keen interest in their apostolic work that he often undertook the long journey there himself, in order to check on their needs himself and to give them any help they might require. As soon as he realized that the number of workers for this new part of the Lord's vineyard needed to be increased, he was ready to send help from St. Vincent. Thus it came to pass that his new colony of Benedictines soon grew to a community of 10 priests and as many brothers, strong enough to start thinking of the establishment of a canonical priory. The original plan was to build the monastery at the place where they had settled at the beginning, near St. Cloud, along the western banks of the Mississippi. However, this plan had to be abandoned, after the Brothers Rothkopf, the owners of the property of 160 acres, lost it; whether it was by trickery, justly or unjustly, we must leave the judgment to others.

The priests discussed the matter and then came to the decision to choose a suitable site for their monastery in the so-called Indian Bush, in a large forest, along a small but romantically situated lake. The abbot considered it only right to report about this step for the further expansion of the Order to the West also to his noble benefactor in Bavaria, since he had always taken such an active interest in Abbot Wimmer's foundation. For his part, King Ludwig showed that he was always willing to pay honor where honor was due. For this reason he honored Abbot Wimmer not only with his contributions, but also by writing to him in his own hand, like the following, for example, which also shows the noble spirit of the prince:

Ludwigshohe in the Palatinate

July 4, 1856

Rev. Abbot, your letter of May 30 was very interesting to me, and it makes me very happy that the abbey of St. Vincent is flourishing, as does the fact that my work on behalf of elevating St. Vincent to an abbey has proved successful. It was a fortunate meeting between the two of us in Rome last year. That St. Vincent, a colony of Metten, has already started another one, is welcome news to me. May God

continue to give his blessing to these undertakings. In the Palatinate,
too, piety is increasing. It makes me very happy that that which I
have done for religion has taken root and is prospering. Also thriving
is the monastery I sponsored at Oggersheim, where, I hear, nearly
4000 pilgrims come to the pilgrimage church on the best days. That
the Benedictines were my favorite Order already when I was a boy,
you already know. Kind regards to all members of St. Vincent,

from your very appreciative
Ludwig

The Minnesotan Benedictines first called the place designated for the future
monastery "St. Ludwig on the Lake." However, since they had already received a
title to the so-called "Rothkopf Addition" near the little town of St. Cloud on March
6, 1857, where they had initially planned to settle, calling it, "St. John's Seminary,"
they eventually transferred this title along with the rights of the charter, to this new
settlement by the lake. In 1858, 4 priests and 9 brothers were living at St. Joseph's.
By fall the latter had already constructed a two story log house, 30' long, by the
lake. While working on this they had to buy their groceries at St. Joseph, which was
separated from the lake by 4 miles of dense forest. There they often came in contact
with Indians. One day one of the brothers was driving his wagon, hitched to two
yoke of oxen, toward the lake. In the middle of the forest some Indians approached
him, inspected his load, opened a bag, and took three loaves of bread out, which they
divided among themselves. Then one of them walked toward the frightened brother
and handed him a quarter dollar. Then they let him go his way in peace. Not long
after this when Brother Wolfgang Beck (from Metten) was alone in the log house by
the lake, an Indian entered and said to him, "give me some whisky." The brother did
not have a drop of whisky in the house, and, since he was not able to express himself
in either the Chippewa language nor in English, he had to make himself understood
with gestures. He had already heard about the passion among the Indians for whisky,
so he quickly pointed his guest to a tub full of water that stood in the room, while he
himself grasped a kitchen knife, cut a piece weighing about two pounds from a large
loaf of bread and handed it to the Indian, who left, content with it.

Friends of Brother Peter Muggenthaler had sent a bell from Bavaria to this young
Benedictine colony, which was a big event.

In 1859 the Abbot of St. Vincent undertook his second journey to Minnesota
for visitation. He stopped at St. Cloud and from there went on to St. Joseph, where
in those days there were only a few houses. The brothers who lived there worked
mostly in the "Indian bush" during the week in order to ready a place for their future
monastery. The local superior was Fr. Clemens Staub,[4] a former officer from the spe-

---

[4] Fr. Clement Staub was born in Baar, Canton Zug, Switzerland on 9 August 1819. He made
profession on 15 August 1852 and was ordained to the priesthood on 12 December 1853. He died
on 23 April 1886

cial forces of Switzerland. He received the abbot with greatest joy and after greeting him, asked him to wait a moment, so he could introduce him to his two novices. He opened the door and whistled, and immediately two shiny black bears hurried toward him, which he then introduced to the abbot. The abbot, however, was not very happy with such company at first sight, until Fr. Clemens explained that he had brought the two from the woods when they were still very young. In winter they crawled into the straw pile beside the stable, and in spring they came back out again. They always stayed around the house and were as tame as dogs.

But once they had innocently frightened the whole population of the settlement. This happened one afternoon when most of the settlers were working in the fields, and all of a sudden the church bell started to ring. Such a thing had never happened before in this quiet neighborhood at that time of day. Everyone feared that something bad had happened. Some said, "There must be a fire!" while others called out, "The Indians!" Brother Cook, however, who also was the sacristan, immediately discovered the source of the frightening occurrence. As soon as he had heard the first peal of the bell, he looked over to the church door from his kitchen, and noticed how the bears were beating a hasty retreat through that door. They paused for a moment and, detecting no danger, returned to the church. But they were no longer alone. The brother snuck up behind them, with a stick in his hand. The bears climbed up to the organ loft and starting to swing from the bell rope, playing in the manner of cats.

The constant arrival of more and more immigrants made it possible for our missionaries to replace the often all too shabby log chapels with larger and more dignified church buildings in many locations after just a few years. Thus a second church rose on the site of the first one in Richmond in Stearns County under the direction of Fr. Bruno, a solid, dignified house of God in St. Cloud under Fr. Meinulph Stuckenkemper;[5] in St. Joseph, a stone church 164' long, under Fr. Cornelius; the stone church in Shakopee under Fr. Eberhard;[6] the splendid Assumption of the Blessed Mother Church in St. Paul, which cost more than 100,000 dollars, under Fr. Clemens. In each parish, whenever possible, a Catholic school was established also. At St. Cloud Fr. Magnus Mayer[7] opened a Latin school in 1859.

While his confreres were active in ministry in the far flung areas, the prior, Fr. Benedict Haindl, and his lay brothers were busy laying the foundation for the future monastery at the "hermitage," as they called the log house by the lake in those days. After they had prepared a nice piece of land for farming, they erected a chapel with a large adjacent house, built of quarried stones.

---

[5]Fr. Meinulph Stuckenkemper was born in Waterschloo, Westphalia on 17 January 1837. He made monastic profession on 11 July 1859 and was ordained to the priesthood on 20 July 1861. He died on 3 July 1919.

[6]Fr. Eberhard Gahr was born in Pfatter, Bavaria on 18 September 1832. He made profession on 17 January 1856 and was ordained a priest on 17 May 1857. He died on 31 March 1922 and is buried at Saint Vincent.

[7][original footnote] M.M had passed the philosophical course in Bavaria before he entered the Order.

First house of the Priory at the Lake in Minnesota.

Had Weber come to Stearns County in Minnesota at that time, he would have seen a part of his ballad of the "Thirteen Linden Trees" realized in real life:

> Only recently white men
> Had arrived from distant realms,
> Words of blessing on their lips,
> In their hands the sign of peace;
>
> Serious men, often tested,
> Who in hard disdain for the world,
> Consecrated themselves to work,
> To prayer and to meditation,
>
> Quiet settlers, who labored to
> Cultivate wild ravines,
> And wilder hearts
> With gentle seeds of teaching.
>
> With wisdom and undiscouraged,
> They built with plumb and scale,
> Square and saw and hammer,
> Axe and trowel day by day,
> Till their labor has succeeded
> Building church and monastery strong,
> Till the pious notes of psalms
> Sound from the choir of the brothers.

The colony of the Benedictines in Minnesota, visibly blessed by God, gained in ecclesiastical as well as secular importance year by year, until the Holy Father Pius the IX, of blessed memory, elevated the monastery by the lake to an abbey on August 3, 1866. In December Abbot Wimmer went to Minnesota in order to preside at the election of the abbot. It took place on the 12th of that month and the vote went to Fr. Rupert Seidenbusch,[8] who was prior at St. Vincent at the time. After the papal brief of March 15, 1867 confirming the election arrived, the Most Reverend Aloysius Carrell, bishop of Covington, consecrated the first abbot for Minnesota in the church at St. Vincent on Ascension Day.

By an apostolic brief on February 12, 1875 the vicariate for Northern Minnesota

---

[8]Albert Seidenbusch was born in Munich, Bavaria on 13 October 1830. He made monastic profession as Brother Rupert on 6 January 1852 and was ordained to the priesthood on 22 June 1853. His election as abbot was confirmed by Rome on 15 March 1867 and his blessing followed on 30 May of the same year. He was consecrated as Vicar Apostolic of Northern Minnesota on 30 May 1875, resigned in1888 and died on 23 July 1895

St. John Abbey in Minnesota.

Bishop Rupert Seidenbusch   **Abbot Alexis Edelbrock**

was established. Abbot Seidenbusch, who had by now led his monastic family with great merit for eight years, was named Vicar Apostolic by the Holy See and consecrated Titular Bishop of Halia on May 30, 1875. The orphaned abbey elected the very reverend Alexius Edelbrock as its worthy head on June 2 of the same year, and he was blessed on October 24. Seven years later to the day the new monastery church was consecrated. Fr. Ferdinand Hundt, pastor of St. Peters, Indiana, an alumnus of St. Vincent, dedicated the following stanzas to the occasion:

From St. Vincent's mother abbey, the daughters went forth,
Following the ever new waves of the
German immigrant stream
And the oldest of the daughters
Celebrates today in happy wonder
Already the silver jubilee of a quarter century.

The abbey of St. John is in the great far west
Already the liveliest and strongest of
The branches of the monastic tree.
Its buildings nesting gloriously in
The bay of gentle hills,
And the church's spires are reflected
In the nearby lake.

St. Benedict's, in Kansas.

The borders of present-day Kansas were established in 1854 and the area was organized as a territory; it was accepted into the Union as a state in 1861. Before that it was included in the "Indian Territory," and originally it was a part of that large area of land called Louisiana, which was sold to the United States by France in 1803. The Most Reverend J.B. Miege, S.J. was consecrated titular bishop of Messenia on March 25, 1851 for the church of the region, and named Vicar Apostolic for the "Vicariate east of the Rocky Mountains," which included what is today Kansas and Nebraska. The extraordinary fertility of the soil drew immigrants to Kansas in great numbers. Therefore the bishop tried to make sure at the very start to have their spiritual needs taken care of. With this intention he turned several times to Abbot Wimmer and invited him to establish a settlement of the Benedictine Order in the vast area of his vicariate.

In the summer of 1856 a start was made. Fr. Augustine Wirth,[9] the Superior of the mission, settled at Doniphan with Fr. Lemke, while Fr. Casimir Seitz remained with the bishop at Leavenworth, where he gathered the Catholic Germans of the city into a parish and thus founded the St. Joseph Parish, which was later transferred to the Carmelites. After a short stay the Benedictines became convinced that the younger city of Atchison would soon surpass the older town of Doniphan, due to its more favorable location. In the fall of 1857 the abbot of St. Vincent came to Doniphan for visitation, and the decision was made to move to Atchison. This was a very important step. The latter was a city of great importance. Where the present city of Atchison is now located, with its 15,000 inhabitants, George M. Million from Missouri had built the first log cabin in the summer of 1854. The monastery is situated a ways outside of town, along the western banks of the Missouri, a little over 150' above the river. The layout of the city of Atchison resembles a large amphitheater which rises gently from the river inland for two to five miles, reaching an altitude of 200'. From year to year the abbot would send new priests and brothers to help out at this mission, as the need arose.

By a decree of December 23, 1858, the young monastery was recognized as a priory by the Holy See, and Fr. Augustine Wirth[10] was confirmed as its prior, an office which he fulfilled with laudable energy for ten years. A college for higher learning was added to the monastery. After sufficient space for living quarters and a school was created, the prior decided on a bold plan. He wanted to build a grand church which was to exceed any church of his monastic congregation, both in size and solidity. He

---

[9] [original footnote] The following works of his were published:
  1) *The Pulpit Orator,* 7 vols. Elizabeth, NY 1881
  2) *New and Old Sermons.* Elizabeth, NY. 6 vols., 1885
  3) *The Confessional.* Murphy and Co., Baltimore, 1877
  4) *New May Devotions.* Elizabeth, NY, 1882
[10] Fr. Augustine Wirth was born in Lohr, Bavaria on 17 March 1828. He made monastic profession on 15 August 1852 and was ordained to the priesthood on 8 December 1852. He died on 20 December 1901 as a member of St. Mary's Abbey in Newark.

Abbot Innocent Wolf   **Bishop L.M. Fink**

turned to benefactors for contributions to the building of this sanctuary that was to be a witness to the faith and sacrifices of the donors for centuries to come. Among the magnanimous souls who contributed to the erection of this sanctuary, King Ludwig I of Bavaria was the most generous, followed by the Empress Iturbide of Mexico, among others. The building progressed quite well up to the height of the windows. Even the massive pillars, each made of two stones, were already at the building site, when obstacles occurred which brought everything to a stand still. The prior resigned, and even though the abbot of St. Vincent came to its aid with a sizeable sum of money, the young monastery found itself getting deeper and deeper into financial difficulties over the next ten years, which could not be completely eliminated even after two decades. In spite of all the hopeless jeremiads Abbot Boniface was to hear from this monastery, he never tired of reaching deeply into the till time and again in order to help out, until his inexhaustible patience and invincible magnanimity won out over all unpleasant prophesies.

After it had existed for 20 years, the priory was finally elevated to an abbey by Pope Pius IX in 1876, at the request of the abbot. The Rev. Fr. Innocent Wolf, Th.D.,[11] was elected its first abbot and blessed on March 21, 1877. With this act a weight was lifted off the shoulders of the abbot of St. Vincent, as it were. In addition to this he experienced another joy in Kansas. The abbot considered it one of the greatest honors of his life when he received a letter from the Cardinal Prefect of the Propaganda, requesting him to provide information about the education and moral character of one of his monks, since the latter was being considered for consecration as a bishop. This chosen one was none other than the Reverend Ludwig M. Fink,[12]

---

[11]Fr. Innocent Wolf was born in Schmidheim, Rhenish Prussia on 13 April 1843. He made monastic profession on 11 July 1861 and was ordained to the priesthood on 26 May 1866. His abbatial election was confirmed on 20 October 1877 and his blessing followed on 21 March. He died on 14 October 1922.

[12]Fr. Louis Fink was born in Triftersberg, Bavaria on 12 July 1834. He made monastic profession at Saint Vincent on 6 January 1854 and was ordained to the priesthood on 28 May 1857. He was constituted the first bishop of Leavenworth on 22 May 1877. He died on 17 March 1904 and was buried at the cemetery of the Sisters of Charity of Leavenworth in Xavier, Kansas.

Abtei St. Benedict in Atchison.

St. Benedict Abbey in Atchison.

bishop of Leavenworth, who was consecrated titular bishop of Eukarpia on June 11, 1871.

St. Mary's Abbey at Newark in New Jersey

This abbey came into existence by circumstances that were very different from those that brought about the founding of the other abbeys established by Abbot Wimmer. Indeed, we see in this foundation a complete deviation from his original plan, according to which he did not want to establish any independent houses of his Order in a city. Only his endeavor to have all the monasteries which were located at a distance from St. Vincent elevated to abbeys whenever possible, something which became more and more important to him as he neared the end of his life, could persuade him to take this step. His main motive in doing so was to diminish the area in which his immediate supervision was required, along with the responsibility that went with it.

The abbey at Newark had gradually grown out of St. Mary's parish. The establishment of this parish, however, dates back to the year 1841, when the Reverend Father Nicholaus Balleis built the church and the school on Grand Street, now Howard Street. Fr. Balleis took solemn vows at the venerable Benedictine abbey of St. Peter in Salzburg as early as October 28, 1830, and was consecrated a priest on December 4, 1831. When several American bishops made repeated efforts to get German priests for their dioceses who would care for the German immigrants, Fr. Balleis signed on. Equipped with the necessary documents from the Propaganda in Rome as well as the best references and the permission of his monastic superior, he proceeded to Newark in 1836, in order to share toil and labor with his compatriot, Vicar General Dr. Raffeiner,[13] the founder of St. Nicholas Church. However, they did not in any way limit their concern only to the Germans of the city; rather, their mission district initially encompassed the whole diocese, which included the two states of New York and New Jersey.

Fr. Raffeiner organized parishes in Boston, Albany, Syracuse, Poughkeepsie, Macaupin, Stony-Hill, Manhattanville, etc. Fr. Balleis, on the other hand, dedicated himself completely to his new foundation in Newark since January 1842. What changes have taken place there since then! Did Bishop John Hughes, of blessed memory, have any idea on that cold fall day in 1842 as he was traveling from New York to Newark to consecrate St. Mary's church, that with this action he was laying the cornerstone for a future abbey? The little church stood more or less in an open field at that time; the streets had been laid out, but there were only a few houses here and there, with large empty areas between them. Adjacent to the church was the burial ground for the parish. The classroom and the rectory were built onto the church and were under the same roof. The whole building was

---

[13]Fr. John Stephen Raffeiner was vicar general for Germans in the Diocese of New York and pastor of St. Nicholas Church in Williamsburg (Brooklyn).

St. Mary's Abbey in Newark

constructed of wood.

A strange episode occurred in the history of this church in 1846, which involved Fr. Balleis deciding to move the whole building to a more suitable lot which he had obtained on the corner of High and William Streets. The man, with whom he had contracted for the job, started right away. He lifted the building onto long logs and rollers, and rolled it along about one third of the way. Then, however, he cancelled the contract with Fr. Balleis, and thus left the church and the house stranded on someone else's property. Since Fr. Balleis had assumed all responsibility for this move, one can imagine the dilemma in which he found himself. Only with much difficulty was he able to find another man after two weeks who finished the move successfully. One good thing about it was that the church had ended up situated in such a manner that people could still gain access into the sanctuary by means of some stairs, so that Sunday worship did not have to suffer any disruption. Nevertheless, it was a strange site to see this church on pilgrimage for three weeks, and to hear the Ave Maria bell pealing from different directions as time went on.

A few years later Fr. Balleis, upon his request, received an assistant from St. Vincent. And then, in the year 1856, the parish was formally incorporated into the abbey of St. Vincent. This occurred upon the express wish of Bishop James Roosevelt Bayley, Th.D, former bishop of Baltimore. The foresight and genuine desire to care for the well being of every part of his flock in every way possible, which impelled this man, is clearly evident in the following letter to Abbot Wimmer:

Newark, NJ, May 12, 1857

Most Reverend Sir!

I am happy about the willingness with which you met my request by sending several priests of your Order to this place in order to take over the parish ministry at the German parish of St. Mary's in this city. I addressed this request to you because I am hoping that you will take measures to transplant a branch of the Benedictine Order to Newark. For this purpose I will transfer to you the property on High Street which Fr. Balleis had purchased, as well as the burial ground on Grand Street, so that it will forever stay with your Order for the benefit of the parish...

It is my hope and my expectation that as a result of the coming of your Order, religion in this city will attain such vigor and such growth that on this foundation a monastery will arise in a short time, to which an institution of learning will soon be associated for the education of young men, especially for those who show a calling for a priestly vocation...

I assure you that I will joyfully do everything in my power to work with you on behalf of this good work which is so necessary for the salvation of our large Catholic German population, which is still continuing to grow. Also trust that the most complete agreement regarding the planning and execution of the details of this undertaking will exist between us, since we both have one and the same goal, that is, the flourishing of our holy religion.

With sincere respect and devotion I remain,

Your obedient servant
+ James,
Bishop of Newark

To the very Reverend Boniface Wimmer, Abbot of St. Vincent, Latrobe, PA

Everything promised the best hopes for the near future. Already a committee had been elected from the parish that would consult with the new priest about the building of a new church, when suddenly the sad news arrived on May 28 that Fr. Valentine Felder, the pastor, had been run over and killed by the horse-drawn trolley in New York City. However, Abbot Wimmer took care of immediately providing a successor, and the building of the church proceeded quickly. It distinguished itself inside and out by the excellence of its workmanship as well as it architectural style. What the bishop had referred to in his letter was becoming reality step by step. In the course of a few years a new parochial school was built matching the style of the church. Later an institution of higher learning was added and, in connection with that, a monastery; all of which already gave this complex the appearance of an abbey. With the consent of the reverend bishop, the abbot of St. Vincent eventually petitioned the Holy See for the designation of abbey for the place; this was granted by a decree of

Abbot James Zilliox   **Abbot Hilarius Pfrängle**

December 19, 1884. The election of an abbot took place at St. Vincent on February 11 and the Reverend James Zilliox, Th.D[14] was elected. He accepted the election and was blessed; but before the year was over, he had already resigned due to poor health.[15] The newly elected Reverend Hilarius Pfraengle, Th.D.,[16] took his place.

---

[14][original footnote] From his pen: *Album Benedictinum, Prodiit e typographaeo S. Vincentii in Pennsylvania 1880. — Octavo. — p. 450.*

[15]Abbot James Zilliox had been born in Newark in 1849. He made profession at Saint Vincent in 1866, was ordained to the priesthood in 1873. He served as novice master and prior at Saint Vincent before being elected as abbot of St. Mary's in 1885 but resigned in November 1886. He died in 1890.

[16]Abbot Hilary was born in Butler, PA in 1843, made monastic profession at Saint Vincent in 1862, and was ordained as a priest in 1866. After obtaining a doctorate degree in theology in Rome, he served as director of the college at Saint Vincent from 1872 until his election as abbot to succeed Abbot James in Newark.

CHAPTER TWENTY TWO
St. Mary's Abbey at Belmont, North Carolina.
A Negro[1] Mission in the year 1877.
Mary, Help of Christians, North Carolina.

In the southwestern part of the State of North Carolina, where the so-called Blue Ridge with the outstanding elevations of Kings Mountain and Spencer Mountain offers a romantic view, one can find many a pleasant area where a monastery or an institution of learning might be located, much like the venerable old abbeys of Europe, the contemplation of whose historic ruins fills the Christian with melancholy. Far from the numbing tumult of city life, a monastery could be a spring of blessings for the surrounding area like a fertile oasis. But who would establish one? Perhaps a wealthy philanthropist? No, for these usually make their bequests only to populous cities or their surroundings. Monastics themselves? Most of today's Orders find their work, as well as their base of support, only in cities, or at least in large parishes. That monks might go out into the woods, ax in hand, in order to build their cells and turn the wilderness into fertile fields, many people think to be only the stuff of legends and of days long gone, such as the story of St. Sturmius, perhaps, who in 744 with his seven companions founded the monastery of Fulda in a dense forest. The abbot of St. Vincent thought to the contrary, saying, "History repeats itself; what happened in former times can happen again now."

However, one must add to these sayings also, "*Mutatis mutandis.*"[2] His brothers know how to swing an axe; they change many a stretch of woods into fertile fields; they construct buildings of wood and stone. However, as regards the way of life of the old anchorites, it is not only times that have changed, but people as well. The needs and demands of today's life style are increasing in all countries according to the rule that supply creates demand, and, conversely, demand fosters supply. Accordingly, one could expect that founding a monastery and a school in the midst of woods far from cities would involve many difficulties and great expense. Divine Providence, though, knows

---

[1] The English terms "Negro" and "colored" are literal translations of Father Oswald Moosmüller's German. These terms are usually regarded as pejorative today, but they were not so when Father Oswald wrote his biography of Boniface Wimmer. More acceptable terminology today would be "African-American," but this was a term that did not exist in either German or English in 1891 when the biography was written.

[2] Latin: the necessary changes having been made.

how to direct the steps and how to bring the appropriate man to the right place.

It was near the end of the year 1872 that the Reverend J.J. O'Connell, Th.D., purchased the Caldwell place in the area described above, in Gaston County in North Carolina. This property consisted of 500 acres but had been neglected for years as far as cultivation went. After a few years Dr. O'Connell came to the decision to use his property for the establishment of a monastery. He presented this offer to the reverend Bishop Dr. Gibbons who at that time was in charge of ecclesiastical affairs in the state of North Caroline as Vicar Apostolic. The bishop took advantage of this opportunity with joy, since his whole vicariate had only two thousand Catholics among a population of one and a quarter million. He did not want to lose any time and immediately took steps to put the plan into action. For this purpose he first turned to the School Brothers of Baltimore and, when these refused acceptance, he contacted Abbot Wimmer in order to win him over for his plan. The latter accepted and for reasons that were most characteristic of all of his undertakings, that is, "because of the poverty and isolation of the Catholics in North Carolina."

The main goal he had in mind was to establish an outpost for the faith in an area where the Catholic Church was known only in the distorted image presented by its opponents. "To do good to those who revile us," was his aim.

Fr. Hermann Wolfe, M.D., O.S.B.,[3] was sent to the Caldwell place in the spring of 1876 with 4 lay brothers, in order to make a start. In February 1877 he received the help of Fr. Joseph Keller and two additional brothers. Three months later the abbot himself visited the new settlement, called it "Maria-Hilf" (Mary, Help of Christians) and provided the means for the building of a chapel. Then an educational institution was founded under the leadership of Fr. Stephan Lyons. The first students came from Richmond.

In the meantime the donor of this foundation himself took the habit of St. Benedict. Since then he has occupied himself with literary activities, and two interesting works witness to his talent.[4] Thanks to Fr. Placidus Pilz's knowledge of construction, two fine looking buildings for monastery and college rose up, which were further enlarged as the years passed. The abbot of St. Vincent endeavored to build up the house Mary Help of Christians in every possible way. He supplied the institution with capable instructors, and it gave him great satisfaction that as a result of this the number of students increased year by year.

In this manner it came to pass that that which many considered wasted effort and useless expense proved to be a brilliant success in the course of a few years. Today Abbot Wimmer is admired for the calculated wisdom, the far reaching eye, and the sacrificial zeal with which he looked beyond all difficulties and envisioned success, at a time

---

[3] Fr. Herman ((1816-1884), who was ordained a priest in 1867 and made vows in 1868, had served as a doctor in the Confederate army during the Civil War and had converted from Lutheranism. See Oetgen, *Mission to America,* 159-160.

[4] [Original footnote] 1) *Catholicity in the Carolinas and Georgia: Leaves of its History,* by Rev. Dr. J.J. O'Connell, O.S.B. (1820-1878). New York: Sadleer, 1879 (80 , XVIII, 647). 2) *Conferences on the Blessed Trinity.* 1885.

Mary-Help-of-Christians Abbey in Belmont.

when even those most closely involved in this undertaking predicted certain failure. His patient perseverance won the victory here also, so that the Holy Father Leo XIII elevated this monastery to an abbey already on December 19, 1884, by means of a brief and gave it the title, Mary Help of Christians. Until then, this monastery had been only an affiliate or external station of St. Vincent; therefore there were no monks incorporated into it. All priests and brothers who worked there were only sent there [temporarily] by the abbot of St. Vincent and were subject to being recalled.

However, after the house was elevated to an abbey by papal decree and permission for the election of an abbot was given, there were two ways in which the organization of the new monastic community could be handled. In one case, a chapter first would be constituted at Mary Help of Christians by having the monks who wished to join the new abbey transfer their vows there, with the permission of the abbot of St. Vincent. In this way, these alone would have the right to elect their abbot. In the other scenario, the capitulars of St. Vincent might consider the fact that the new community as well as its abbot would come from among them; and, since they also had born the burden of the work and the expense for the new foundation, they were entitled to make use of their right to choose the new abbot. [In this second case] the number of monks entitled to vote would be 106. The abbot and the chapter of St. Vincent decided on the latter course of action. Accordingly, the election was carried out at St. Vincent on February 11, 1885, under observance of the relevant canonical prescriptions. In the first *scrutinium*, O.M.[5] received the required number of votes and was consequently proclaimed the first abbot of Mary Help of Christians. The elected one was on a mission 1000 miles from the monastery and had not appeared in person for the election. Because of this he was informed of the proceedings by telegraph; and he replied immediately by the same route, thanking his confreres for the honor but declining the position. The abbot of St. Vincent did not pay any attention to this telegram, for he hoped that in the course of the two months which church law allows the elected one for reflection, he would probably be able to talk him into accepting. After he had finally been convinced to the contrary, it was decided to use the first method for a second election.

Accordingly, Mary Help of Christians Abbey got its own community after a few months when a sufficient number of the monks, twelve, that is, agreed to transfer their

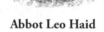

Abbot Leo Haid

---

[5]This would refer to Oswald Moosmüller himself.

vows there, with the approval of the abbot. By doing so, these monks earned the exclusive right to participate in the upcoming abbatial election. The election was held on July 13 of the same year, and Fr. Leo Haid[6] received the majority of the votes. After his confirmation by the Holy See arrived, he began his tenure and with the greatest success. The richly blessed work of Abbot Leo soon received such favorable recognition that he was entrusted with the administration of the apostolic vicariate of North Carolina, and already on July 1, 1888, he was consecrated titular bishop of Messena.

Savannah and Skidaway Island, Georgia.

In 1876 the city of Savannah suffered great affliction due to the terrible plague of yellow fever. Among the many victims whom death overtook was the Reverend Gabriel Bergier, superior of the Benedictines on Isle of Hope, near Savannah, as well as Dom Gregory Enright, a cleric, and M. McDonald, a brother aspirant. These three died in October 1876. The above monastery had been founded by two priests who had come to Savannah from Pierre-qui-vire Abbey in France, upon invitation by the Most Reverend Bishop W.H. Gross, D.D., in order to found a mission for Negroes there. As early as May 1874, right after their arrival, they started to organize a parish and to open a parochial school. They built a small church, which in no time was filled with the faithful each Sunday. It was very gratifying to watch how their efforts received such a favorable reception among the people of color.

The following year they established a novitiate on the Isle of Hope. But when the shepherd was smitten, the flock scattered. After death had visited the house of the Benedictines, two of the clerics joined their confreres in Indian Territory, which belonged to the same congregation. Three brothers and one scholastic stayed behind. In this time of affliction and distress, the very reverend bishop turned immediately to the superior of Pierre-qui-vire in order to obtain priests who would continue the work begun earlier. The care for the colored congregation he had temporarily assigned to a diocesan priest. The reply was not long in coming; but the request was declined. Without hesitation the bishop then wrote to the abbot of St. Vincent in December 1876 and attempted to persuade him to assume the care of the orphaned mission. At the same time he offered him a 717 acre farm on the nearby Skidaway Island which would be very suitable for the establishment of an agricultural school for Negro boys.

The two factors prominently involved in this offer, namely the poverty of the Negroes and the development of the agricultural land, could not fail to have an effect on Abbot Wimmer. He presented the matter to the Chapter and the mission was adopted. In February 1877 there were already two priests on the way to Savannah.[7] Although the distance between there and St. Vincent is more than 1,000 miles, the

---

[6] Michael Haid (1849 – 1924) had been born in Westmoreland County, not far from Saint Vincent, made monastic profession in 1869 as Brother Leo, and was ordained priest in 1872.

[7] These two were Fr. Oswald Moosmüller and Fr. Maurice Kaeder. See the account in Oetgen, *Mission to America*, 162-164, which also supplies the names of other monks who were engaged in the mission.

abbot nevertheless appeared on the Isle of Hope and on Skidaway as early as the following May, in order to see for himself what could be done for the colored people. He left his instructions and promised to send additional help, depending on the needs and progress of the mission. Above all he inculcated in his priests and brothers the mandate, "Educate the Negro boys in agriculture; that is best for them and for the country." At considerable expense he had all the necessary buildings constructed: a beautiful little church, living quarters, a school, and farm buildings. He sent several priests and brothers there, and visited the mission in person four times within the time span of the ten years from 1877 to 1887. He made the last visit shortly before the beginning of his [final] illness.

If someone asked him at times if he expected this mission to bear any fruits, he would reply that one must be willing to make sacrifices for such a noble purpose, one had at times to be able to work for an idea the fruits of which might not become visible in the present, one had to consider it an honor to be permitted to participate in such an apostolic endeavor. Abbot Wimmer followed the progress of the mission with greatest interest. The plan was to make religion the foundation for the education of the Negro boys. Most of the boys who were taken into the school had not yet been baptized. The class work was to be limited to the basics of reading, writing, arithmetic, and singing. Every day at certain hours all students had to work in the fields, in the garden, or in the workshops. All were to be convinced, by theory and practice, of the necessity and the usefulness of farming. Abbot Wimmer often maintained that, "The farmers are the conservative element of a country; the more independent farmers there are in a country, the better it is for the entire population." Therefore, he rightfully considered the plan of instructing them in agriculture to be of the greatest benefit, not only for the poor colored boys but for the nation as a whole.

Three years after the establishment of this institution, there were 2 priests there, 6 brothers, and 25 colored boys. In addition there was also a cleric, who after having passed the examination administered to him by the school superintendent, was put in charge of the newly established public school for colored children on the Island, which was attended by 56 students. *Utinam!*[8]

It was known not only at St. Vincent but in more distant circles, that Abbot Wimmer had a special affection for the mission on Skidaway, and that he felt fortunate to be in a position to support it in every way. His motivation for this was primarily the saying, "Amen, I say to you, whatever you did for one of these least brothers of mine, you did for me" (Matthew 25: 40). When at times he heard that one or the other of the brothers on the island did not share his opinion regarding the honor of participating in this meritorious work nor in the hope of a favorable outcome, he was quick to remind him of the temptations of

---

[8]Latin: would that [it had succeeded]!

Negro School in Savannah.

the Israelites in the desert.

What Abbot Wimmer did for the poor Negroes on Skidaway Island by the establishment of the above mentioned school placed a shining pearl in his crown. What little has been said about this mission in these lines brings only a part of his efforts and sacrifices to light; for the report was stopped here, because someone[9] who had participated in this mission for ten years, set a limit, "Thus far and no further." This is meant to give an opportunity to anyone else who might want to immortalize the merits of him who took it upon himself to continue this good work and to further it, to start there where this description was broken off.

---

[9]This apparently would refer to Fr. Oswald himself.

CHAPTER TWENTY THREE

**The founding of a canonical priory for the Bohemians.
Establishment of a mission in Ecuador. Anniversary celebrations.
The end of the Archabbot's life. The election of his successor.**

Saint Procopius, Chicago, Illinois.

For twenty years now there were several Bohemians among the monks at St. Vincent.[1] Since in recent times the immigration of Bohemians continued to increase, several bishops found it necessary to turn to Abbot Wimmer in order to obtain Bohemian priests for their dioceses. As a result, Benedictines came to serve the Bohemian parish in Allegheny City, Bohemian missions in Nebraska, as well as the Polish parish in Pittsburgh, among others. Finally, the Abbot came to believe that everyone would be better served if the Bohemian Benedictines would be given a central location for themselves where they could take in Bohemian candidates and educate them for their future profession. When circumstances then worked out in such a way that he was to take over St. Procopius Church in Chicago, he made the decision, with the consent of the archbishop, to establish the projected monastery in conjunction with this church. To this house he sent five priests, who served the parish and also established a Latin school. After that, he addressed his last petition to the Holy See to obtain the establishment of a canonical priory, in conjunction with St. Procopius Church in Chicago. His request was granted, and the response arrived at St. Vincent during his last illness, in the form of an Apostolic Brief.

Bahia, Ecuador.

The founding of a Benedictine mission in Ecuador constitutes the final chapter of the biography of the late Archabbot Wimmer. Although the actual establishment was carried out only by his successor, the correspondence of the most reverend bishop of Puertoviejo indicates how extensively Abbot Wimmer was involved in this project.

The reader may now ask, how did Abbot Wimmer get to Ecuador? Actually, he did not go there himself; however, two seminarians from St. Vincent, Pfefferkorn and Kruse, corresponded with the Most Reverend Bishop Peter Schumacher, Th. D., of the Lazarite Order. He eventually accepted them into his diocese and announced their

---

[1] The term Bohemians here refers to those from Bohemia or, in German, Böhmen. One of the results of World War I was that this area and these people were gathered into a new political entity entitled Czechoslovakia. More recently Czechoslovakia was dissolved and what was once called Bohemia has become the Czech Republic.

arrival to Abbot Wimmer by way of the following letter:

Ecuador, Puertoviejo, April 12, 1887

Most reverend, esteemed Archabbot!

I have the pleasure of being able to inform you that the two young gentlemen, Kruse and Pfefferkorn, have arrived here safely. Thanks be to the
dear Lord and also to you, reverend abbot, for the favor you have shown
to this poor diocese. The kindness you have shown us and the praise for
your apostolic zeal offered by the new arrivals raises my hopes that you
will offer a helping hand to us in the future also. The seed bed is large,
but there is a lack of laborers who could tend it.

Since you and your esteemed companions have, with God's visible
blessings, accomplished such great things for the Church in North America, you would place a crown on your achievements if you were to extend the same to Catholic Ecuador. To submit my thoughts on this matter
to you, I am looking forward to the moment when I will have the honor to
speak to you personally; and I have decided to undertake a journey to
North America for this purpose in the course of this coming summer. In
the meantime I have the honor of greeting you most respectfully.

Yours most devotedly in Christ,
+Peter Schuhmacher
Bishop of Puertoviejo

In June 1887, the bishop of Puertoviejo honored St. Vincent with his visit. All
those who had the good fortune to meet the distinguished guest described him as a true
apostle, who could not fail to leave enthusiasm for his mission at St. Vincent, which
would in time bear fruit. That he had won the good will of the chapter was already
demonstrated by the enthusiastic participation in the celebration of his feast day (June
29), which was observed during his stay here. Unfortunately the health of the late archabbot, which was already noticeably declining, did not permit his involvement with the
important plans for undertaking new missions. For this reason the bishop considered it
more appropriate to repeat his concerns in writing, which he did in the following letter:

New York, July 5, 1887

Most reverend Archabbot!

After careful deliberation I have decided to start on my trip to Europe. However, before I act on this decision and leave America for some time, I take the liberty to humbly present to you again, this time in writing, my requests and desires for my poor South American Mission. I do so in the hope that this will give you, most reverend archabbot, time and opportunity to examine my proposals in depth and come to the most suitable decision. May the dear Lord by his grace make up for what my feeble words are lacking, in order to give you a clear picture of the scope and importance of the work to be undertaken, and at the same time lead you to decide in our favor. However, may everything be for the greater glory of God, whatever the final result of my efforts may be.

First, most reverend archabbot, I would like to take the liberty to show you a brief and concise picture of my diocese by describing its geographic location, its climatic conditions, as well as the religious and moral condition of its inhabitants. The Diocese of Puertoviejo, which is entrusted to me, encompasses the region along the western shore of the Republic of Ecuador. It is bordered in the south by the Province of Guayaquil, and in the North it touches the neighboring republic of New Granada or Columbia. It consists of two provinces, namely Esmeraldas and Manabi. The capital of the latter, Puertoviejo, is also the residence of the bishop. Extensive and almost impenetrable virgin forests separate the above provinces from the interior of Ecuador; and this natural separation has given them a special character all their own, which distinguishes them completely from the provinces located in the Ecuadorian Plateau.

The interior of the republic, i.e. the highlands of the two mountain ranges of the Andes Mountains, has a moderate climate. The Diocese of Puertoviejo is located in the lower, and therefore warmer, coastal region. However, the climate is considerably moderated by the vicinity of the ocean, on the one hand, and the snow-covered Cordillera, which stretches along the opposite side. Our climate therefore, though part of the tropics, is not like that of Africa. In fact, the sea shore along the Pacific Ocean always offers a pleasant and very healthy climate. The farther inland one penetrates, the more the temperature rises. Only the actual rainy season, which usually starts in January and ends in April, is unhealthy. The pouring rain and flooding rivers often cause certain paludian fevers, which however, rarely take on a malignant course. In fact, with a little caution the danger can usually be avoided.

The extremely fertile soil, favored by the winter rains and the warm temperatures, produces an abundance of the most wonderful natural products. God's benevolent hand has fairly deluged man with his gifts there. The most wonderful and tasty fruits, such as coconuts, bananas, oranges, and countless other ones surround the residences. Nutritious and valuable plants make for good substitutes for the grains and other growing things native to the temperate zone and missing here. The meadows feed many horses and cattle. The virgin forests provide for lucrative exports, though their treasures are far from being fully utilized. Ivory nuts, which are the main harvest, are picked all year long and sold to other countries for a good profit. The most profitable cultivation is that of the cocoa tree, the fruit of which constitutes the main ingredient of chocolate. The production of the so-called Panama hats represent the industry branch [of the economy], since all of these hats come from Ecuador; not a single one is fabricated in Panama, while here women and girls in almost every family carry out this work. Much could be done in these areas to help poorer families to improve their lot.

Oh, how many blessings a company of women religious (nuns) could bring to this area! How much they could contribute to the improvement of the lot of persons of their gender if they would combine their work with providing education. I harbor this confidence based on my acquaintance with the excellent potential among the feminine gender of my diocese. The nuns would only need to set to work in order to soon harvest the most beautiful fruits. I cannot help but share with you, most reverend archabbot, the joy of my heart—I have just received the promise that the venerable Benedictine nuns of Newark will move to Puertoviejo in order to devote themselves to the education of young women there. Will you now admit that it can be said again this time: "God has chosen the weak ones." Well, then, will you let the women beat you to the prize? But forgive my teasing. Scholastica will once again draw Benedict, her reverend brother, into this situation with the strength of her virginal prayer. May the Lord grant it!

I move on to the ecclesiastical and religious life. If I remember correctly, the Diocese of Puertoviejo was established only in 1873. This occurred as a result of the efforts of Garcia Moreno, who labored untiringly for the church. For this purpose the two new provinces, Esmeraldas and Manabi, were combined by separating the latter from Guayaquil and the former from Onito. Until this time the spiritual care of the residents was only minimally provided for by sending priests to these distant provinces as they became available. The unforgettable Garcia Moreno, who had an open and watchful eye for the spiritual needs of his compatriots, was responsible for getting a group of Capuchin priests to settle in the area, and he sent some Christian School Brothers to Manales. It was a great loss for the young diocese when Garcia Moreno was murdered in 1875. As a result, both of the above-mentioned groups withdrew again, since they were now left without the hoped-for support. The most reverend bishop was compelled to leave the diocese of Puertoviejo due to illness. The seminary, barely opened, was closed. And so, the religious development of the area came to a troubling standstill.

When I came to the diocese in August 1885, I found that the majority of the twenty three parishes were orphaned. Even in the capital there was only one priest at the cathedral. It was a diocese like probably no other in the Church—without a seminary, without schools, indeed, almost without any ministry. With the help of a few young priests and theologians, who had come along with me from Quito, I opened a high school for young boys without delay. I also succeeded in establishing a high school for girls, led by three excellent ladies. The success everywhere exceeded my expectations. The youth of both genders showed themselves to be teachable, talented, and receptive to the salutary influence of the religious education. In Puertoviejo I have introduced something like a monastic life with my young companions. The loyalty of our young boys and young men has made our efforts well worth our while. Teaching gives us a pleasant occupation. In the city itself, an eager priest has revived the religious life. The church, once empty, is now filled on Sundays and holy days.

A small group of devout believers has been formed who receive the Holy Sacraments monthly. Wonderful young men have hurried over from the interior of Ecuador, from Germany, and from the United States in order to prepare themselves for the priestly state, some in Quito, where there is an excellent seminary, some in Puertoviejo itself. However, we are lacking a religious Order; the clergy are lacking the support of a religious family, which could sustain them and help them in the toils and hardships of the priestly vocation. The people in general still have preserved their deep faith, which only needs stimulation, instruction, and especially a good example, in order to bear the most beautiful fruit. However, the evil one has scattered his seeds. There is also a darker side, and my report would not be faithful were I to keep silent about this.

Particularly destructive and damaging has been the work of the so called Spiritism in the diocese in warring against the Catholic faith and the foundation of morality. It rejects the teaching of Jesus as imperfect and replaces it with supposed messages from the spirit world. These, be they actually true or made-up lies, all proclaim that the Son of God and the Catholic Church count for nothing, and that everyone may believe and teach what suits or pleases him.

In regard to moral law, Spiritism posits as its fundamental principle that it is the right and purpose of man to follow his natural instincts and not deny himself any pleasure. Then, in order to calm any possible pangs of conscience or apprehension, this same Spiritism asserts that there is no eternal punishment in hell, nor are there any evil spirits. Rather, after death, there follows a comfortable life in the company of friendly spirits, which engage in pleasant past times. At most one or the other may be in need of some additional cleansing, by having his soul continue life on earth through incarnation in a human or animal body. Religious indifference, moral decline, wanton disrespect of any law, are the sad fruits of these devilish teachings.

Political chaos has also contributed mightily toward unleashing evil passions and impeding religious life. However, more about this topic another time. I see that my letter has gotten longer than it should be, and for that reason I am closing with the humble request that you and all most honored members of your community give serious consideration as to whether you can offer us any help.

Whoever decides to follow me will have to be prepared for a life filled with renunciation from the beginning and expect no reward or consolation other than the conviction that he is working and suffering for the glory of

God and for the salvation of abandoned souls. Should, as I am hoping, with the grace of God, a small group of apostolic men from among your monks be willing to join me, I would accept this help not only with thanks, but offer them everything possible to ensure the success of their efforts. I hope, most reverend archabbot, that you will have made a decision by the time I return from Europe at the end of this month, or at the latest, the beginning of next month, and that this will be in my favor. In this hope, I remain most devotedly.

Yours in Christ,
+Peter Schumacher
Bishop of Puertoviejo

Accordingly, three priests, one cleric, two scholastics, and two brother-candidates from St. Vincent set out for Ecuador in the summer of 1888 and settled at Bahia. Bahia is a small town of about 800 inhabitants and lies along the shore of the Pacific Ocean, near the equator.

1400th Anniversary Celebration.

In the year 1880 the Abbot of St. Vincent undertook his fourth journey to Rome, chiefly with the intention of participating in the celebration of St. Benedict's 1400th birthday at Monte Cassino. After having renewed his strength at the tomb of the saintly founder of his Order, he returned, and the following year celebrated his fiftieth jubilee of ordination at his own monastery. Several most reverend bishops, as well as many diocesan priests and members of his Order brought him congratulations. Of the many poems that were composed in his honor, the title of the most memorable was:

"A Forget-me-not, lovingly woven into the wreath of the jubilee of His Grace, the most reverend Boniface Wimmer, Abbot of St. Vincent and President of the American Cassinese Congregation, from the Archabbey of Mount St. Martin in Hungary".

Another enthusiastic jubilee poem was composed by the very reverend Ferdinand Hundt, Pastor of St. Peter's in Indiana. Permit me to quote a few of the seventeen verses here:

It is a song of praise to God the Lord, the father of all light,
The source of all that's good, when sings the bard
On this day of Golden Jubilee the praise of noble deeds,

Montecasino

That you, O, son of Benedict hast brought about.

In witness and reward of our great salvation's grace,
The heads of two of your sons are crowned with mitres,
And at your right and on your left, an abbot takes his place.
And half a thousand is the number of your confreres.

Thus, for this new land you rose to be the patriarch
Of all the Orders, the oldest and most noble,
The Order that already stood around the cradle of Christianity,
That spread faithful learning spread from sea to sea in Christian lands.

Not for the narrow circle of your fellow members only,
But for the Church at large throughout this whole wide land,
You have become a Boniface, a man of grace and blessing;
The walls of this grand edifice bear resounding witness thereof.

Both science and the arts you favored; a loyal friend the poor found
you to be.
And in your love's kind rays you warmed many noble hearts.
And all the praise that beams upon your brow today,
It is the due of gratitude, it is the blessing of our hearts.

Abbot Boniface's Golden Jubilee and Last Illness.

Two years later another Jubilee followed, because now a half century had passed since the abbot had professed solemn vows as a Benedictine at Metten. Surrounded by a great number of his spiritual sons, as well as many friends and patrons from far and near, the aged abbot celebrated his fiftieth jubilee of profession on December 29, 1883. This festive occasion inspired several most reverend prelates and priests, former alumni of St. Vincent Seminary, to obtain from the Holy See the title of archabbot for the respected jubilarian. Even though there were no new rights or

Archabbot Wimmer

St. Vincent from East.

duties connected to this title, it nevertheless would be considered a sign of honor and recognition for all his accomplishments.

As soon as the festivities were over, the archabbot started on the necessary preparations for elevation to the status of abbey the two houses in Newark and Belmont, or "Garibaldi", as the latter was still known, in North Carolina. How he brought this, his last endeavor, to a happy conclusion, is described elsewhere.[2]

Soon after this, the evening of this life of many accomplishments began to approach. Unmistakable symptoms of a painful, lengthy, and incurable illness became evident, so that he was never again able to leave the walls of his monastery during the last twelve months of his life. His robust frame seemed to shrink to half its size as a result of his illness, and he could apply to himself the words of Fr. Alto Hörmann, when he says:

> "Evermore tired I'm getting, and older.
> The experience makes me colder,
> And my autumn is fast approaching.
> Many a sorrow I've borne,
> By many a conflict been torn,
> Many a good deed I've been offering."

The last year was a time of great suffering for the archabbot, who for half a century had worked tirelessly, with unshakable courage and unimpeded health, on fulfilling his responsibilities as a priest and as a monk. Being confined to his sickbed for months on end was a severe trial for his active temperament. However, he who had gone through many a fire in his eventful life transcended this trial victoriously also, for he understood suffering as a Christian should, namely, purification of the soul from the dross of earthly things, as Fr. Alto expresses so strikingly by in *Aners Rückkehr*:[3]

> Heavier, heavier becomes the burden.
> O, my God! Shall I lament,
> Since you yourself hast borne the cross,
> Borne it unto death?
> O, it is getting bitter for me, harsh,
> Yet, the Cross is my inheritance,
> My salvation's pledge.
> Come, sweet, sacred burden,
> You, my glory, you my honor,
> Be my consolation at the grave.

---

[2] The account about the abbey in Newark is given in chapter twenty one and the account about Belmont in chapter twenty two.

[3] The English translation appeared as *Anêr's Return*, New York: P. O'Shea, 1869. These quotations come from chapter XVI, from a song called "The Knight's Traveling Hymn."

St. Vincent from West.

For about a year he was confined to his sickbed; all hope for recovery was gone; the most experienced physicians from near and far put fourth their best efforts to prolong his days, but in vain. The hand of death lay on him, and he was aware of it. He had fought the good fight and kept the faith; and now, rest from his labors and an incorruptible crown awaited for him. The once so robust figure had shrunk to a weak, thin skeleton. On December 8, 1887, on the Feast of the Immaculate Conception, Archabbot Boniface Wimmer completed his earthly course while the high mass was being sung in the church.

The following most reverend bishops were present for the funeral mass on December 13: Most Reverend Richard Phelan, D.D., Coadjutor from Pittsburg-Alleghany; Most Reverend Tobias Mullen, D.D., of Erie; Most Reverend Joseph Rademacher, D.D., of Nashville; Most Reverend William O'Hara, D.D., of Scranton; Most Reverend Camillus Paul Maas, D.D., of Covington.

Furthermore the following abbots were in attendance: Right Reverend Alexius Edelbrock, O.S.B, St. John, Minnesota; Right Rev. Innocent Wolf, D.D; O.S.B., of Athchison , Kansas; Right Rev. Leo Haid, O.S.B, of Belmont, North Carolina; Right Rev. Hilarius Pfrängle, D.D., O.S.B., of Newark, N.J., Right Rev. Fintan Mundwiler, O.S.B, of St. Meinrad, Indiana;

In addition, approximately 100 priests participated in the funeral. After the Requiem the Most Reverend Bishop O'Hara gave a touching eulogy. The body was placed in a metal coffin, which was enclosed within a coffin of cedar wood, and then was lowered into a vault under the large stone cross which stands at the center of the nearby cemetery, located on the highest hillock in the surrounding area. May he rest in peace.

That, then, was the life of Archabbot Boniface Wimmer. If we cast a summarizing glance over the same, the foremost impression that shines stronger than everything else is his generosity. This was expressed in many ways, for the suffering of others affected him deeply, and he was always ready to help where he could. Friends as well as strangers, Catholics as well as Protestants, all were given proof of that. Although it is true that no one lives unto himself, the number of those who pursue doing good for others with the zeal of Abbot Wimmer is always in the minority. How he cared for poor students and tended to needy travelers had been described in detail above. One thing still needs to be mentioned, however, namely that he accepted not a few missions mainly because of the poverty of the parishes, and he never tired of supporting the priests of such parishes for many years. Some parishes that his priests had either newly established, or for which they built, enlarged, or renovated, he in time transferred back to the respective bishops, as soon as they were able to staff them with their own priests. It would not be difficult to name fifty such parishes.

For this reason Fr. Alto's words rightfully apply to him:

"Wandering, he cast good seed abroad;
Who him knew, his name
With thanks and blessing speaks.
Though he didn't see the fruit mature,
Now the harvest's sheaves
His garner grace."

Two equally bright stars in his life were the steadfastness and the perseverance with which he endeavored to reach his goal once he had set it for himself. Every person seeks to transform his vision into reality. The thoughts of every person, when made known and spread about by word and deed, bring to bear an influence, bring about an effect, either for good or for evil, and this influence may last to the end of time, when the full measure of the merit or the harm done will be revealed.

In this account an attempt has been made to record how Archabbot Wimmer followed his vision to establish Benedictine monasteries in America, patterned after those of the Middle Ages, and to indicate with what steadfastness and perseverance he worked on the actualization of his plan.

The accomplishments he leaves behind bear powerful witness that the Lord has blessed his untiring activities. By founding a Benedictine Congregation consisting of five abbeys, in which more than 200 priests and as many brothers work in the service of God, Abbot Wimmer has achieved the goal of his life's work. The words of the psalmist apply to him:

"Funes ceciderunt mihi in praeclaris: etenim haereditas mea praeclara est mihi!"

"Pleasant places were measured out for me; fair to me indeed is my inheritance."
(Vulgate Ps. 15:6; NAB 16:6)

Abbot Boniface's Successor.

If the kind reader has followed the description of the establishment and progress of the blessed Archabbot Wimmer's foundation with some interest until this point, he may also wish to learn who carried on the good work as his successor.

Two months after the death of the blessed founder, the election of his successor took place. Of all the capitulars who were eligible to vote, two thirds were present in person. The rest, unable to come due to great distances or other circumstances, were represented by procurators. Abbot Alexius Edelbrock of St. John, Minnesota, presided. The first two ballots did not yield an absolute majority. However, in the third *scruntinium* the name of Abbot Innocent Wolf, Th. D., from Atchison, Kansas, emerged from the voting urn with the necessary majority. The result was immediately communicated to him by telegraph, and after only a few hours he sent the following reply: "Thank you for your confidence, but am unable to accept." Thereupon, a new vote was taken and the majority vote went to Fr. Andrew Hintenach. The result of this vote brought about great joy and general satisfaction. As soon as the chosen one declared his acceptance, all present went to the church, to thank the Lord with the singing of a solemn *Te Deum.*

The newly elected abbot was born in Schollbrunn, in the grand-duchy of Baden, on May 12, 1844, and received the name "Tobias" at

Abbot Andrew Hintenach

Baptism. His parents later settled in Baltimore, and eventually his older brother (Fr. Athanasius) was accepted at St. Vincent College, where the young Tobias also set foot for the first time on August 15, 1854. Taking the religious name, Andrew, he professed simple vows on July 11, 1861, and three years later, solemn vows. He received priestly ordination on April 12, 1867. Since that time, Fr. Andrew was active in the monastery, partly as a professor, partly as Master of Novices, and then as Prior, with the exception of eight months during which he ministered in the small parish of Tuscumbia in Alabama. Now that all participants recognize in this election the guidance of all-gracious Providence, they look toward the future with full trust, and they confidently expect a successful continuation of the good work.

Made in the USA
Columbia, SC
16 May 2020